Learning Spaces

Diana G. Oblinger, Editor

ISBN 0-9672853-7-2
©2006 EDUCAUSE. Available electronically at
www.educause.edu/learningspaces

An EDUCAUSE *e-Book*

Learning Spaces

ISBN 0-9672853-7-2
©2006 EDUCAUSE. Available electronically at
www.educause.edu/learningspaces

An EDUCAUSE *e-Book*

An EDUCAUSE *e-Book*

CHAPTER 1

Space as a Change Agent

Diana G. Oblinger
EDUCAUSE

Spaces are themselves agents for change. Changed spaces will change practice.[1]

Learning is the central activity of colleges and universities. Sometimes that learning occurs in classrooms (formal learning); other times it results from serendipitous interactions among individuals (informal learning). Space—whether physical or virtual—can have an impact on learning. It can bring people together; it can encourage exploration, collaboration, and discussion. Or, space can carry an unspoken message of silence and disconnectedness. More and more we see the power of *built pedagogy* (the ability of space to define how one teaches) in colleges and universities.

This e-book collection—chapters, examples, and images—presents learning space design from the perspective of those who create learning environments: faculty, learning technologists, librarians, and administrators. Other books focus on architectural and facilities issues; this e-book collection makes no attempt to duplicate them, despite their importance. This e-book focuses on less often discussed facets of learning space design: learner expectations, the principles and activities that facilitate learning, and the role of technology. Three trends catalyzed this collection:

▶ Changes in our students
▶ Information technology
▶ Our understanding of learning

Today's students—whether 18, 22, or 55—have attitudes, expectations, and constraints that differ from those of students even 10 years ago. Learning spaces often reflect the people and learning approach of the times, so spaces designed in 1956 are not likely to fit perfectly with students in 2006.

Many of today's learners favor active, participatory, experiential learning—the learning style they exhibit in their personal lives. But their behavior may not match their self-expressed learning preferences when sitting in a large lecture hall with chairs bolted to the floor. The single focal point at the front of the room sends a strong signal about how learning will occur. A central theme of this e-book is how to reconceptualize learning spaces to facilitate active, social, and experiential learning.

Students are also highly social, connecting with friends, family, and faculty face-to-face and online. They say they find great value in being with other people and want their college experience to promote those connections. Yet the way they establish and maintain their personal and professional networks may be anything but traditional. Facebook.com, instant messaging, and cell-phone photos coexist with conversations over coffee.

To most faculty and administrators, students appear to have no fear of technology. Mobile phones, digital cameras, and MP3 players constitute today's backpack. Browsing, downloading, and messaging happen anywhere and anytime.

Another characteristic of students has an impact on space: time constraints. The majority of today's students work part time (often 30 or more hours per week), commute, and have outside responsibilities. Even traditional-age, residential students exhibit the most common student characteristic: lack of time. With student attention pulled in multiple directions, how can learning spaces bring students and faculty together, ensuring that the environment promotes, rather than constrains, learning?

Information technology has changed what we do and how we do it. It would be hard to identify a discipline in which IT is not a necessity. Collecting, analyzing, displaying, and disseminating knowledge typically involves IT. Retrieving information has become an IT function; students consider the Internet, not the library, their information universe. And, rather than trying to know everything, students and faculty rely on networks of peers and databases of information. What impact, if any, should this have on learning space design?

Technology has also brought unique capabilities to learning. Whether by stimulating more interaction through the use of personal response systems or by videoconferencing with international experts, IT has altered learning spaces.

What we know about how people learn has also changed our ideas about learning space. There is value from bumping into someone and having a casual conversation. There is value from hands-on, active learning as well as from discussion and reflection. There is value in being able to receive immediate support when needed and from being able to integrate multiple activities (such as writing, searching, and computing) to complete a project. And, there is value from learning that occurs in authentic settings, such as an estuary or on a trading floor. How do we turn the entire campus—and many places off campus—into an integrated learning environment?

As we have come to understand more about learners, how people learn, and technology, our notions of effective learning spaces have changed. Increasingly, those spaces are flexible and networked, bringing together formal and informal activities in a seamless environment that acknowledges that learning can occur anyplace, at any time, in either physical or virtual spaces. We have also come to understand that design is a process, not a product. Involving all stakeholders—particularly learners—is essential.

This e-book represents an ongoing exploration. We know that space can have a significant impact on teaching and learning. Exactly how we bring together space, technology, and pedagogy will continue to evolve. I hope you will find this exploration of learning spaces helpful as you and your institution work to ensure learner success.

Acknowledgments
I'd like to thank this e-book's authors for their insightful contributions. I'd also like to thank Cyprien Lomas and Chris Johnson for their help identifying many of the cases that make this collection so valuable.

Endnote
1. Joint Information Systems Committee (JISC), *Designing Space for Effective Learning: A Guide to 21st Century Learning Space Design*, p. 30, <http://www.jisc.ac.uk/uploaded_documents/JISClearningspaces.pdf>.

About the Author
Diana G. Oblinger is a vice president at EDUCAUSE, where she directs the EDUCAUSE Learning Initiative (ELI). Previously Oblinger served as the vice president for information resources and the chief information officer for the 16-campus University of North Carolina system and as a senior fellow for the EDUCAUSE Center for Applied Research (ECAR). Prior to that she was the executive director of higher education for Microsoft Corporation and led the Institute for Academic Technology for IBM. Oblinger was on the faculty at Michigan State University and the University of Missouri–Columbia, where

she also served as an academic dean. Oblinger has authored and edited numerous books and publications, including the award-winning *What Business Wants from Higher Education* and the first EDUCAUSE e-book, *Educating the Net Generation*, with James L. Oblinger.

CHAPTER 2

Challenging Traditional Assumptions and Rethinking Learning Spaces

Nancy Van Note Chism

Indiana University-Purdue University Indianapolis and Indiana University

▶ A student relaxing in the grass with a laptop
▶ Several hundred students listening in a lecture hall
▶ Students working together at an outdoor table
▶ A student studying in his residence hall lounge
▶ A student reading a book in a window well
▶ A group of students mixing solutions in a laboratory

These learning scenarios occur whether we arrange the spaces or not. We can facilitate deeper and richer learning when we design spaces with learning in mind.

Learning takes place everywhere on a college campus. In fact, learning arguably happens everywhere—on city sidewalks, in airplanes, in restaurants, in bookstores, and on playgrounds. Human beings—wherever they are—have the capacity to learn through their experiences and reflections.

Institutions of higher education are charged with fostering specific kinds of learning: higher-order thinking abilities, communication skills, and knowledge of the ways of disciplinary experts, to name a few. Educators must create structures that support this learning. Space can have a powerful impact on learning; we cannot overlook space in our attempts to accomplish our goals.

Torin Monahan used the term "built pedagogy" to refer to "architectural embodiments of educational philosophies." In other words, the ways in which a space is designed shape the learning that happens in that space.[1] Examples surround us. A room with rows of tablet arm chairs facing an instructor's desk in front of chalkboards conveys the pedagogical approach "I talk or demonstrate; you listen or observe." A room of square tables with a chair on each side conveys the importance of teamwork and interaction to learning. (See Figures 1 and 2.)

Figure 1. Traditional Class

Figure 2. Remodeled Class

Strange and Banning[2] asserted that "although features of the physical environment lend themselves theoretically to all possibilities, the layout, location, and arrangement of space and facilities render some behaviors much more likely, and thus more probable, than others." Because we habitually take space arrangements for granted, we often fail to notice the ways in which space constrains or enhances what we intend to accomplish. Chism and Bickford[3] listed a number of typical assumptions:

▶ Learning only happens in classrooms.
▶ Learning only happens at fixed times.
▶ Learning is an individual activity.
▶ What happens in classrooms is pretty much the same from class to class and day to day.
▶ A classroom always has a front.
▶ Learning demands privacy and the removal of distractions.
▶ Flexibility can be enhanced by filling rooms with as many chairs as will fit.
▶ Higher education students are juvenile:
  ▷ They will destroy or steal expensive furnishings.
  ▷ They need to be confined to tablet arm chairs to feel like students.
  ▷ They are all small, young, nimble, and without disabilities.
▶ Amplification is necessary in large rooms only to make the instructor or technology audible.

Changing Our Assumptions

Why challenge these assumptions? Because of

▶ literature on the influence of physical space on human activity,

▶ cognitive theory, and

▶ descriptions of the new student demographics.

Space and Activity

The influence of physical space on human activity has been studied from both psychological and physical perspectives. The field of environmental psychology explores such topics as place attachment, psychological comfort with space, and the motivational and inspirational effects of space. Those who study space from a physical viewpoint are interested in the effects on activity of light, temperature, and physical closeness. From the literature applied to learning spaces in higher education, we can extrapolate some general patterns.

Strange and Banning[4] emphasized the ways in which the physical aspects of a campus convey nonverbal messages—welcoming or discouraging, valuing or disrespecting—even more powerfully than verbal messages. They cited research that links the physical attractiveness and lighting of a space to the motivation and task performance of those in the space. Graetz and Goliber[5] summarized research that links lighting to psychological arousal, overheated spaces to hostility, and density with low student achievement. Scott-Webber[6] reviewed research on how space makes us feel and related it to knowledge creation, communication, and application, arguing that space configurations exert powerful influences on these activities.

Cognitive Theory

Advances in learning theory[7] have clear implications for the ways in which learning most likely takes place. The emphasis today is on active construction of knowledge by the learner. The importance of prior experience, the fitting of knowledge into existing schema or the establishment of new schema, and the active processing of information are all components of this model that emphasize high learner involvement. Environments that provide experience, stimulate the senses, encourage the exchange of information, and offer opportunities for rehearsal, feedback, application, and transfer are most likely to support learning.

Additionally, social constructivists point out that the social setting greatly influences learning. Picture the limitations of the standard classroom or study carrel in terms of these ideas. The decor is sterile and unstimulating; the seating arrangements rarely allow for peer-to-peer exchange; and the technology does not allow individual access to information as needed. Rather, the room supports a transmission theory whose built pedagogy says that one person will "transfer" information to others who will "take it in" at the same rate by focusing on the person at the front of the room.

Moving beyond classrooms to informal learning spaces, the typical unadorned corridors where students pass from class to class and sit on benches looking forward in parallel or sit on the floor outside classroom spaces say something similar: students do not learn until they are in the "learning space" where a teacher presents information. The segmentation of faculty offices from classrooms increases this distance and lack of agency on the part of students and reinforces the transmitter image of the faculty member. Rather than appearing to be a co-learner, the faculty member is set apart. Similarly, computer labs that do not provide for multiple viewers of a monitor or libraries that do not permit talking convey a built pedagogy contrary to the ideas of social constructivism.

Demographics of the Student Population

Descriptions of the characteristics of traditional-age college students provide a rationale for challenging our space use. The entry of large numbers of previously underrepresented students—students from ethnic cultures that stress social interaction, older students, students blending work and learning—also calls for environments in which social interchange and experiential learning are valued. This demographic picture also favors standard adult furniture over juvenile tablet arm desks.

The argument doesn't include just nontraditional students, however. Characterizations of Net Generation students[8] extend similar considerations to current traditional students in reinforcing the need for social space and technology access. Brown[9] listed these implications for space, depicting a different built pedagogy than normally present in higher education. He cited the preference of Net Gen students for:

▶ Small group work spaces
▶ Access to tutors, experts, and faculty in the learning space
▶ Table space for a variety of tools

- Integrated lab facilities
- IT highly integrated into all aspects of learning spaces
- Availability of labs, equipment, and access to primary resources
- Accessible facilities
- Shared screens (either projector or LCD); availability of printing
- Workgroup facilitation

The advent of distance courses has done much to dispel the idea that learning happens only in a classroom, yet the reality of how dated our standing assumptions are continues to unfold. Podcasting of lectures can both extend the lecture hall and make its spatial arrangement far more specialized than normally assumed. As Mitchell[10] pointed out, "If you get wireless reception under a tree, there really isn't any need to be in a classroom." Smaller places for debriefing, project work, discussion, and application of information become paramount. Outdoor spaces, lobby spaces, cafés, and residence halls all need to be considered in terms of how they can support learning.

Intentionally Created Spaces

Spaces that are harmonious with learning theory and the needs of current students reflect several elements:

- **Flexibility.** A group of learners should be able to move from listening to one speaker (traditional lecture or demonstration) to working in groups (team or project-based activities) to working independently (reading, writing, or accessing print or electronic resources). While specialized places for each kind of activity (the lecture hall, laboratory, and library carrel) can accommodate each kind of work, the flow of activities is often immediate. It makes better sense to construct spaces capable of quick reconfiguration to support different kinds of activity—moveable tables and chairs, for example.
- **Comfort.** At a recent town hall meeting on the campus of Indiana University-Purdue University Indianapolis (IUPUI), faculty were startled to hear two of four student panelists confess that they had dropped classes because of uncomfortable chairs in the classrooms. Such testimony takes our normally casual attitude about comfort into the realm of attrition. Campus seating must take into account different body sizes and the long periods of time students must sit without moving. Discomfort makes a compelling distraction to learning. We should also provide surfaces for writing and supporting computers, books, and other materials. The small, sloping surfaces

on most standard tablet arm chairs are inadequate for these purposes. The chairs also presume a standard space for the girths of the occupants and their arm reach.

▶ **Sensory stimulation.** Antiseptic environments consisting of white rectangles with overhead lights and bland tiled floors create a mood for the occupants of these spaces. Human beings yearn for color, natural and task-appropriate lighting, and interesting room shapes. The current generation of students, attuned to home remodeling television shows and examples of stimulating spaces in the coffee shops and clubs they frequent, seem particularly sensitive to ambiance. One study[11] found that the majority of students, male and female, continually rearranged their living spaces to be more attractive. In evaluating a model learning space, they noted the paint colors, carpeting, and lighting without prompting.

▶ **Technology support.** As Oblinger,[12] Oblinger and Oblinger,[13] and Brown[14] pointed out, the current generation of students expects seamless technology use. Their older counterparts and teachers would appreciate the same capability. As technology changes, smaller devices will probably travel with users, who will expect wireless environments, the capacity to network with other devices and display vehicles, and access to power. Rather than cumbersome rack systems and fixed ceiling-mounted projectors, learning spaces of the future will need more flexible plug-and-play capabilities.

▶ **Decenteredness.** Emphasizing the principles of socioconstructivism, spaces must convey co-learning and co-construction of knowledge. Implications for architecture include thinking of the whole campus as a learning space rather than emphasizing classrooms. Within the classroom, it means avoiding the message that the room has a front or a "privileged" space. Outside the classroom, it means providing ubiquitous places for discussion and study. It means that the flow of spaces—from library to faculty or administrative offices to classrooms and the corridors and outdoor passageways in between—must be rethought in terms of learning. Spaces should center on learning, not experts.

Consider the following examples of experiments with spaces centered on learning:

▶ **The studio classroom.** This arrangement introduces flexible furniture arrangements, decenters the room from teacher to student activity, and stresses collaboration. From the early models at Rensselaer Polytechnic Institute to current spaces at North Carolina State University (http://www.ncsu.edu/PER/SCALEUP/Classrooms.html, ch. 29) to current models at the University of Dayton (http://ltc.udayton.edu/faculty/studio.htm, chs. 3, 4, 13) and Stanford University (http://wallenberg.stanford.edu/, ch. 36), such spaces are becoming more common. An example of an extended studio model is the Math Emporium at Virginia Tech (ch. 42). The new auditorium design employed at Iowa State University is another example described in this book (ch. 22).

▶ **Information Commons/Collaboratory.** Increasingly, campus libraries are recognizing the need for study spaces that permit interaction among students. Furniture, computer displays, and space arrangements all support group work. Examples can be found at <http://www.brookdale.cc.nj.us/library/infocommons/ic_home.html>. Examples of information commons arrangements described in this book include those at the University of Georgia, Duke University, Northwestern University, and The Ohio State University.

▶ **Living-learning spaces.** Moving academic work into student residences through scheduling classes or other learning activities within living facilities integrates courses with student life. The ArtStreet project (http://artstreet.udayton.edu/, ch. 13) at the University of Dayton integrates studios, a café, living facilities, and galleries in one complex. New campus residences elsewhere include meeting rooms for classes right in the living facilities.

▶ **Corridor niches.** No longer simply passageways, corridors in some buildings serve as study and meeting space. See the case study in this book on the ES Corridor Project at IUPUI for an example. An additional example in this book is found in the commons spaces near faculty offices and informal study spaces at Hamilton College.

Opportunities and Barriers

Our current learning spaces present several opportunities, as well as substantial barriers. The opportunities include enrollment growth and the competition for students—factors already leading to construction of new facilities with modernized learning spaces, as well as climbing walls. Technology, which allows ubiquitous access to information and learning environments, also enables different uses of physical space. Yet traditional space standards on the books of most colleges and universities direct those planning and constructing new facilities in "old paradigm" ways of thinking. Moreover, faculty who are uninformed of new advances in learning theory or unwilling to make adjustments in their normal approaches pose significant barriers to change. Tight fiscal conditions, especially in public and small private institutions, also constrain what can be done.

Moving Forward

In their recent study of institutions that do exceptionally well in engaging their students, Kuh et al.[15] discovered that the physical environment is an important characteristic of such campuses. One of the main recommendations from their study is that institutions "align the physical environment with institutional priorities and goals for student success." To exploit the potential for physical space to advance learning, conversations about campus priorities must include space as a critical factor affecting learning. The perceived urgency of the conversation changes dramatically when framed in terms of learning impact rather than student comfort or preference.

Helping the campus community understand how spatial arrangements preclude or support retention, graduation, pedagogical innovation, and a host of campus priorities is an essential first step. From governing boards and legislatures (in the case of public institutions) to central administration, facilities planners, maintenance operations, faculty, and students, all must realize that good space is not a luxury but a key determinant of good learning environments.

Understanding then must lead to advocacy on a number of issues:

▶ Changing antiquated space standards and decision-making processes
▶ Dispelling long-held assumptions about students and space ("I learned in hard chairs in the heat, and they can too," "Students will steal anything not nailed down," "Students will ruin anything upholstered or carpeted with their carelessness," "Windows distract students from paying attention")
▶ Putting learning considerations at the heart of space-planning conversations
▶ Arguing for resources for space renovation and construction

The cultural change required in thinking of space in a new way should not be underestimated. We need to ask such basic questions as "Should rooms have a front and a back?" "Should faculty offices be separate from classroom facilities?" "Should food and talking be allowed in the library?" As Scott-Webber[16] pointed out, our sense of space is one of the most primal of human instincts. Deeply engrained attitudes about space in colleges and universities mean it will take patience and persistence to make changes, particularly more radical ones.

We also need to rethink the finances of space. Many public campuses, for example, have no base funding allocations for furniture replacement. Furniture is generally funded with the construction of a new building or when major renovations take place, but routine replacement of furniture and updating of lighting and decor depend on the chance administrator with a little end-of-the-year cash. It is not unusual to see 40-year-old chairs in classroom buildings. In addition, universities often have no designated funding source for informal learning spaces. On most campuses, it is not clear who has authority for these spaces, especially hallways or lobbies—which most people do not think of as learning spaces anyway.

Fortunately, physical space is one aspect of campus need that lends itself to collaboration with donors. While naming physical spaces has long been a standard practice of campus development units, enlisting community partners in the design and construction of learning spaces, even renovated spaces, is one way to approach the frequent lack of funding. An example is the Education–Social Work Corridor project at IUPUI (see the case study in this book), constructed with donations from nearly 30 businesses in Indianapolis. Furniture manufacturers also increasingly show interest in fostering innovation. The partnership of Herman Miller and Estrella Mountain Community College in Phoenix offers another example of how to create good spaces through partnerships (see the case study in this book).

Finally, we need more research on the impact of existing and experimental spaces on learning. We need basic research on the influence of the physical environment on creativity, attention, and critical thinking. We need applied research on the effect of different kinds of lighting and furniture on comfort, satisfaction, and interaction. We need to study carefully the model environments we have created to determine how they influence students and faculty so that we can construct future ones in ways most likely to foster our goals. Fortunately, this research is growing in volume and quality. Professional associations and furniture manufacturers, architects, and academic scholars all are making contributions to what will hopefully become an important body of literature.

Hope for the Future

If campuses exist to foster specific kinds of learning, they should inspire and foster this work physically as well as intellectually. Choosing chairs should receive the same kind of attention to learning as choosing textbooks; decisions on building layouts should be made with the same focus on learning as developing curricula. In short, a campus should proclaim that it is a location designed to support a community of scholars. It should say this physically—from the inscriptions on its buildings to the spaces for study and reflection created by its landscaping, from the placement of furniture for team work and intellectual discourse to the way in which light is used to support energy and creativity. No longer can we assume that any old furniture and any old room arrangement will do—we know better. Like all academicians, we should ensure that current knowledge informs practice.

Endnotes

1. Torin Monahan, "Flexible Space and Built Pedagogy: Emerging IT Embodiments," *Inventio*, vol. 4, no. 1 (2002), <http://www.doit.gmu.edu/inventio/past/display_past .asp?pID=spring02&sID=monahan>.

2. C. Carney Strange and James H. Banning, *Educating by Design: Creating Campus Learning Environments That Work* (San Francisco: Jossey-Bass, 2002), p. 15.

3. Nancy Van Note Chism and Deborah J. Bickford, eds., *The Importance of Physical Space in Creating Supportive Learning Environments: New Directions in Teaching and Learning*, no. 92 (Winter 2002) (San Francisco: Jossey-Bass, 2003), <http://www .josseybass.com/WileyCDA/WileyTitle/productCd-0787963445.html>.

4. Strange and Banning, op. cit.

5. Ken A. Graetz and Michael J. Goliber, "Designing Collaborative Learning Places: Psychological Foundations and New Frontiers," in *The Importance of Physical Space in Creating Supportive Learning Environments: New Directions in Teaching and Learning*, Nancy Van Note Chism and Deborah J. Bickford, eds., no. 92 (Winter 2002) (San Francisco: Jossey-Bass, 2003), pp. 13–22, <http://www.josseybass.com/WileyCDA/WileyTitle/ productCd-0787963445.html>.

6. Lennie Scott-Webber, *In Sync: Environment Behavior Research and the Design of Learning Spaces* (Ann Arbor, Mich.: Society for College and University Planning, 2004).

7. John D. Bransford, Ann L. Brown, and Rodney R. Cocking, eds., *How People Learn: Brain, Mind, Experience, and School* (Washington, D.C.: National Academies Press, 1999), <http://www.nap.edu/html/howpeople1/>; and Marilla D. Svinicki, *Learning and Motivation in the Postsecondary Classroom* (Bolton, Mass.: Anker Publishing, 2004).

8. Diana G. Oblinger, "Boomers, Gen-Xers, and Millennials: Understanding the 'New Students,'" *EDUCAUSE Review*, vol. 38, no. 4 (July/August 2003), pp. 37–47, <http:// www.educause.edu/ir/library/pdf/erm0342.pdf>.

9. Malcolm Brown, "Learning Spaces," in *Educating the Net Generation*, Diana G. Oblinger and James L. Oblinger, eds. (Boulder, Colo.: EDUCAUSE, 2005), <http://www.educause.edu/LearningSpaces/6072>.

10. "Designing the Space: A Conversation with William M. Mitchell," *Syllabus*, September 1, 2003, <http://www.campustechnology.com/article.asp?id=8105>.

11. Chism, Coles, and Associates, *ES Informal Learning Spaces: A Study of Use*, June 2, 2005, PowerPoint presentation, <http://www.opd.iupui.edu/uploads/library/APPD/APPD8980.ppt>.

12. Oblinger, op. cit.

13. Diana G. Oblinger and James L. Oblinger, eds., *Educating the Net Generation* (Boulder, Colo.: EDUCAUSE, 2005), <http.//www.educause.edu/educatingthenetgen>.

14. Brown, op. cit.

15. George D. Kuh et al., *Student Success in College: Creating Conditions That Matter* (San Francisco: Jossey-Bass 2005), p. 314.

16. Scott-Webber, op. cit.

About the Author

Nancy Van Note Chism is the associate vice chancellor for academic affairs and associate dean of the faculties at Indiana University-Purdue University Indianapolis, as well as a professor of higher education at Indiana University. She is a past president of the Professional and Organizational Development Network in Higher Education and was previously the director of Faculty and Teaching Assistant Development at The Ohio State University. She has written about learning spaces in *The Importance of Physical Space in Creating Supportive Learning Environments* and coedited the volume with Deborah J. Bickford for Jossey-Bass (2003).

CHAPTER 3

Seriously Cool Places: The Future of Learning-Centered Built Environments

William Dittoe
Educational Facilities Consultants, LLC

"Whoa, dude, this is a seriously cool place!" With that remark we knew we were on to something special. But what? The comment came from a young man upon his entry into the Studio, a prototype learning environment embedded within the newly opened Ryan C. Harris Learning Teaching Center (LTC) at the University of Dayton in Ohio. While the United States has numerous learning centers, many were created to help faculty teach with technology. The University of Dayton's LTC is different; it combines several functions traditionally disconnected and scattered throughout campus in order to promote collaboration or "to practice what we preach." Offices placed in close proximity surround communal spaces to encourage collaboration. The Studio, a café called the Blend, and large furniture-filled pathways provide opportunities to gather, discuss, and continue learning.

Many important lessons came from simple observation of the daily occurrences at the LTC. Faculty and students seemed to act differently in the Studio. They exhibited a new freedom to be creative and more actively engaged and to continue the learning process as activities flowed into other parts of the complex. These observations, many of them serendipitous, allowed new insight into the attributes of flexible, fluid space. The Studio provided opportunities to discover concepts of educational connections and links later used to develop learning space prototypes in a new residence hall.

The provost's office, in its continuing quest for academic excellence, quickly recognized an opportunity to continue its exploration of prototype spaces. The second floor of a new residence hall was set aside for additional classrooms. It became a test bed for an educational model involving intense student-faculty interaction, interdisciplinary teaching, and redefined "seat time." A new space

©2006 William Dittoe

2

model combined the studio concept with other teaming, seminar, and assembly areas. Pathways—spaces that normally function as hallways—were expanded to support continued learning opportunities, promote impromptu gatherings, and provide individual places for quiet reflection (see Figure 1). Faculty offices immersed in the complex encourage further interaction. The entire complex serves as a model for engagement and interaction, team teaching, and interdisciplinary themes. The assessment now under way is providing valuable information linking learning and the built environment.

The first user of the Marianist Hall Learning Space was an innovative interdisciplinary program at the University of Dayton called Core. First year students take two tightly integrated courses in a 12-credit-hour sequence that integrates history, philosophy, and religious studies chronologically and thematically along with selections from literature and the visual and performing arts. English composition uses materials from all of the disciplines in honing the students' writing skills.

Second year students choose one of three social science courses and one course in either philosophy or religious studies. They also take one arts studies course. These three courses build on what the students learned in the first-year courses, focusing on contemporary issues.

We are learning that space, properly conceived and built, is essential to learning. Just how is the Marianist Hall Learning Space used? A story told through a user's eyes might give some insight into just how students and faculty interact.

Figure 1. Example of a Collaboration-Friendly Pathway

Marcy

"Ummmff." Marcy groaned and hit the snooze button one more time. She then pulled the pillow over her head and wished she were home. Finally, she roused herself, reluctantly slipped into her bunny slippers, and pulled on a warm University of Dayton sweatshirt. After a quick brush of hair and teeth, and with eyes only half open, she made her way to the small café in her residence hall, clutching a notebook and laptop computer.

"Hey, Sam…Hey, Carol." She worked her way past new friends and grabbed some much needed caffeine. Marcy made a slight face at the first sip. "Not Starbuck's, but okay." She trudged up the steps, laptop and notebook balanced with her coffee cup and bunny slippers flopping, to begin her first day in Core.

She paused at the top of the stairs and glanced at a small greeting sign, *Welcome to Marianist Hall Learning Space.* Then she looked ahead and realized this was something different. No tight and congested hallways. No classrooms lined up like a series of bland boxes and crammed with tablet arm chairs. She blinked and tried to understand what she was supposed to do. The complex stretched ahead with pockets of intriguing spaces running off this direction and that—leading to where? she wondered. Her eye followed the sinuous curve of the ceiling to a far point that ended in a deep-brown wall. Comfortable looking chairs and sofas grouped around coffee tables invited her to sit for a while with her steaming coffee. The small table lamps cast a welcoming glow, more homelike than institutional. "I'll need to come here to study," she thought, making a mental note of the tables available to spread out books and the access to wireless. Marker boards were everywhere, and a quick glance showed a wide variety of projectors, speakers, and other forms of technology (see Figure 2). Maybe she could even meet with her study group here. And look at all the busy people! She recognized Professor Cummings, a member of her welcoming committee, talking with a group of students, some of whom she already knew.

"Hi, Marcy," said the professor, then turned and saw Sara. "Hey, girl! You're going to be an English major. What are you doing with us history geeks?" George shuffled up to join them. His disheveled hair seemed a natural extension of his odd mixture of clothes. He also wore a perpetual look of bewilderment that successfully masked his quick mind. "Well, the philosophy guru has arrived," said Sara. George bowed graciously. "Morning, ladies." They then pulled up some of the rolling soft seats and chatted about what the first day might hold.

Figure 2. Marker Boards, Wireless Access, and Technology

Later that week Marcy was in her residence hall living area with her roommates sharing war stories about their first adventures in college life.

"How did your day go, Tom?" He was not in the Core program but enrolled in the typical humanities program that held classes throughout campus. Tom frowned and shrugged. "It was, like, forever. Had history, English, and psych all the same day. That's 150 minutes of just sitting and listening to people talk at you. We did get to discuss things for a bit, but I mean, like, over two hours of just sitting in a chair!"

"Sounds like high school, man," chimed in Bruce. As others wandered in, Marcy mulled this over and thought of her day. She actually had gone early to study. Since her Core companions seemed to have a similar idea and also arrived a bit early, she met with her group. After a quick glance at her watch, she hurried downstairs and got a latté from the café, thus beginning her day. She, like Tom, had English, philosophy, and smatterings of history. She also had a bit of art and literature mixed in that day. But, she thought, this was apparently different from other students. How? she wondered. She found out over the next few weeks—and the difference was remarkable.

A few weeks later Marcy felt at home with her fellow students, her professors, and especially the place. The students had quickly assumed ownership of the space. They policed each other and felt free to move furniture and arrange the area as it best served the immediate purpose. There were no squabbles about who was responsible for what. Marcy and her friends—and she found that she included many of the faculty as friends—were not only learning, they actually enjoyed each day.

Professors Donna Gray and Renaldo Garcia were in the studios quite early, reminiscing. A year ago, during the first few days of trying out the new learning space, they had pondered a bit and then had come up with an idea. "Let's just switch rooms!" they had exclaimed at the same time. They would never have been able to do this in a conventionally scheduled array of classrooms. Donna needed Studio 117 that day as it had four plasma screens, one on each wall. Ron's class was going to do some research on the Web and then compare findings on the whiteboards (see Figure 3). Since then, changing rooms had become part of their daily routine, as it had for many other faculty. Now they freely traded spaces and often teamed up by having impromptu classes together.

Today Donna made a quick switch with Ron, walked into Studio 117, now dubbed "The Sports Bar" by students with too much time on their hands. She punched in her password, detached the wall-mounted remote control, and put in her CD. She then fired up the electronics and smiled. "What till they get a load of this!" she thought.

That day was memorable to Marcy and her companions—and was becoming typical. She was encouraged to think, explore, create. It began as other days; get up early and get a latté from the café. She would worry about her diet later, she

Figure 3. Whiteboards in a Studio Setting

thought. She then went to the learning space, as she found it a quiet place to organize her day. "Am I actually forming good habits?" she wondered. She smiled. If so, she hoped the latté would neutralize it. Her friends slowly trickled in; by 7:30 a.m. most of her group had arrived. Funny, she mused, the other students, those attending "real" classes in typical classrooms across campus, didn't seem to arrive early. She shrugged and greeted her friends—or her community of learners, as her professors called them. Intriguing, she thought, that her professors also stressed that they were part of this community. Are they still learning also?

Today was a bit different. She started with Dr. Gray's lecture on Islam and Mohammed. The professor normally didn't lecture, but today she had prepared a series of photos, film clips, and cuts to Web sites that sprang up on the plasma screens. The 24 students sat in a circle, swiveling around as the scenes rotated with action (see Figure 4). Within 20 minutes they had been through a condensed history of Islam, its fundamental beliefs, and its prophets. The presentation also incorporated cuts from CNN, the History Channel, and various newspapers. The surround sound heightened the effect. Even though Professor Gray occasionally said "whoops" and corrected small glitches, the overall effect was powerful. The professor then further softened the lighting and asked the students to reflect quietly on what they had just experienced.

During this time a presentation in the adjoining studio focused on the history of Christianity. Professor Garcia used twin projectors simultaneously and occasionally

Figure 4. Plasma Screens in a Studio Setting

highlighted the talk with points written on the large, writable wall surface. The sun crept in through the window, muted by the shades, and fell across the tabletops. The low up-lighting in the room provided a rich environment to experience some 2,000 years of history. The professor then called his students to reflect on the presentation.

In the Commons, a multiuse space at the far end, visiting sociology professor Cindy Metzger was speaking with the third Core cohort about Buddhism. After her presentation, strengthened by visual images, she had her group sit and try to meditate.

Twenty minutes later the entire learning space had become a hub of intense activity. Each of the cohorts of about 25 had dispersed in groups of four or five to prepare for an afternoon debate on the topic "Does religion or spirituality bring peace to the world—or the opposite?" Some of the students elected to stay in the studios and use the resources there: wall and portable marker boards, projection equipment, and access to the Web. A few groups snuggled into the table booths within a secluded area. Some pulled the flexible seating together and used both laptops and portable marker boards. (See Figure 5.) Coffee runs were frequent, and an occasional pizza materialized. At 2:00 p.m. the professors called a 10-minute break while the Commons was rearranged to hold the "Great and Profound, Earthshaking Event," as someone had scrawled on one of the marker boards. Three of the students had disappeared into their rooms and returned wearing

Figure 5. Class Collaboration in a Common Area

improvised robes to further enhance the general ambiance. The rest of the day the student presentations were imaginative, provocative, and at times a bit silly. Some had brought in compelling information from various digital resources. The student presentations used the available technology. There were no winners—just a great amount of learning.

That evening after dinner, the students—and the faculty—were exhausted. Nonetheless, they returned to the Commons at 7:00 p.m. to attend a guest lecture. The topic, by mere coincidence, was "Religion: a path for world peace—or otherwise."

Two days later Marcy was pondering some of the issues brought up by the debate and other recent discussions. "I just don't get this one point," she thought. "It's got to be the foundation for what Dr. Garcia was explaining about the Gnostic philosophy, so I'd better get it. This concept seems to be extended even into our current times." She then remembered the information her group had pulled up on the Internet. They had accessed the Web during a break as they huddled together in the pathway. "Cool!" George had exclaimed as he tapped into a science fiction film site. Marcy had gotten up and crossed over to the faculty offices a few feet away. Ron Garcia had been talking with one of his colleagues.

"Pardon me, professor, but could you...?" Moments later Marcy, Professor Garcia, and Dr. Schramm were sitting in the alcove sofas and drew a crowd. Forty-five minutes later Marcy understood the concept and also had some new horizons opened about the connections between early church history and contemporary philosophy. More connections were made the next evening as they sat in the Commons to watch an obscure but important movie by a Mexican filmmaker from the 1960s. "Why was Mexico so antireligion for a while?" Marcy wondered. This led to her exploring the topic on her own. This, in turn, brought a developing interest in Latin American history and culture. She eventually ended up taking a minor in Spanish to go with her marketing degree.

Toward the end of the semester Marcy stretched and shuffled down the hall to start her day in the learning space. She nodded to some of her friends going off to what she now considered to be drudgery courses in history, English, and other subjects given at traditional areas of the campus. Stopping at the entry, latté in hand, she looked again at the inviting area filled with the soft sounds of conversation. She smiled and thought, "I'm sure glad I don't have to go to class today."

The Learner-Centered Difference

The story of Marcy and her companions, although fictional, is based on reports, observations, and assessments under way at the Marianist Hall Learning Space at the University of Dayton. Many of the observations correlate with the writings of teaching and learning scholars. We are just beginning to understand how important physical space is to learning and how radically different true learning-centered campuses will look in the future. The question is, just how will they be different?

In the story, Marcy, her friends, and the faculty used the space in new and different ways to achieve student success. George Kuh et al. contended that the two most important influences on student learning are interacting with faculty, staff, and peers in educationally purposeful ways and having a high degree of effort directed toward academic tasks.[1] Vincent Tinto stressed the importance of learning extending beyond the classroom into corridors and walkways.[2] Tinto and others contended that students are more likely to succeed in settings that assess skills, monitor progress, and provide feedback. Numerous educators stress the importance of students' social involvement and the social context of learning. Faculty are encouraged to become more engaged because they "influence the quality of students' experiences through their interaction inside and outside the classroom."[3] Marcy and her colleagues experienced these teaching and learning opportunities more frequently and far more productively than would have occurred within the traditional credit-hour course offerings held in traditional classrooms.

The key, therefore, is to provide a physical space that supports multidisciplinary, team-taught, highly interactive learning unbound by traditional time constraints within a social setting that engages students and faculty and enables rich learning experiences. This space will be far different from the traditional classroom and, while many significant designs contain parts of the solution, few examples of the envisioned pedagogical model exist. To provide the proper space for teaching and learning, we need more than a single place—educational activities are organic; they ebb and flow. (See Figure 6.) What we really require is a complex of spaces—interconnected and related spaces designed to support learning. These spaces will be flexible and functional and pay greater attention to aesthetics than traditional 20th-century classrooms. This design concept extends beyond the places normally designated as "academic" such that the entire campus can become a learning space. These principles guided the design of the Marianist Hall Learning Space at the University of Dayton.

Figure 6. Flexible Teaching and Learning Opportunities

We are still in the embryonic stages of exploring design concepts that will ultimately shape the campuses of the future. While there are no real experts yet, many dedicated people are exploring ways to continually improve teaching and learning, assisted by talented and creative architects and planners in the design of spaces that support their visions. Students continuously challenge and motivate institutions' focus on learning excellence. The transformation of learning spaces holds immense challenges and presents opportunities not yet imagined. Our understanding of how students learn will continue to evolve, and the design of space will, at times, struggle to keep up. At other times, creative space will lead and challenge its users to break free of traditional restraints. We may never find the ideal learning space; the adventure is in trying to get there.

Endnotes

1. George D. Kuh et al., *Student Success in College: Creating Conditions That Matter* (San Francisco: Jossey-Bass, 2005).

2. Vincent Tinto, "Taking Student Learning Seriously: Rethinking the University of the Future," in *Charting the Course: Earl V. Pullias Lecture Series on the Future of Higher Education*, 26th Annual, Fall 2003, (Los Angeles: Center for Higher Education Policy Analysis, USC Rossier School of Education), <http://www.usc.edu/dept/chepa/documents/pullias/2003PulliasBooklet.pdf>.

3. George Kuh, "Improving the College Experience: Using Effective Educational Practice," *NSSE Viewpoint* (November 2001), <http://nsse.iub.edu/pdf/viewpoint.pdf>.

About the Author

William Dittoe is a member in Educational Facilities Consultants, LLC, a firm specializing in planning built environments that support the mission of learning-centered institutions. Dittoe has been involved with the design of educational spaces for more than 40 years, with expertise in campus planning, classrooms, residence halls, and recreational and sports centers. For the past 10 years he has assisted learning-centered institutions in the design of learning environment prototypes. He regularly conducts institutional workshops and has given numerous presentations at regional and national conferences. His topics include the fundamental shifts in student expectations, campus culture, and pedagogy and their significant impact on facilities.

CHAPTER 4

Community: The Hidden Context for Learning

Deborah J. Bickford and David J. Wright
University of Dayton

This chapter focuses on a powerful context for learning: community. Community catalyzes deep learning and should be a critical consideration when planning physical and virtual learning spaces. In higher education, however, specialization has a long and comfortable history—in the way our disciplines are partitioned and also in the way our institutions are organized. Tradition encouraged specialists to attend to their individual areas: faculty developed pedagogy and curriculum; information technologists made decisions about technology; and facilities managers designed and developed classrooms and other spaces. As Boyer and Mitgang[1] see it, "Too often, the academic and professional worlds are marked by vocationalism, the fragmentation of knowledge, and territoriality." While such specialization has led to some innovations, we have fallen short of the full power and potential of aligning our efforts in pursuit of learning. More than a decade ago, Boyatzis, Cowen, and Kolb[2] reflected on this less than ideal condition of higher education:

> Why we conduct education as we do is a puzzling question. How to do it better is a big challenge. For us, the idea that learning should be the primary purpose of education has been a beacon—we might all agree that learning is a purpose of education—but is it the primary purpose?

The importance of community to learning is implied but rarely stated as a significant context in higher education. Were community not important for learning, colleges and universities would have little reason to exist—people could learn efficiently by reading and interacting with tutors. Research on learning theory, how the brain works, collaborative learning, and student engagement has taught us that people learn best in community.[3] Fostering community is critical to learning, regardless of whether an institution is primarily online, commuter, or residential. We answer Boyatzis, Cowen, and Kolb's challenge of finding ways to conduct education better by suggesting a focus on community and community building and by seeking ways in which community can enhance learning through three strategic levers:

▶ Improving the process of developing learning spaces
▶ Using information technology to enhance communication and collaboration
▶ Using community to improve pedagogical, curricular, and cocurricular environments

Why Community?

Although learning involves individual behavioral changes, the context in which those changes occur is a social environment involving many people. All aspects of education—including the planning of space design—should acknowledge community. Just as a learning paradigm focuses on the importance of learning, we argue for a community paradigm that emphasizes the role social interactions play in facilitating learning and improving student engagement. through community, learning can grow. Given that physical and virtual learning spaces play critical roles in enabling or deterring community,[4] it is essential that educators reevaluate the role of virtual and physical space as a way to improve student (as well as faculty and staff) learning and engagement in community.

Defining Community

The term *community* here refers to the social context of students and their environs. A community is a group of people with a common purpose, shared values, and agreement on goals. It has powerful qualities that shape learning. A community has the power to motivate its members to exceptional performance. M. Scott Peck[5] defined community as "a group whose members have made a commitment to communicating with one another on an ever more deep and authentic level." It can set standards of expectation for the individual and provide the climate in which great things happen.[6] These qualities characterize what Kuh and colleagues[7] described as conditions that matter for student success in college. Higher education is replete with descriptions of communities—research communities, learning communities, communities of practice—in fact, the entire enterprise can be viewed as a community.[8] A real community, however, exists only when its members interact in a meaningful way that deepens their understanding of each other and leads to learning. Many equate learning with the acquisition of facts and skills by students; in a community, the learners—including faculty—are enriched by collective meaning-making, mentorship, encouragement, and an understanding of the perspectives and unique qualities of an increasingly diverse membership.

Why Care?

Society should care about learning in community for two primary reasons. First, learning is a social process that works best in a community setting, thus yielding the best use of societal resources. According to Peter Ewell,[9] evidence documenting the importance of community in learning is "overwhelmingly positive, with instances of effective practice ranging from within-class study groups to cross-curricular learning communities." Despite multiple theories about how people learn, they agree on one point: the critical role of interaction. In particular, social cognitive learning theory argues for a rich environment in which students and faculty share meaningful experiences that go beyond the one-way information flow characteristic of typical lectures in traditional classrooms.[10] Second, learning in community will have an important role in preparing students for their work-life to come. College graduates must succeed in professional environments that require interactions with other people. Some companies today call for graduates with different perspectives to collaborate across traditional disciplinary and business lines.[11] Indeed, because of the volume and volatility of information today, as well as the proliferation of information-sharing mechanisms,[12] knowledge may be seen as vested in a distributed network across communities of practice, not in individuals.[13] In other words, community-centered education will help prepare graduates to live and work in a world that requires greater collaboration.

Diminished Learning in Community

Community has always been a purported cornerstone of higher education.[14] Historically, higher education in Western civilization occurred at community-centered institutions. Early universities and colleges were private, residential, and almost exclusively connected to a religious founding organization.[15] Civic engagement was cultivated.

As large public institutions have expanded to accommodate federal- and state-mandated support of larger enrollments, efficiency has become more important in structuring processes, leading to larger class sizes. Some describe this as production-oriented education, with colleges and universities operating like manufacturing firms with students as throughput and graduates as the products.[16] Universities' fixed costs from the high proportion of labor result in the cost of attending college rising faster than inflation. This creates pressures for cost-cutting, for example, by increasing class sizes.

Additional factors have exacerbated the loss of community. Increasing demands on faculty for research productivity outside the classroom,[17] increasing numbers of commuter students, and an increasingly secularized society have contributed to the erosion of the social interactivity that characterized the earlier, English system based model of higher education. During the mid-20th century, as classrooms became larger, the level of social interaction diminished within the classroom, with the student role becoming increasingly one of a scribe. The sense of community within higher education has become increasingly obscured, with negative consequences for both faculty and students. Eugene Rice reported the negative impact on young faculty of diminishing community,[18] and Gerald Graff pointed out that the lack of interactivity diminishes students' expectations for their educational experience.[19] It also contributes to a tension between a "student culture" and an "academic culture," according to Arthur Levine.[20] Some commentators have observed an unspoken pact—faculty don't expect much of students so that they can concentrate on the growing demands of research, and students don't demand rigorous instruction so that they can concentrate on their social lives.

Whether due to the absence of deep engagement between students and faculty or to their desire for peer interaction, students have begun to develop student-centered communities with their peers.[21] While this trend satisfies the need for community, this interaction often lacks academic learning as the focal point. With the rise of information technologies, including cell phones and instant messaging, students communicate with each other to an unprecedented degree,[22] but this networked generation is only part of a community.

Today an increasingly connected student body devotes less and less time to structured, instruction-driven learning. It is therefore appropriate to reevaluate the role of community as a way to improve student, faculty, and staff engagement and learning. We believe we can rebuild community, thereby strengthening learning through

▶ learning space design,
▶ information technology, and
▶ pedagogical, curricular, and cocurricular design for learning.

Community as a Context for Learning

For several decades we have been creating spaces that promote mass production of classroom instruction predicated on a model in which education involves transferring information. Using the same model to develop learning spaces perpetuates that outcome. As Albert Einstein once suggested, the definition of insanity is doing the same thing over and over again and expecting a different result. We need to explore how building community enables the creation of spaces for learning (and conversely, how creating learning-centered spaces can enhance our ability to build community); how technology can foster community and information exchange; and how community in pedagogical, curricular, and cocurricular design fosters learning.

Spaces for Learning in Community

It is a new era; we need new "places that foster connections rather than compartmentalization."[23] For several reasons, we need a community of faculty, administrators, facilities managers, architects, students, student development professionals, technologists, and other stakeholders to participate in a process of dialogue and discovery, creating spaces to reengage faculty and students in the pursuit of learning. The complexity of projects defies the ability of one perspective to capture the necessary requirements and contingencies involved. No one group has enough information to make informed decisions—team learning is needed.[24] Renovating current infrastructure and building anew happen infrequently, and the results are expected to endure for a very long time, so it is important to increase the chances of getting it right. In addition, the investment is substantial. More subtle reasons trump these arguments, however:

▶ First, organizational silos result in a lack of awareness and acceptance of the interconnectedness of roles on campus. We cannot design effective spaces for learning unless we recognize that many stakeholders hold a valuable piece of the puzzle—their input is essential.

▶ Second, given how infrequent and expensive projects can be, we need to learn from each successive project, even though the players will likely change. Community learning can foster organizational learning and the ability to continually improve, based on input and assessment from past projects.

▶ Finally, and perhaps most strongly, major paradigmatic change in higher education alters our needs in far-ranging ways. Standard operating procedures are no longer effective—we need to learn anew and from each other. Barr and Tagg's influential 1995 *Change* article[25] suggested the impact of paradigm shift on all dimensions of campus life:

> Roles under the learning paradigm, then, begin to blur. Architects of campus buildings and payroll clerks alike will contribute to and shape the environments that empower student learning.

The learning paradigm invites us to realize that all space is learning space, and community involvement is essential to its creation. How, then, do we engage community in co-creating the built environment? We offer five steps to harness the full potential of community:

▶ Invite stakeholders to participate.
▶ Select and empower a talented leader.
▶ Understand and appreciate differences in perspective.
▶ Eliminate roadblocks to community learning.
▶ Balance patience and performance.

Stakeholders

Inviting people with different perspectives to contribute to collective decision making can be time-consuming in the development phase but ultimately is less time-consuming than leaving them out. As Margaret J. Wheatley[26] pointed out, "It doesn't work to just ask people to sign on when they haven't been involved in the design process, when they haven't experienced the plan as a living, breathing thing." Involvement, and rewarding involvement (especially cross-unit collaboration), are essential to having people bring their full selves to the task of making change.

The Leader

To tap into the potential of community, the leader must be someone who can build community and create a safe environment for participation and team learning. The leader should have vision, empathy, and an ability to listen and appreciate different perspectives. The leader should empower others. These are but a few of the essential qualities for leadership. Once selected, the leader should be empowered to carry out the necessary tasks.

Different Perspectives

Cultural differences between stakeholder groups, combined with power differentials and hierarchy, could limit certain members from sharing perspectives needed for breakthrough thinking.[27] Insights on appropriate space use often come to those closest to the "action"—in this case, students and faculty. Students and even faculty are often overlooked when seeking input on space design. Even if brought up in the discussions, student ideas can be ignored in favor of ideas coming from people in positions of power. Communities reach full potential with participants who understand differences in perspective and encourage sensitivity to those differences. Every voice needs to be heard and respected.

Roadblocks

Several potential roadblocks exist. Differences in the values and communication styles of college and university subcultures (for instance, faculty, student development, enrollment management, facilities managers, students, and so on) can inhibit collaboration. Personality and group dynamics, as well as differences in knowledge and expertise, can also present roadblocks. How can the group weight expertise appropriately to leave room for new perspectives while honoring expertise that has worked in the past? Other roadblocks can come from processes and systems that can prevent people from finding common ground. Take, for instance, the challenges of developing an integrated living-learning center within the structure of traditional budgets that call for money to flow through either academics or residential areas. If the "living units" are physically located above the "learning spaces" and the funding for maintenance of spaces follows traditional silos, whose budget pays for a shower leak that drips from the living space into the learning space? Creating one budget for the hybrid project prior to construction could go a long way toward encouraging cooperative behavior and a sharing of risk on the part of stakeholders.

Patience and Performance

Creativity cannot be scheduled or commanded. Often, patience is needed to allow new ideas to flourish. On the other hand, extensive discussion and debate in the name of patience, while edifying, can be time-consuming and costly, eroding construction budgets. Replicating what has been done in the past is not the most effective approach when charting a new paradigm; it can lead to designing spaces for yesterday's needs—ultimately, a very costly mistake. The community needs to find the delicate balance between patience and performance.

In short, we need meaningful community to create new learning spaces that can enhance community. This team approach, directed by a talented architect who understands the importance of putting learning in the center on campus, "can transform a building from one that discourages community to one that dramatically promotes it."[28] The sidebar demonstrates how spaces designed to enhance community can appear, using the example of new construction that created a suite of academic spaces within a residence hall—Marianist Hall at the University of Dayton in Ohio.

Spaces Designed to Enhance Community: Marianist Hall

A learning space housed within an undergraduate residence building—Marianist Hall at the University of Dayton—demonstrates design principles that foster community. In the studio classroom shown in Figure 1, the presence of reconfigurable furniture and the absence of a lectern or "front of the room" allows active learning approaches that focus on student interactions and involvement. Multiple plasma screens connected to a variety of audiovisual sources and writing surfaces on contoured walls provide flexible presentation options. Portable marker boards can be carried or wheeled by students to and from adjacent team rooms. Lighting and audiovisual adjustments are made using a simple, quickly operated LCD touch-screen panel. Glass doors and windows along corridor walls create a more transparent and inviting environment such that learning and teaching do not occur "behind closed doors."

Figure 1. Studio Classroom

Wide corridors or pathways connect studio classrooms and smaller meeting spaces in Marianist Hall at the University of Dayton. The pathways are wide enough to accommodate traffic as well as enable group conversations. A CopyCam (PolyVision) can digitally capture and share whiteboard images on the Web. Comfortable furniture is arranged to foster social interaction while also being conducive for studying. Wireless access points allow students to connect notebook computers to the Web. Studio classrooms, seminar rooms, and faculty offices open into this pathway to create a spacious environment that welcomes continued dialogue between class changes. (See Figure 2.)

Figure 2. Marianist Hall Pathway

Although large enough to accommodate classes, the Commons in the Marianist Hall Learning Space is used as a flexible pathway space to encourage multiple classes to meet for a joint experience such as a play, performance, or debate. The Commons can also be used for group presentations and static works associated with academic or cocurricular programs (see Figure 3). When classes are not in session, the space becomes an extension to the pathways connecting other rooms and becomes a favorite area for studying, faculty-faculty or faculty-student meetings, and impromptu gatherings. Comfortable furniture and soft lighting ensure the space more closely realizes the needs of the learners. Glass walls provide an inviting visual cue to students for interaction with faculty in their adjacent offices.

Figure 3. The Commons

Technology, Community, and Information Exchange

Communication is key to building and sustaining a community of learners.[29] Information technology (IT) solutions offer an outstanding platform for connecting and sharing information among community members in or outside the classroom. Technology is broadening the scope of when and where learning occurs; planning for new or renovated physical spaces must consider the role of IT. At one extreme, physical learning spaces may no longer be necessary if an academic program is delivered online, while at the other extreme, face-to-face classes can occur in a variety of physical spaces that take advantage of technology in or out of the space. At these extremes and all the hybrid possibilities in between, technology should be used to foster learning by building community as well as creating and sharing knowledge within the group while allowing interaction to take place in and outside the formal classroom setting.

IT can foster community in several ways. Most notably, communication outside the classroom can become richer and more extensive using tools such as e-mail, instant messaging, threaded discussions, blogs, and wikis. Another very important consideration is the use of IT to build student understanding outside the classroom, thereby freeing classroom time for more active pedagogical approaches. Faculty frequently struggle over wanting to spend time with active learning methods while covering a prescribed list of topics in the allotted time. By using IT solutions to share course content outside scheduled class time, faculty can use the face-to-face time in the classroom for more active learning approaches. Therefore, classrooms need to be designed with much greater flexibility for a wide variety of pedagogical approaches.[30]

Many institutions are investigating or implementing mobile computing for their students.[31] Students can research or author while networking to build community. Mobility and academic requirements for technology access are important considerations,[32] since learning occurs in a variety of spaces. At the University of Dayton (UD), all incoming students are required to purchase a university-supplied notebook computer. The UD student computer initiative was implemented to ensure that students gain the IT skills needed for the modern workplace and to align with the needs of building and sustaining community. Students choose among several models provided by a partnering vendor, but in each case the hardware and software meet institutional requirements and ensure that students have a common computing platform. Surveys indicate that 70 percent of UD students use their notebooks in one or more classes each semester in their first year. Many UD classes require notebooks; those classrooms have been equipped with tables and wired network connections to each seat or wireless access for the entire room.

Communication tools such as enterprise-level e-mail and calendaring as well as learning management systems are important tools, but there is a surprising lag in the widespread development and adoption of applications that allow the spontaneous and ad hoc teaming that characterize an active community. The potential of peer-to-peer tools such as Virtual Office from Groove Networks (http://www.groove.net) show promise for teaming, as does powerful, inexpensive, mobile computing hardware that is always connected to the Internet.

Despite the fact that technology is always changing (and that presumably additional teaming and collaborative applications will be developed), physical space planning should embrace the idea that face-to-face classroom meetings will become less didactic and more active, allowing for student participation and engagement in authentic learning approaches. With more powerful communication outside the classroom, space planning will ask how best to serve community needs as opposed to delivery needs.

Pedagogical, Curricular, and Cocurricular Design

Students can participate in many activities to create the social interactions necessary to establish and build community (see the sidebar). Community can and does form in the absence of significant faculty participation. However, faculty can have a tremendous positive impact on shaping, contributing to, and expanding the environment in which students learn.[33] It therefore makes sense to coordinate and improve pedagogical approaches, the curriculum, and the cocurricular experiences of students with the goal of creating a more learning-friendly community characterized by engagement.

Examples of Activities That Foster an Engaged Academic Community

Pedagogical approaches that foster community	
Example	**Implications for Learning Environment Design**
Students experience a community-friendly learning environment from the beginning of the first class.	Community-centric ambience of physical and virtual spaces should be readily discerned by faculty and students, from room lighting and decoration to learning management system usability.
Faculty and students learn about each other and from each other.	Mechanism for learning each other's names available in and out of the classroom. Students and instructor(s) post interests, photos, and backgrounds on course Web site.
Students participate in discussion in class.	Classroom "front" is deemphasized (removing the lectern, for example) to create open, discussion-friendly space. Choice and placement of furniture allows students to see and hear each other.
Active learning activities in class use cooperative techniques.	Students are seated in proximity to each other but with flexibility for movement and space between chairs for instructor mobility.
Team-based projects are conducted outside class and culminate in student-led presentations.	Room technology enhancements and lighting controls should be immediately intuitive to student presenters.

In-class activities are augmented by completing a significant fraction of course expectations online.	Courses use a learning management system that provides delivery of course materials online and enables exchange of messages, threaded discussions, announcements, homework assignments, quizzes, and grades.
Classroom visitors, such as civic leaders or alumni, can broaden classroom community and enrich discussion.	Rooms are easy for visitors to find and have extra seating and tables of adequate quality so as to send a positive image of the institution. Time in class can be used to make meaning out of the material rather than conduct "housekeeping" tasks.
Video or telephone conference-based technologies enable discussion with experts in the field from inaccessible locations, such as overseas.	Conferencing equipment is placed in room, with remote or on-site technical management and setup.
In-class integration of study skills and best practices nurture collaboration and improve student learning.	Space redesign should be connected to faculty development efforts that focus on learning-centered pedagogies.
Student-faculty interactions can occur immediately before and after a class.	Broad pathways (not corridors) connect classrooms, with ample room for discussion and whiteboard use during class changes without impeding traffic flow.
Students meet with faculty in office spaces that are easy to find and conducive to dialogue.	Building signage is clear and in keeping with universal design principles, to be accessible to all. Faculty office suites are large enough for meetings, with sufficient seating and board space.

Curriculum that fosters community	
Example	**Implications for Learning Environment Design**
First-year academic programming introduces students to college life, rigorous academics, appropriate lifestyle choices, and high expectations.	Innovative programming demands nontraditional spaces, such as first-year introductory seminars, that do not fit well in rooms designed for lectures.
Connections are made between learning and living, such as creating course sections taken by student residential cohorts.	The distinction between academic (classroom) and residential buildings begins to blur, such as the integration of learning spaces in residential halls.
Matriculating students are prepared for an academic program by collaborating online using a virtual orientation Web site.	Orientation activities begin before students arrive on campus using a sophisticated Web site and managed programming, such as common readings and discussion postings.
Academic advising involves extensive personal interactions to form deeper mentoring relationships.	Students and faculty interact and share information from a pool of Web-based resources such as course listings and audit reports, allowing face-to-face meetings to be more substantial.
Tutoring programs are offered for at-risk students and students with learning support needs.	Learning support centers and associated rooms for tutoring, supplemental instruction, and testing services are inviting, roomy, and equipped with whiteboards and computer access.
Students participate in faculty-sponsored research projects.	Research laboratories, libraries, and faculty work spaces become learning spaces and should include physical provision for interpersonal interactions and brainstorming meetings.
Student research projects culminate in presentations on campus and may be offered for credit.	Large atriums or presentation halls are available for on-campus conferences and workshops.
Programs include extensive civic engagement such as service-learning projects that integrate with the curriculum.	From classroom to college towns and beyond, the physical environment can enable interactions between on- and off-campus visitors.

Integration of multicultural and inclusive awareness helps increase participation by all community members and ensures diverse perspectives.	Public spaces contain artifacts of a wide range of cultures and tell the story of community from the perspective of different societies.
Interdisciplinary courses are taught across traditional academic units, for example, connecting liberal education to professional preparation.	Learning spaces should be designed to foster faculty and student interactions from multiple backgrounds, such as new interdisciplinary buildings.
Faculty team-taught courses stimulate in-class discussion across disciplines.	Don't assume a classroom will contain only one teacher or perspective.
Faculty learning communities collaborate to design innovative curricula, sequenced courses, and new learning-living activities.	Learning and teaching centers should be large enough to accommodate collaborative discussions and foster professional development for leadership and learning/teaching improvements.
Common readings create links between courses students deem unconnected and integrate with extracurricular events such as artistic performances.	Physical and virtual learning environments must create the times and places for interaction that create student engagement in common readings or other events such as artistic performances.
Group tours and field trips are encouraged to introduce students to a wider world of learning.	Academic and residential areas are well served with public transport, parking, walkways, and accessibility friendly traffic flow on and off campus, and campus culture supports value of out-of-classroom experiences to learning.
Design, law, consulting, and manufacturing clinics connect student projects with area business and individual needs.	Large and flexible suites of spaces permit collaboration with regional partnering clients and for students to conduct and present project work.
Internships and cooperatives are linked to courses.	Physical or virtual mechanisms exist for students to interact with academic programs during off-campus experiences.
Academic departments offer regular open seminars and socials to connect scholars and students.	Large seminar rooms are available for departmental and cross-departmental events, with adequate facilities for receptions.

Cocurriculum that fosters community

Example	Implications for Learning Environment Design
Orientation and preorientation events introduce students to the campus culture and help define standards of behavior and norms of civility.	Campus-wide architecture, landscaping, interior design, and even Web presence provide an ambience that immediately conveys openness, community, sociability, and safety.
Students live in residential housing closely associated, physically and culturally, with the campus. They can live together in thematic or curricular cohorts.	From campus master planning to student residential programming, housing should be integrated into a campus culture that sees the "living" part of a college education as linked to the academic experience.
Social and cultural activities explore and build on the institution's heritage, mission, and connection with alumni as well as the community.	A wide variety of physical spaces create places for campus involvement, including recreational and intramural sport facilities, religious and cultural gathering spaces, and a wide variety of formal and informal avenues for artistic representation.
Students participate in volunteer work to expand their understanding of social responsibilities and to develop leadership skills.	Meeting spaces and administrative centers house programs that develop student leadership and connect student clubs and organizations to service-learning opportunities.
Cocurricular activities involve students, faculty, and staff in shared dialogue.	Inviting, comfortable, and flexible spaces should be available for clubs and organizations so that more involved participation occurs with connections to academics, such as reading clubs to discuss popular books or hot topics.
Studying occurs anywhere and at any time.	Public and residential spaces, from the library to laundromats, can be made amenable to studying, including wireless network installation. Many factors such as safety, lighting, and noise control play into suitability for studying.

Students collaborate on team projects outside the classroom and participate in group study sessions.	Public areas such as dining and foyer spaces are considered social spaces. They are spacious, inviting, and accessible at times when students need to meet.
Students participate in experiential learning opportunities while on campus.	On-campus employment and student-run businesses should be created to expose students to a variety of relevant real-world business and administration learning experiences.
Students participate in campus management decisions to create a sense of ownership and responsibility.	Broaden student involvement in campus planning and administrative decision making and respect their unique and critical viewpoint.

Perhaps the most effective way faculty can appreciate the possibilities of a learning community is to experience professional development opportunities that give them the opportunity to experience being a student again. Learning communities are increasingly common in faculty development programs, providing a valuable learning process for knowledge workers.[34] These learning communities allow open dialogue and sharing among faculty—and other contributors to the educational enterprise—to help frame questions such as "Who are our students?" and "How can we help them learn?" Learning communities help make teaching community property.[35]

Learning and teaching centers such as the Ryan C. Harris Learning Teaching Center at the University of Dayton offer powerful mechanisms for stimulating institutional change that encompasses pedagogical, curricular, and cocurricular approaches (see the sidebar on example activities). The diverse range of activities includes experimental classrooms, faculty learning communities, grant support and consultation, support of student learning, and measurement of student learning outcomes. These centers foster partnerships between student development and faculty. They can prepare faculty to facilitate learning in community and prompt them to consider the value of cocurriculum in student learning.[36] Guided by leaders that articulate and implement a community-centric mission, learning and teaching centers serve as valuable change agents for the pedagogical, curricular, and cocurricular innovations that foster community and transform colleges and universities into learning-centered organizations.[37]

Conclusion

In this chapter we focused on the role community plays in learning. We explored three sets of strategic levers that can enhance learning through community processes: the design of spaces that support learning; the use of information technologies; and the design of structures for learning that encompass pedagogy, curriculum, and cocurricular programming.

Alignment with mission is key to success. A community-centered mission signals to the entire campus that actions for the greater good supercede parochial actions. A community-centered mission speaks to the importance of working through conflict rather than avoiding it. At the University of Dayton, the heart of our mission is a dedication to integrating learning and living in community. As a Catholic and Marianist institution, we are committed to educating through community. Even so, embracing community and its inherent messiness can be challenging.

No one group can move a campus to recognize the value and importance of community as a medium for learning. Leadership at all levels must invite people with different perspectives to the table when formulating new approaches and making decisions. A community-centered mission helps stress the importance of the issue.

Promoting community approaches could imply that there is no role for individual effort or learning. Nothing could be further from the truth. As Peter Senge put it, "There is commonality of purpose, a shared vision, and understanding of how to complement one another's efforts.... Alignment is the necessary condition before empowering the individual will empower the whole team."[38] Emphasizing the value of creating communities of practice does not obviate the need for the excellent educative efforts of individual faculty and staff, just as encouraging students to develop skills in teamwork does not imply that they no longer have to prove individual capability. Not all activities benefit from community approaches, but overall, higher education underestimates their value. Community can and does make a difference when we learn to channel interests and focus people's efforts so that the shared vision becomes an extension of the personal visions of the diverse groups of people involved.[39]

Of great significance is the question of how to integrate learning in community into an institutional assessment plan. If we view community as a context for learning, it should be carefully monitored and improved. With less-than-obvious metrics, community is not a single entity but the sum of many factors. As we become purposeful and conscious of what makes spaces more supportive of learning, we need to analyze new and existing spaces and ask how community contributes to the learning that occurs.[40]

Endnotes

1. Ernest L. Boyer and Lee D. Mitgang, *Building Community: A New Future for Architecture Education and Practice* (Princeton, N.J.: The Carnegie Foundation for the Advancement of Teaching, 1996), pp. 148–149.

2. Richard Boyatzis, Scott Cowen, David Kolb, and Associates, *Innovation in Professional Education: Steps on a Journey from Teaching to Learning* (San Francisco: Jossey-Bass, 1995).

3. George D. Kuh et al., *Student Success in College: Creating Conditions That Matter* (San Francisco: Jossey-Bass, 2005).

4. Carney C. Strange and James H. Banning, *Educating by Design* (San Francisco: Jossey-Bass, 2001), pp. 9–33.

5. M. Scott Peck, *Meditations from the Road* (New York: Simon and Schuster, 1993).

6. George Manning, Curtis Kent, and Steve McMillen, *Building Community: The Human Side of Work* (Cincinnati, Ohio: Thomson Executive Press, 1996), p. 3.

7. Kuh et al., op. cit.

8. Larry A. Braskamp, Lois C. Trautvetter, and Kelly Ward, *Putting Students First: How Colleges Develop Students Purposefully* (Bolton, Mass.: Anker Publishing, 2006); and William M. McDonald and Associates, *Creating Campus Community: In Search of Ernest Boyer's Legacy* (San Francisco: Jossey-Bass, 2002).

9. Peter Ewell, "Organizing for Learning: A New Imperative," *AAHE Bulletin*, vol. 50, no. 4 (December 1997), pp. 52–55.

10. Marilla D. Svinicki, *Learning and Motivation in the Postsecondary Classroom* (Bolton, Mass.: Anker Publishing, 2004).

11. Shirley Ann Jackson, "Presidential Address: The Nexus: Where Science Meets Society," *Science*, vol. 310, no. 5754 (December 2005), pp. 1634–1639.

12. Brian L. Hawkins, "Information Access in the Digital Era: Challenges and a Call for Collaboration," *EDUCAUSE Review*, vol. 36, no. 5 (September/October 2001), pp. 50–57, <http://www.educause.edu/ir/library/pdf/erm0154.pdf>.

13. John Seely Brown and Paul Duguid, *The Social Life of Information* (Boston: Harvard Business School Press, 2000).

14. Frank H. I. Rhodes, *The Creation of the Future: The Role of the American University* (Ithaca, N.Y.: Cornell University Press, 2004).

15. Roger L. Geiger, "The Ten Generations of American Higher Education," in *American Higher Education in the Twenty-First Century: Social, Political, and Economic Challenges*, Philip G. Altbach, Robert O. Berdahl, and Patricia J. Gumport, eds. (Baltimore: The Johns Hopkins University Press, 2005); and John R. Thelin, *A History of American Higher Education* (Baltimore: The Johns Hopkins University Press, 2004).

16. John Tagg, *The Learning Paradigm College* (Bolton, Mass.: Anker Publishing, 2003).

17. Murray Sperber, "How Undergraduate Education Became College Life—and a Personal Apology," in *Declining by Degrees: Higher Education at Risk*, Richard H. Hersh and John Merrow, eds. (New York: Palgrave Macmillan, 2005).

18. R. Eugene Rice, "Making a Place for the New American Scholar," AAHE Pathways Project, working paper, March 1996.

19. Gerald Graff, *Clueless in Academe: How Schooling Obscures the Life of the Mind* (New Haven, Conn.: Yale University Press, 2003).

20. Arthur Levine, "Worlds Apart: Disconnects Between Students and Their Colleges," in *Declining by Degrees: Higher Education at Risk*, Richard H. Hersh and John Merrow, eds. (New York: Palgrave Macmillan, 2005).

21. Diana G. Oblinger and James L. Oblinger, "Is It Age or IT: First Steps Toward Understanding the Net Generation," in *Educating the Net Generation*, Diana G. Oblinger and James L. Oblinger, eds. (Boulder; Colo.: EDUCAUSE, 2005), <http://www.educause.edu/educatingthenetgen/>.

22. Robert B. Kvavik, "Convenience, Communications, and Control: How Students Use Technology," in *Educating the Net Generation*, Diana G. Oblinger and James L. Oblinger, eds. (Boulder, Colo.: EDUCAUSE, 2005), <http://www.educause.edu/educatingthenetgen/>.

23. Boyer and Mitgang, op. cit., p. 148.

24. Peter M. Senge, *The Fifth Discipline: The Art and Practice of the Learning Organization* (New York: Currency Doubleday, 1990).

25. Robert Barr and John Tagg, "From Teaching to Learning—A New Paradigm for Undergraduate Education," *Change* (November/December 1995), pp. 12–25.

26. Margaret J. Wheatley, *Leadership and the New Science* (San Francisco: Berrett-Koehler, 1992).

27. Deborah J. Bickford, "Navigating the White Waters of Collaborative Work," in *The Importance of Physical Space in Creating Supportive Learning Environments: New Directions in Teaching and Learning*, Nancy Van Note Chism and Deborah J. Bickford, eds., no. 92 (Winter 2002) (San Francisco: Jossey-Bass, 2003), <http://www.josseybass.com/WileyCDA/WileyTitle/productCd-0787963445.html>.

28. Boyer and Mitgang, op. cit., p. 147.

29. Arthur W. Chickering and Zelda F. Gamson, "Seven Principles for Good Practice in Undergraduate Education," *AAHE Bulletin*, vol. 39, no. 1 (March 1987), pp. 3–7.

30. Phillip D. Long and Stephen C. Ehrmann, "Future of the Learning Space: Breaking Out of the Box," *EDUCAUSE Review*, vol. 40, no. 4 (July/August 2005), pp. 42–58, <http://www.educause.edu/apps/er/erm05/erm0542.asp>.

31. David G. Brown and Karen R. Petitto, "The Status of Ubiquitous Computing," *EDUCAUSE Review*, vol. 38, no. 3 (May/June 2003), pp. 24–33, <http://www.educause.edu/LibraryDetailPage/666?ID=ERM0331>.

32. Bryan Alexander, "Going Nomadic: Mobile Learning in Higher Education," *EDUCAUSE Review*, vol. 39, no. 5 (September/October 2004), pp. 28–35, <http://www.educause.edu/apps/er/erm04/erm0451.asp>.

33. Richard J. Light, *Making the Most of College: Students Speak Their Minds* (Cambridge, Mass.: Harvard University Press, 2001).

34. Milton D. Cox and Laurie Richlin, eds., *Building Faculty Learning Communities: New Directions for Teaching and Learning*, no. 97 (Spring 2004) (Mississauga, Ontario: John Wiley & Sons Canada, Ltd.); and Etienne C. Wenger and William N. Snyder, "Communities of Practice: The Organizational Frontier," *Harvard Business Review* (January/February 2000), pp. 139–145.

35. Pat Hutching, *Making Teaching Community Property: A Menu for Peer Collaboration and Peer Review* (Washington, D.C.: American Association for Higher Education, May 1996); and Parker J. Palmer, *The Courage to Teach: Exploring the Inner Landscape of a Teacher's Life* (San Francisco: Jossey-Bass, 1998).

36. Delivee L. Wright, "Program Types and Prototypes," in *A Guide to Faculty Development: Practical Advice, Examples, and Resources*, Kay H. Gillespie, Linda R. Hilsen, and Emily C. Wadsworth, eds. (Bolton, Mass.: Anker Publishing, 2002).

37. Sondra K. Patrick and James J. Fletcher, "Faculty Developers as Change Agents: Transforming Colleges and Universities into Learning Organizations," in *To Improve the Academy*, Mathew Kaplan, ed. (Stillwater, Okla.: New Forums Press and the Professional and Organizational Development Network in Higher Education, 1998).

38. Senge, op. cit., pp. 234–235.

39. Ibid.

40. To further explore this concept, see chapter 13 in this book, "Assessing Learning Spaces," by Sawyer Hunley and Molly Schaller.

About the Authors

Deborah J. Bickford is the associate provost for academic affairs and learning initiatives at the University of Dayton. As director of the Ryan C. Harris Learning Teaching Center, she collaborates with colleagues to create a laboratory for innovation in learning and teaching. She is a professor of strategic management in the School of Business Administration and has taught various courses in the areas of strategy and leadership. Her current research interests focus on the impact of physical space on learning and on connected and active learning. With Nancy Van Note Chism, she coedited *The Importance of Physical Space in Creating Supportive Learning Environments* for Jossey-Bass (2003).

David J. Wright is the director of curriculum innovation and e-learning at the University of Dayton. In this capacity he directs a number of technology units including the eLearning, eMedia, and IT training labs in the Ryan C. Harris Learning Teaching Center. Wright oversees many of the faculty development programs and e-learning initiatives at the University of Dayton. He is chair of the Southwestern Ohio Council for Higher Education, Faculty Development Committee. Wright has worked on numerous grant and contract funded research projects, including work for the National Aeronautics and Space Administration (NASA), National Science Foundation (NSF), and National Institutes of Health (NIH). He also has taught extensively with technology in biology courses. Wright earned his doctorate from the University of Iowa.

CHAPTER 5

Student Practices and Their Impact on Learning Spaces

Cyprien Lomas
University of British Columbia

Diana G. Oblinger
EDUCAUSE

Students will spend much of their academic lives in classrooms, laboratories, and libraries—the places where education happens. Such learning spaces impart a feeling of the campus culture to students. But is the culture they sense one of a previous era or one that meshes with their habits? This alignment is important because well-designed learning spaces and enabling technologies encourage students to spend more time on campus, increasing engagement and improving retention.

Understanding the traits and habits of students (and potential students) should shape the discussion of learning spaces. A quick scan of any campus will reveal students hanging out alone or in small groups while reading, taking notes, writing, chatting, or simply enjoying campus life. There may be another layer of activity beyond the obvious, however, enabled by cell phones, iPods, personal digital assistants (PDAs), and laptops. Both student habits and their technologies raise questions. For example, if students carry laptops to class, does this affect how we equip the rooms? Will the generation that has grown up with video games, camera phones, and home theater systems be satisfied with what we can offer in classrooms? What spaces will give students the most educational value?

Student Habits

Today's college students have been described as preferring learning experiences that are digital, connected, experiential, immediate, and social. Constantly connected, they seem to have no fear of technology or interacting with people they have not met face-to-face. Although they communicate a great deal online, they still want direct interaction with others. They appear to prefer learning-by-doing rather than learning-by-listening and often choose to study in groups. Much to the consternation of adults acculturated to lectures, they become impatient in situations where they don't feel engaged.

While many student attributes may be important to educators, five characteristics seem particularly applicable for learning spaces:

▶ Digital
▶ Mobile
▶ Independent
▶ Social
▶ Participatory

Digital

Many students under 20 years of age are adept with technology, according to faculty and staff standards. They have adopted practices that are quickly becoming the norm, such as instant messaging, text messaging, Googling, and social networking. Students' comfort with the Internet means it isn't "technology" to them—it may be a way of life.

Students are used to entertainment environments with rich images and high-fidelity sound. Most students have played video games since childhood; almost all have been exposed to them. In addition to sophisticated story lines and opportunities for collaborative play, games employ stunning visual and sound effects along with complicated story lines. Students may have technically advanced home entertainment systems featuring large, high-resolution displays and elaborate sound systems. Video-game consoles can generate complex graphical data rendered in close to real time. Home theater systems rival movie complexes.

While students have access to more networked technology than their predecessors, many are not technophiles—or even good with technology. Comfort with technology does not guarantee proficiency. Students recognize that technology often provides the fastest and best way to get something done, so they have developed social structures to solicit answers from friends and acquaintances. As a result of these social networks, new technologies and practices are adopted and discarded quickly.

Mobile

Aided by devices like laptops and iPods, students bring their preferred environments to campus with them. Most students carry at least one connected device, and most have MP3 players on which they will have spent significant amounts of money and effort to ensure that they have the perfect song collection at all times. In addition, student use of cell phones is almost ubiquitous. Many have had cell phones for more than half their lives. Although functional and effective, cell phones may have joined cars as status symbols—owners customize models with personalized ringtones and colorful add-ons.

Students take advantage of the ability to communicate with one another, connect to the Internet, and access information at all times through laptops and cell phones. Short message service (SMS) and instant messaging let them maintain constant contact with one another. Students share information about their current locations, activities, and companions on an almost constant basis, not just with text but by sharing pictures, movies, and audio.

Handheld devices have impressive displays. All but the most basic cell-phone models include full-color screens capable of displaying pictures and video. Cell-phone carriers are exploring agreements with media providers and other partners to use the capabilities of their devices for playing podcasts and MP3s, for example. Phones able to create and share podcasts were recently announced, and GPS and mapping software are being integrated into handheld devices.

Independent

The Internet has given rise to a new set of competencies. Individuals surf the Internet to uncover facts, chase down links of interest, and then aggregate and synthesize information. This self-reliance reveals that many of today's students are self-directed, internally motivated, and inquisitive. They choose when to pay attention—and what to attend to.

Students will spend hundreds of hours in class. While they might not have much choice where they spend their class time, they do control how they behave in these spaces. Given their facility with cell phones, iPods, laptops, and other mobile devices, new in-class practices are evolving.

Once freed from the classroom, students gravitate to the spaces most appealing to them. Comfortable and customizable spaces quickly become candidates for frequent use between classes. The informal learning that takes place outside classes occurs in libraries, information commons, coffee shops, and any other locations where students can gather.

Social

Using video cameras or similar devices and aided by MySpace-type environments, students can capture and share experiences with friends and strangers alike. This social side of students manifests when they share knowledge of new technologies; most learn new things when their friends show them how.

Students are quite comfortable with group work and interactions. One of the traits of the Net Generation is the ease with which they can form and re-form working groups.

Many students will have spent time in highly social, engaging online game environments. Unlike the physical space students typically inhabit, these spaces can be configured to match students' preferences.

An interesting emerging practice that fits with students' social inclinations is the Nokia Lifeblog, an Internet community that allows owners of Nokia mobile phones to document and share every aspect of their lives in real time. The phones allow users to capture photographs, sounds, and other artifacts, then instantly share them with family, friends, and the general public. Content could be breaking news or the discovery of the latest food hotspot. And because Lifeblog is an Internet community, a lurker can quickly become a colleague by contributing comments and sharing experiences.

While the Nokia Lifeblog community represents a small subgroup of Nokia owners, the practices they employ are not unique. The Internet enables social software, open sharing, and serendipitous discovery of small groups of people with common interests, often in very specific and esoteric subjects.

Participatory

"Open source" is not just a way of developing software; it is a mindset about participation. Bloggers embody the do-it-yourself (DIY) spirit. Lack of easy-to-use tools required bloggers to find their own solutions; many of the early bloggers got their start using blogging software they created. The DIY attitude extends to their creation and consumption of content on the Internet. Reputation, as well as recommendations and referrals, are of paramount importance. Curiosity, debate, and consensus are all valued traits in the blogging world. Many of today's students possess these traits.

Many technologies used by students have a low barrier to participation and a fun contribution process. For example, Digg.com makes it easy to share opinions and rank the top stories of the week. Flickr makes it easy to share photos with friends, family, and the rest of the world. When users explore the Flickr Web site, they are encouraged to upload their favorite photographs. But Flickr goes beyond just photo sharing; options include geotagging photos. A photo can include tags that pinpoint its exact latitude and longitude. Integration with an application such as Google Maps allows users to populate locations with their own tags and documentation; tagging permits the sharing of a personal history associated with any space.

Classrooms and Formal Spaces

Classes are the most visible components of campus life. Lectures typically involve a single "expert" delivering content to students through a combination of diagrams, text, and narration. Classrooms have relatively straightforward requirements: line of sight, good acoustics, and a focal point at the front of the room. Even in formal learning spaces, however, instructors can take advantage of emerging student practices in a variety of ways.

Students are constantly connected, yet classrooms may seem disconnected. Classrooms need not be isolated from the rest of the world—ubiquitous access brings additional capabilities. A class can "travel" to any location in the world through the Internet, have experts "visit" them, or browse available resources. Remote instrumentation and laboratories make it possible for students and faculty to run experiments or control a device without leaving the room.[1] Used effectively and thoughtfully, technology in the hands of the instructors can bring new dimensions to the class.

Many instructors find that interspersing interactivity, discussion, and group work in lecture engages learners. Physical constraints, however, such as the ability of students to turn around in their seats, can limit the success of these techniques. Some lecturers assign students to groups, producing seating maps of their lectures to help facilitate group forming and save time. In other cases, the room is designed for student collaboration. Seats are arranged in paired rows with specially design chairs that allow students to face each other for collaboration (For example, see chapter 22 on LeBaron Hall, a large lecture hall at Iowa State University). Other spaces are outfitted with movable tables, chairs, and whiteboards so that seating can be reconfigured to suit the activity.

Technology can greatly enhance interactivity in the classroom. For example, student response systems solicit and track student progress throughout a class by enabling anonymous polling. Many expect to see cell phones used as student response systems in the next few years. Another option is to allow students to "take control" of the computer and present during class. Facilities that have wireless keyboards and mice make it easy for students to present from where they sit. Space and pedagogical models, such as SCALE-UP (see chapter 29), are designed around interactivity. The round tables, student teams, and the ability to see others create a highly interactive, participatory environment.

Mobile technologies can also be used to engage students in learning. Using laptops or Tablet PCs combined with a wireless network, students can search for additional information on the Web, engage in collaborative editing, or use learning objects to illustrate specific points. Lectures or discussions can be captured and the podcasts replayed later.

Informal Spaces

Students spend a large proportion of their time outside class. Students and faculty value the time spent with peers discussing academic work or other topics. Spaces that catalyze social interaction, serendipitous meetings, and impromptu conversations contribute to personal and professional growth. Many different types of communication devices, including laptops, enhanced cell phones, and PDAs, when equipped with ubiquitous wireless access, allow almost any space to become a gathering space that students can use for studying, collaborating, and socializing. These informal spaces, often combining food services and wireless access, are ideal for casual activities including searching the Internet, catching up on e-mail, or chatting with friends. Students are no longer confined to computer terminals; indoor and outdoor spaces can become study areas or a social space as long as the Internet and power are available.

MIT's Steam Café, for example, encourages serendipitous connections among students and faculty through the space design, the use of technology, and food services (see chapter 27). The University of Dayton has integrated informal learning spaces with classrooms and a residence hall to enable frequent contact and interaction among students and faculty (see chapter 3).

The emergence of learning commons provides another example of how out-of-class time is being enriched with learning opportunities (see chapter 7). The Information Commons at Northwestern University (see chapter 30), the USITE/Crerar Computing Center and Cybercafé at the University of Chicago (see chapter 40), and Emory's Cox Hall Computing Center (see chapter 8) exemplify the integration of space and services based on an understanding of how students work and live.

Creating spaces for spontaneous meetings is particularly important. "Think stops" are places for individuals to stop, relax, and meet others. Often marked by a chalkboard or whiteboard, these locations encourage impromptu meetings and conversations. The ES Corridor Project at Indiana University-Purdue University Indianapolis (IUPUI) illustrates how valuable these spaces can be, even if they were created with limited funds (see chapter 21). And, given the ability for Internet-savvy individuals to self-organize, think stops in the future may no longer need distinctive physical attributes—they may be virtual instead.

With applications like Flickr and Google Maps, students can tag their campuses with personal histories, giving them novel ways to make campus spaces—new or old—their own. A recent posting on a University of British Columbia (UBC) student portal prompted a discussion about the best places on campus to sleep. In the future, will technology-enabled geographic locators aid discussions like these?

What Colleges Can Do

Based on student habits, colleges and universities should consider several learning space principles that mix space, technology, and services.

Participation

Today's students often learn better by doing rather than by listening. As a result, classroom, laboratory, and studio designs that provide students with ample opportunities to participate will become more common. Whether the form of participation is discussion or construction, designs should enable interaction, transparency (seeing others engaged in work), and group work. Participation may be physical (such as constructing a model) or virtual (videoconferencing). When considering the technologies to support, remember that students no longer just consume information, they construct it—in multiple media formats.

Connections

Learning is a social process. Often the most memorable college experiences involve connections with others, whether students or faculty. All indications point to the importance of learning spaces that facilitate connections. Those connections are not just verbal or spatial—they are visual, enabling people to see others and feel as though they are part of something bigger (see chapter 10), such as observing a class at work in a laboratory. In other cases visual connections enable one-on-one conversations, such as a student seeing a faculty member in the café and stopping to chat. Connections can be virtual as well, where students work with others who are not physically colocated (through videoconferencing, for example) or who are separated by time (through asynchronous communication).

Connections may be from the campus to the outside world (a view of a natural landscape, for instance) or by allowing the outside world to view the campus.

Connections can also be made with information. Displays can highlight departmental activities or provide a glimpse of world news, stock prices, or environmental conditions. For example, Hamilton College's Science Center (see chapter 20) highlights many green features of the center. External and internal environmental conditions can be monitored along with operating the geothermal and heat-recovery systems.

Proximity

Because of the importance of student-faculty interaction, faculty offices are being located close to student spaces. Multiple departments are housed together to encourage interdisciplinary collaboration. Some campuses are establishing subcampus environments that bring specific departments together. Interaction, collaboration, and engagement can be stimulated by placing people in proximity to each other. Placing student study areas in close proximity to classrooms can be helpful as well.

Integration

Students blend the physical and virtual worlds, moving seamlessly between living and learning environments. When they express themselves, they are increasingly likely to mix audio or images with text. When they have a problem to solve or assignment to complete, the steps are integrated rather than sequential. Colleges and universities can model spaces after students' integrative behavior.

Whether on residential or commuter campuses, students mix classes, study, group work, eating, and sleeping. Increasingly institutions are designing spaces that allow students to work, socialize, and sometimes sleep. Information commons and computing labs such as Emory's Cox Hall Computing Center provide multi-use spaces. Others repurpose between-building space for student use, such as Michigan Technical University's Center for Integrated Learning and Information Technology (see chapter 25).

As seen in information commons, multipurpose spaces integrate services. Students need not move from location to location to complete research or assignments; tools and support personnel are brought together to serve their needs.

Integration also occurs between the physical and virtual worlds. Online tools for team collaboration can be integrated with physical space design, such as Stanford's GroupSpaces (see chapter 35). Within the virtual environment, students integrate multiple media forms. No longer confined to text, students integrate images, video, and audio into assignments; institutions must expand the available technologies to accommodate learners' needs and habits.

Flexibility

Students, like faculty, prefer to control their environment. The ability to rearrange seats or adjust the lighting makes it possible for the same space to be used in many ways, by different groups, throughout the day. A computer lab or classroom may become the site of a jazz concert or a game competition at night. This flexibility also allows customization, enhancing not only space utilization but also convenience.

Flexibility also fosters different teaching and learning styles. Not all faculty can—or should—use the same instructional style. Pedagogies should be tailored to the subject, the learners, and the intended outcomes. Student needs and learning preferences vary as well. Spaces that are flexible, accommodating different approaches and uses, improve the odds for effective learning. Many institutions are finding that students will assume responsibility for self-scheduling and self-policing, so flexibility is not necessarily synonymous with irresponsibility.

Ubiquitous Access

For students whose world is digital, connected, immediate, social, and participatory, access to a wireless network is becoming mandatory. The students' world is not just the physical one in which they find themselves; it is also the virtual one in which they chat with friends, meet people, share photographs, and explore new ideas. Neither learning nor socializing is one-dimensional; the physical complements the virtual, and vice versa. Since learning can occur any place and at any time, there are few—if any—locations where wireless is not valuable.

Because students consume information in multiple formats—text, audio, photographs, and video—and interact with information by modifying it or sharing it, this activity places additional demands on the network. During peak periods, student use may saturate the wireless network, making it important to have wired connections available as well as wireless.

Personal Devices

Most students own a variety of technologies—laptops, MP3 players, cell phones, and more. As technology becomes more ubiquitous and affordable, institutions will find opportunities to deliver information and services in multiple formats and to multiple devices. Convenience is a priority for students, so ensuring that any space can be a learning space—bus, residence hall, sidewalk, or café—by delivering information to personal, handheld devices is important. In the future, some students may choose to carry a USB device (or thumb drive) with their files and applications rather than carrying a laptop (see chapter 9). Student mobility means that students, not just the institution, define the learning space.

Regardless of the technology students use in learning spaces, they will need power—all laptops and MP3 players have a limited battery life. Space planners must take this requirement into account.

Support

Although students have little fear of technology, they are not necessarily proficient with technology, information retrieval, or cognitive skills—what many call *information fluency*. It is not just technology or information resource assistance students need; sometimes that assistance involves writing, student services, and so on. Locating support desks and help systems where students (and faculty) are, rather than just where the unit's home base is found, encourages use. Some IT units locate technical support staff in classroom buildings. Learning commons create one-stop centers, incorporating services from the library, IT, and the writing center. Although they may look different or have a new name, help desks are probably here to stay.

Involve Students

Student use of spaces and technology can easily be misunderstood when viewed from a nonstudent perspective. For example, faculty or administrators might consider lounge seating in a library to be distracting, while students find it the best way to study. Students will likely spend more time in campus learning spaces than anyone else. Learners have a legitimate perspective on what works—and what doesn't. Finding meaningful ways to involve students in planning and evaluating space design is an effective way to ensure that space catalyzes learning.

Conclusion

Students are changing, technologies are changing, and learning spaces are changing. Students will use the spaces that best suit their needs. By examining students' habits and use patterns and then creating spaces that meet their needs, we have an opportunity to make our institutions more student-centered and appealing. At UBC, the motto is *Tuum est*, which in Latin means "It's yours." By creating the spaces that our students will use, we can give students the opportunity to make the university their own.

Endnote

1. EDUCAUSE Learning Initiative, "7 Things You Should Know About Remote Instrumentation" (Boulder, Colo.: EDUCAUSE, 2006), <http://www.educause.edu/ir/library/pdf/ELI7013.pdf>.

About the Authors

Cyprien Lomas is the director of the Learning Centre in the faculty of Land and Food Systems at the University of British Columbia. He oversees the integration of IT, instructional support, and teaching and learning. Lomas is also an EDUCAUSE Learning Initiative (ELI) Scholar in Residence and studies the fit of emerging technologies and practices in institutional strategies. Current projects include analysis of social software, tagging, and the use of rich media (including digital storytelling and podcasting) in the educational context and within formal, informal, and virtual learning spaces.

Diana G. Oblinger is a vice president at EDUCAUSE and directs the EDUCAUSE Learning Initiative (ELI). Previously Oblinger served as the vice president for information resources and the chief information officer for the 16-campus University of North Carolina system and as a senior fellow for the EDUCAUSE Center for Applied Research (ECAR). Prior to that she was the executive director of higher education for Microsoft Corporation and led the Institute for Academic Technology for IBM. Oblinger was on the faculty at Michigan State University and the University of Missouri–Columbia, where she also served as an academic dean.

CHAPTER 6

The Psychology of Learning Environments

Ken A. Graetz
Winona State University

He emerged into the strangest-looking classroom he had ever seen. In fact, it didn't look like a classroom at all, more like a cross between someone's attic and an old-fashioned tea shop. At least twenty small, circular tables were crammed inside it, all surrounded by chintz armchairs and fat little poufs. Everything was lit with a dim, crimson light; the curtains at the windows were all closed, and the many lamps were draped with red scarves. It was stiflingly warm, and the fire that was burning under the crowded mantelpiece was giving off a heavy, sickly sort of perfume as it heated a large copper kettle. The shelves running around the circular walls were crammed with dusty-looking feathers, stubs of candles, many packs of tattered playing cards, countless silvery crystal balls, and a huge array of teacups.[1]

The Environmental Psychology of Teaching and Learning

This enchanting description of a classroom at the fictitious Hogwarts School of Witchcraft and Wizardry captures three fundamental ideas from the environmental psychology of teaching and learning. First, all learning takes place in a physical environment with quantifiable and perceptible physical characteristics. Whether sitting in a large lecture hall, underneath a tree, or in front of a computer screen, students are engulfed by environmental information. Specific targets within the environment draw the students' attention, such as armchairs, scarves, and teacups, and they continuously monitor the ambient properties such as the light of the lamps, the smell of the kettle, and the warmth of the fire. In any learning environment students are awash in environmental information, only a small fraction of which constitutes the sights and sounds of instruction.

Second, students do not touch, see, or hear passively; they feel, look, and listen actively. Students cannot attend to all the environmental information bombarding them at any given time; their ability to gather and understand incoming information is limited. Through automatic and controlled processes, students select information for consideration. They try to understand what they are sensing by piecing bits of information together from the bottom up and by applying existing thoughts and preconceptions from the top down. A classroom with circular tables and comfortable armchairs may look strange because it deviates from expectations formed through prior experience. Students may direct their attention to particular targets in the learning environment that they find more interesting, important, or unfamiliar than others. For some, it might be the instructor's engaging chemistry demonstration. For others, it may be the silvery crystal ball on the shelf. In any learning environment, students manage their limited cognitive resources by actively selecting environmental information for further consideration and by using existing knowledge structures to interpret this information in ways that have worked previously.

Third, the physical characteristics of learning environments can affect learners emotionally, with important cognitive and behavioral consequences. Although emotional reactions to environmental stimuli have been shown to vary widely across individuals and activities, most students would probably find learning difficult in a classroom that is stiflingly warm. Conversely, environments that elicit positive emotional responses may lead not only to enhanced learning but also to a powerful, emotional attachment to that space. It may become a place where students love to learn, a place they seek out when they wish to learn, and a place they remember fondly when they reflect on their learning experiences. In higher education, we hope to provide such places for our students to learn, even as we build yet another large lecture hall and attempt to squeeze our students into crowded, noisy, and uncomfortable spaces. Clearly, some learning environments are more comfortable and offer fewer distractions than others. In any learning environment, physical characteristics that cause discomfort can be expected to interfere with learning; environments that produce positive emotional states can be expected to facilitate learning and the development of place attachment.

The areas of psychology that relate most directly to classroom design and learning environments are environmental, educational, human factors (engineering), and social psychology. Previous research on the effects of such environmental variables as light, temperature, and noise on learning has yielded some predictable results that are addressed through traditional classroom design. Learning appears to be affected adversely by inadequate light, extreme temperatures, and loud noises—variables maintained within acceptable ranges in most college classrooms. Other results, however, reflect the often complex, subtle, and surprising interplay between the learner and the learning environment. Years of research on the impact of environmental variables on human thoughts, feelings, and behaviors indicate that other variables often moderate the effects of environmental variables. In a summary of the research on educational environments, Weinstein[2] concluded that environmental variables can impact learners indirectly and that the effects of different physical settings often depend on the nature of the task and the learner. For example, distracting noises appear to slow reaction time and degrade performance to a greater degree in older versus younger adults[3] and for introverts to a greater degree than extraverts.[4]

Research on the impact of information technology on learning environments is not as voluminous. The presence and application of technology changes the learning environment, both directly and indirectly. This chapter focuses on the psychological underpinnings of three such changes with major implications for the design of college learning environments:

▶ the increased presence of personal, networked devices (for example, wireless laptops and cellular phones) in the classroom,

▶ the migration of course content to the Web and the subsequent transition in classroom activity from information delivery to collaboration, and

▶ the increasing importance of virtual learning environments.

Devices and Distraction in College Classrooms

Laptops and other mobile devices have great potential to enhance and transform instruction and are being used effectively in many college classrooms.[5] Today's students use their devices in class to take notes, access materials and applications, and find relevant information. When all students in a classroom can access networked tools simultaneously, many collaborative learning and just-in-time teaching opportunities emerge. There is a dark side to the presence of personal, networked devices in class, however—when students use them to engage in activities unrelated to coursework.

Students have always found ways, other than listening to the instructor, to pass the time during class. Crossword puzzles, doodling, and daydreams have occupied students' minds during more classes than we care to admit. At first glance, it appears that the wireless laptop, PDA, iPod, and cellular phone are simply the crossword puzzles of today's college classrooms. As suggested by the comments below, however, the issue is more complex. Yesterday's students did not have 24 × 7 online access to all of the content presented during a typical lecture-based class, did not find the crossword puzzle being tackled by the student sitting next to them particularly distracting, and were not themselves as tempted by a crossword puzzle as by instant messaging or an immersive online game. In addition, a handful of students in a large lecture hall working on crossword puzzles did not change the physical environment for instructors:

> When a teacher is up there reading his slides and I can go home and look at them later. Solitaire can be a temptation—let alone my e-mail messages that I'm checking. It's kind of a blunt truth, but sitting in the back of the classroom, it's not just me. You look around and all you see is Solitaire, e-mail.[6]

> The computers interfere with making eye contact. You've got this picket fence between you and the students.[7]

In addition to the sensory richness of Web sites and online games, today's mobile devices convey social information, one of the most powerful targets of attention. We seem particularly attuned to this information, whether studying people's faces and body movements or listening to people talk. In addition, the software applications used to mediate communication are designed to grab the user's attention. Microsoft MSN Messenger, a popular instant messaging client, provides a visible and audible signal when a member of your buddy list starts the application and when a message is received. It has a "nudge" feature that presents a distinctive sound and animation when you want to attract the attention of a buddy, shaking the messaging window back and forth on the buddy's screen. It has a "wink" feature that allows you to send animations to a buddy, such as the large set of knuckles illustrated in Figure 1 that appear to rap on the inside of your buddy's screen. Even if students make every effort to pay attention to the instructor, instant messaging applications are designed to capture their attention, and the social information conveyed is probably too alluring for most students to ignore.

Figure 1. MSN Messenger "Wink"

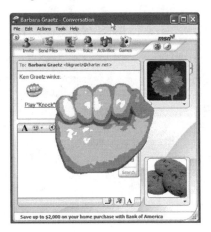

To better understand the potential of today's mobile devices to distract students, it may be helpful to review some of the basic principles of attention.[8] Attention is perhaps best represented not as a single process but as an organized set of procedures through which we select specific environmental stimuli or inputs for cognitive processing.[9] It is commonly held that only one input is processed consciously. This could be called the *attended input*. All other environmental stimuli (for example, background noise, the temperature of the room) are processed unconsciously. These are the *unattended inputs*. Unconscious monitoring detects changes in inputs to which we are not attending consciously, but that might be important. What constitutes an important change is probably determined by another process, referred to here as the *attention controller*, which may push the information into conscious awareness.[10] This might result in the selection of a new attended input, a shift in attention perceived as either controlled and selective or unexpected and distracting.

We have all experienced the sudden conscious awareness of an unattended input. The so-called cocktail party effect[11] occurs when you hear your name mentioned somewhere in a crowded room as you engage in a discussion with someone else. Even as you attend to the discussion, presumably you monitor other sounds in the room unconsciously. Your attention controller detects an important stimulus—your name—which causes you to shift your conscious attention away from your discussion.

Using these basic concepts, the distracting nature of mobile devices in the classroom can be recast. Given two potential inputs, the instructor or a laptop screen displaying a game of Solitaire, some students select the instructor as the attended input and the laptop as the unattended input. Those who are trying to listen to their instructor and find their attention captured by their own or another student's laptop screen are distracted by that device. This can be problematic in a classroom environment, as it interferes with students' ability to process course-related information and prevents them from obtaining an outcome (specifically, learning) they desire and expect to receive, a common cause of frustration, anger, and aggression.[12] This emotional response is probably more pronounced when students are distracted by others' devices over which they have no control.

As much as we hope that all students select their instructors as the primary target of their attention during class, we know that some choose the game of Solitaire, relegating the instructor to the status of unattended input. This is often described erroneously as distraction. In fact, these students are not distracted by their devices; they have selected them for attention. If anything, these students may find themselves distracted by the instructor. This is probably what passes as multitasking for many students. They attend to e-mail, instant messages, and other unrelated, device-based information during class, while monitoring the instructional stream unconsciously. Their attention controllers are set to respond to important signals, such as the phrase, "This will be on the test." In the classroom version of the cocktail party effect, students' attention then snaps to the instructor.

Although the challenge in this case is one of student motivation, not distraction, the two are closely related. As more students decide to instant message or play online games during class, the volume and variety of potentially distracting environmental information increases, making it more difficult for motivated learners to attend to the instructor. What impact does this have on classroom design? First and foremost, instructors must be able to engage students in the learning process during class time, and classrooms must be designed to facilitate that engagement. It is difficult for students to attend to other activities when they are talking to an instructor, working on a group activity, or using their devices for academic purposes. Instead of banning instant messaging in class, instructors might be supported in their use of this and other social technologies to facilitate class-related discussion and collaborative work.

Attempting to prohibit the use of devices in class through edict or infrastructure (for example, installing an Internet kill switch) is costly and does little to address the underlying problem. It is preferable to design classrooms and classroom computing policies that allow instructors to exercise greater social control. In the case of laptops in the classroom, screens should be easily visible to instructors as they walk around the room, and instructors should be able to display any student's laptop screen to a public screen at a moment's notice. In large classes, software that allows instructors to view thumbnail images of each student's screen (for example, DyKnow Monitor or SMART SynchronEyes) may also be useful. Although most instructors are probably not interested in spending time on what feels like student surveillance, the mere presence of these methods combined with clear classroom policies offers a good classroom management solution that lets students continue using their devices for academic purposes.

Through their behavior, some students are telling us that they feel neither the need nor the desire to pay close attention to the instructor during some classes. Generally speaking, this is nothing new. However, those responsible for designing learning spaces should be aware that today's incarnation of this problem requires additional study. Today's devices are colliding with yesterday's methods. What takes place in a college classroom is changing, due in large part to the very information technology that gives some instructors and administrators cause for concern. The classroom is no longer a place where information is delivered to passive students. A growing number of students get that information elsewhere and do not expect to hear it repeated verbatim in class. Instead, the classroom is becoming an interactive, collaborative environment where knowledge is created actively by students, many of whom have devices that are as much a part of them as their own skin and that can be a very important part of this process.

Collaboration in the Classroom

Although planning for data projection and network access is an important part of today's classroom design process, information technology is likely to have an even greater indirect effect on how fixed-site classrooms are used in the future. The migration to the Web of the content traditionally delivered by instructors in lecture format is helping shift the function served by brick-and-mortar classrooms from information delivery to collaboration and discussion. Collaborative learning refers to a wide variety of "educational activities in which human relationships are the key to welfare, achievement, and mastery," wherein faculty "help students learn by working together on substantive issues."[13] Surveys indicate that lecture is still the most common instructional method used by college educators in the United States.[14] Nonetheless, the transition from lecture to collaboration is well under way.

What impact does this have on classroom design? This fundamental change will challenge designers to create environments that facilitate collaborative activities. Instead of theaters where students watch instructors perform, classrooms must be flexible meeting places. Bruffee[15] described the ideal classroom for collaborative learning:

> A level floor, movable seats, chalkboards on three or four walls, controlled acoustics (acoustical tiled ceilings and carpeted floors), and no central seminar table (or one that can be pushed well out of the way without threatening an attack of lumbago). An alternative is six to ten movable four- or five-sided tables of roughly card-table size.

This description implies a maximum class size of 50 students. The question of classroom density is an important one: Researchers have explored the psychological and educational effects of classroom density, both spatial (the size of the room) and social (the number of students). In their meta-analysis of 77 different studies on this issue, Glass and Smith[16] concluded that higher social density results in lower student achievement. When designing collaborative classrooms, a good social density benchmark is three to five groups of 6 to 12 students each. Spatial density should be such that both students and instructors have enough room to move easily from group to group (specifically, 4 to 7 feet between groups). Designers should also pay careful attention to the degree to which students feel crowded in a classroom. The experience of crowding in educational settings appears related to personal space violation.[17] Research suggests that groups of students can be expected to work together most effectively at personal distances of 2 to 4 feet without feeling crowded.

Although class size is a limiting factor when implementing certain collaborative learning activities comfortably, small group collaboration and discussion are easier to manage in large classes than many instructors realize. Informal small group techniques like think-pair-share,[18] wherein students think briefly about a question posed by the instructor, discuss their thoughts with a student sitting next to them, and then share their joint thoughts with the class, are feasible in large classes[19] and can be facilitated by technology. More formal activities such as jigsaw groups and structured controversy can also engage students in large classes.[20]

Classroom response systems or "clickers" are used by a growing number of instructors to gather student feedback and stimulate in-class discussion. In classes that allow group network access, a wide variety of groupware tools can support collaboration in groups of all sizes. DyKnow Vision allows students to view and annotate instructor whiteboard activity in real time. Instructors can then invite students to the virtual whiteboard, displaying their work to the entire class. GroupSystems is a suite of tools for supporting idea generation, organization, and evaluation in face-to-face and distributed groups.

Virtual Learning Environments

Today's students spend an increasing amount of their time peering at computer screens. These virtual environments have physical characteristics that are just as real as those of a dormitory room or a brick-and-mortar classroom, and students can become just as attached to them. On one end of the continuum are virtual worlds that emulate a natural, multidimensional environment. Many students subscribe to massive multiplayer online games such as *World of Warcraft*, wherein they develop personas or "avatars," travel from town to town, acquire property, meet other people, and solve problems. On the other end of the spectrum are the online work spaces that students use every day, such as course management systems and campus portals. Somewhere in between are applications such as Facebook and MySpace, or persistent, customizable, social spaces that lack the immersive qualities of virtual worlds but are more open, recreational, and social than campus work spaces.

Although many administrators and instructors are familiar with course management systems and campus portals, fewer have experience with virtual worlds and may question their academic relevance. A good example of a virtual world used as a classroom is *Second Life*, an online environment designed to support creativity, collaboration, commerce, and entertainment. Although members can play games in world, the environment itself is not a game in the traditional sense. Instead, it is an open environment (what some call synthetic reality) where members can interact with each other and build things (for example, buildings, games, clothing, furniture) for use within the virtual world. A growing community of educators uses *Second Life* for instructional purposes. In fall 2005, the School of Architecture at The University of Texas at Austin used *Second Life* in the course Designing Digital Communities, and Southern New Hampshire University used it in Introduction to International Business. Figure 2 shows a snapshot of my *Second Life* avatar, Hoptoad Flan, enjoying a relaxing moment.

Figure 2. *Second Life* Avatar Hoptoad Flan

What impact does this have on classroom design? First, campuses can expect the boundaries between virtual and brick-and-mortar learning environments to continue to blur. Students and instructors will need access to their virtual learning environments while seated in their brick-and-mortar classrooms. Second, as campuses accept the notion that virtual spaces are actually classrooms, they can begin to apply the same care and consideration to decisions about course management systems and campus portals as they do to decisions about new construction and renovation. Of utmost importance is the usability of these virtual spaces.

A popular model of usability[21] identifies five criteria for defining a usable system:

▶ *Learnability* refers to the speed and ease with which a novice user can achieve proficiency with the system.

▶ *Efficiency* refers to the degree to which the system supports the performance of an experienced user in the shortest amount of time and with the fewest steps.

▶ *Memorability* refers to the degree to which a user, particularly an intermittent or casual user, can remember how to accomplish a task using the system, the steps of which were learned previously.

▶ *Errors* refer to the number of mistakes and missteps made by users.

▶ *Satisfaction* refers to the users' overall emotional experience when using the system.

Careful, objective usability analyses of common digital environments should be conducted and problems should be addressed using similar decision-making processes and with the same sense of urgency that campuses apply when addressing poor conditions in brick-and-mortar classrooms.

College Classrooms of Mystery and Enchantment

As students enter a virtual or brick-and-mortar learning environment, they form a cognitive impression of that space and experience an associated emotional response, just as Harry Potter did when he entered his Divination classroom. People's preference for specific environments appears to depend on their cognitive impression. Kaplan and Kaplan[22] suggested four cognitive determinants of environmental preference:

▶ *Coherence,* or the ease with which a setting can be organized cognitively
▶ *Complexity,* or the perceived capacity of the setting to occupy interest and stimulate activity
▶ *Legibility,* or perceived ease of use
▶ *Mystery,* or the perception that entering the setting would lead to increased learning, interaction, or interest

An interesting addition to this list might be the concept of *enchantment.* Bennett[23] described enchantment as the experience of being "both caught up and carried away." When enchanted by what we are experiencing, we are held spellbound, our senses seem heightened,[24] and we are caught in a moment of pure presence that we try to maintain.[25]

Students probably find today's brick-and-mortar college classrooms quite coherent and legible. They make perfect sense to those who expect to sit, facing forward, and listen quietly. Virtual learning environments may lack some of this coherence and legibility but are probably perceived as more complex and mysterious. What of enchantment? Our students are enchanted by works of art, musical performances, and breathtaking landscapes, but do they find our learning environments enchanting? We can all recall our favorite classroom and our favorite place to study as students. We all relate to Harry Potter walking into a classroom on the first day of school and experiencing a sense of awe and wonder at the feathers, stubs of candles, packs of tattered playing cards, and silvery crystal balls on the shelves. It is possible to build learning environments from both brick-and-mortar and bits-and-bytes that draw students in and elicit a sense of mystery and enchantment. As we respond to the increased presence of networked devices, the transition from lecture to collaboration, and the growing importance of virtual environments and build the classrooms of the future that facilitate usability, engagement, collaboration, and learning, we would do well to remember what it was about learning environments that enchanted us and commit ourselves to preserving, restoring, and creating those experiences for our own students

Endnotes

1. J. K. Rowling, *Harry Potter and the Prisoner of Azkaban* (New York: Scholastic Press, 1999), p. 101.

2. Carol S. Weinstein, "The Physical Environment of School: A Review of the Research," *Review of Educational Research*, vol. 49, no. 4 (Autumn 1979), pp. 577–610.

3. Richard J. Jennings, Robert Nebs, and Kay Brock, "Memory Retrieval in Noise and Psychophysiological Response in the Young and Old," *Psychophysiology*, vol. 25, no. 6 (1988), pp. 633–644.

4. Russell G. Goon, Eugene J. McCown, and James W. Broyles, "Effects of Noise on Sensitivity of Introverts and Extraverts to Signals in a Vigilance Task," *Personality and Individual Differences*, vol. 6, no. 2 (1985), pp. 237–241.

5. Linda B. Nilson and Barbara E. Weaver, eds., *New Directions for Teaching and Learning. Enhancing Learning with Laptops in the Classroom* (San Francisco: Jossey-Bass, 2005).

6. "AskTheStudents.com: 4 Views from the Frontline," *Chronicle of Higher Education*, December 9, 2005, <http://chronicle.com/weekly/v52/i16/16b01501.htm>.

7. "Law Professor Bans Laptops in Class, Over Student Protest," USAToday .com, March 21, 2006, <http://www.usatoday.com/tech/news/2006-03-21-professor -laptop-ban_x.htm>.

8. The cognitive science of attention and consciousness is a large area of study. There is considerable debate within the field over the processes involved. The model and ideas presented here are generalizations and represent only one approach. Those interested in learning more should consult Harold E. Pashler, *The Psychology of Attention* (Cambridge, Mass.: The MIT Press, 1998); Raja Parasuraman, ed., *The Attentive Brain* (Cambridge, Mass: The MIT Press, 1998; and Elizabeth A. Styles, *The Psychology of Attention* (East Sussex, U.K.: Psychology Press Ltd., 1997).

9. Arnold L. Glass, Keith J. Holyoak, and John. L. Santa, *Cognition* (Reading, Mass.: Addison-Wesley Publishing Company, 1979).

10. Ibid.

11. E. Collin Cherry, "Some Experiments on the Recognition of Speech, with One and Two Ears," *Journal of the Acoustical Society of America*, vol. 25, no. 5 (September 1953), pp. 975–979, <http://scitation.aip.org/dbt/dbt.jsp?KEY=JASMAN&Volume=25&Issue=5>.

12. Leonard Berkowitz, "Frustration-Aggression Hypothesis: Examination and Reformulation," *Psychological Bulletin*, vol. 106, no. 1 (1989), pp. 59–73.

13. Kenneth A. Bruffee, *Collaborative Learning: Higher Education, Interdependence, and the Authority of Knowledge*, 2nd ed. (Baltimore: The Johns Hopkins University Press, 1999).

14. Donald A. Bligh, *What's the Use of Lectures?* (San Francisco: Jossey-Bass, 2000).

15. Bruffee, op. cit., p. 259.

16. Gene V. Glass and Mary L. Smith, "Meta-Analysis of Research on the Relationship of Class Size and Achievement," *Educational Evaluation and Policy Analysis*, vol. 1, no. 1 (1979), pp. 2–16.

17. Yakov M. Epstein and Robert A. Karlin, "Effects of Acute Experimental Crowding," *Journal of Applied Social Psychology*, vol. 5, no. 1 (1975), pp. 34–53.

18. Frank Lyman, "The Responsive Class Discussion," in *Mainstreaming Digest*, A. S. Anderson, ed. (College Park, Md.: University of Maryland College of Education, 1981).

19. James L. Cooper and Pamela P. Robinson, "Getting Started: Informal Small-Group Strategies in Large Classes," in *New Directions for Teaching and Learning—Strategies for Energizing Large Classes: From Small Groups to Learning Communities*, Jean MacGregor et al., eds. (San Francisco: Jossey-Bass, 2000), pp. 17–24.

20. Karl A. Smith, "Structured Controversy," *Engineering Education*, vol. 74, no. 5 (1984), pp. 306–309.

21. Jakob Neilson, *Usability Engineering* (San Francisco: Morgan Kaufman, 1993).

22. Stephen Kaplan and Rachael Kaplan, *Cognition and Environment: Functioning in an Uncertain World* (New York: Praeger, 1982).

23. Jane Bennett, *The Enchantment of Modern Life: Attachments, Crossings, and Ethics* (Princeton: The Princeton University Press, 2001), p. 5.

24. John McCarthy and Peter Wright, "The Enchantments of Technology," in *Funology: From Usability to Enjoyment*, Mark A. Blythe et al., eds. (The Netherlands: Kluwer Academic Publishers, 2004), pp. 81–90.

25. Philip Fisher, *Wonder, the Rainbow, and the Aesthetics of Rare Experiences* (Boston, Mass.: Harvard University Press, 1998).

About the Author

Ken A. Graetz is the director of e-learning at Winona State University, where he is engaged in the development of learning opportunities for WSU faculty and staff members, e-learning project management and support, and numerous research and development projects. His research interests include team and group dynamics, social cognition, psychometrics, and computer-supported collaborative work. Graetz received a PhD in psychology from the University of North Carolina at Chapel Hill in 1992.

CHAPTER 7

Linking the Information Commons to Learning

Joan K. Lippincott
Coalition for Networked Information

What exactly is an information commons? Just a new name that institutions give to renovated library spaces? A library reference area that has been spruced up with new furniture and equipped with a large number of computer workstations? Or something more? Are some entire libraries information commons? Is there any genuine meaning in the change in terminology from "information" commons to "learning" commons? This chapter explores the concept of the information commons, describes some of its features, and focuses on the links between information commons and learning. The information should help those involved in planning information commons make choices that ensure the space supports the academic mission of the institution.

Characterizing the Information Commons

Many institutions are renovating their libraries to become information commons or learning commons. Frequently, the information commons occupies one floor of a library facility, generally a main service floor, which often includes or replaces the library's reference area. Most information commons are currently in library spaces that have been renovated; a minority are in totally new buildings. A small number of information commons are in nonlibrary buildings.[1]

These renovated facilities have become enormously successful, if gate count statistics are used as a measure. At Indiana University, for example, the main library gate count almost doubled from the year prior to the opening of the in-formation commons to the second full year of its existence.[2] Although statistics such as gate counts illustrate the impact of an information commons, there is more to success than just getting students into the library's facilities. St. Thomas University's librarian explained:

> I see that one rationale for the Commons is to "get the students to the library." In our case, it has been very effective in attracting

students...our gate count was 110 percent higher...so, it will attract students. But that begs the question—once they are in the building, what do we do with them? How do we engage them? The rationale for the learning commons, in my view, is that, properly designed, implemented, and operated, it will enhance student learning and scholarship. That is the real challenge, and the real goal, of the learning commons.[3]

Pervasive Technology

Information commons have drawn students by offering environments that address their needs,[4] bringing together technology, content, and services in a physical space that results in an environment different from that of a typical library. Traditional libraries offer technology, content, and services, so what is new or different about the information commons? The technology in an information commons is intentionally more pervasive than in most traditional academic libraries. If not already a feature of the library, wireless access is added when the information commons is developed. In addition, increased hardwired Internet connections let students access large files, such as multimedia, or offer an alternative to wireless when the network becomes saturated at peak use times.

Some information commons have hundreds of computers configured with a rich application suite as well as space for laptops. The software on the public computers is much more extensive than that available in typical libraries, including word-processing, presentation, and spreadsheet software, at a minimum. In addition, some workstations have statistical packages, geographic information systems (GIS), or multimedia production and editing capabilities. In contrast, workstations in many traditional library reference areas limit what users can do, namely, check the library's catalog or access licensed information products and Web resources, but do not allow for writing papers, manipulating data, or developing presentations. Some view workstations in traditional library reference areas as consuming valuable space where expert help on information resource discovery and retrieval is available and therefore limit the functions to accessing and retrieving information. In an information commons, the underlying philosophy is to provide users with a seamless work environment so that they may access, manage, and produce information all at the same workstation.

Group Spaces

Another major difference between an information commons and traditional libraries is the way in which they accommodate groups. Traditional libraries have focused on providing quiet space for individual study. Occasionally, a few group study rooms are available, but they are considered a peripheral feature of the library. In an information commons, much of the space is configured for use by small groups of students, reflecting students' desire for collaborative learning and combining social interaction with work. Information commons frequently have furniture built to accommodate several people sharing a common computer and provide large tables where several students can use their laptops while working together, comfortable seating areas with upholstered furniture to encourage informal meetings, cafés with food and drink, and group study rooms, often with a computer and screen, so students can work together efficiently on projects. (See Figure 1.)

Figure 1. Group Space in Information Commons at (a) University of Massachusetts Amherst and (b) University of Binghamton

(a)

(b)

Photo courtesy of UMass/Amherst   Photo courtesy of Binghamton University's Information Commons in the Glenn G. Bartle Library

User Services, Not Just Information Services

The range of services in an information commons is broader than in a traditional reference area. Personnel assist with users' technology needs, not just their information needs. Information commons that include multimedia production capabilities also provide support for those specialties. A service desk in the information commons generally is jointly staffed by library and information technology personnel. Students do not have to know the library's or computer center's administrative structure to ask for help; they can ask questions at a central location and receive help with a wide range of problems.

Some information commons carry the notion of one-stop shopping even further, inviting other campus services into the space. For example, the writing center and faculty teaching and learning center are frequent partners in an information commons. Students writing papers or preparing other course assignments need to access and organize information (library functions), use software and equipment (IT functions), and write the paper or put together a project (writing center function). The library, the computer center, and the writing center all support students' work, sometimes from widely disparate locations on campus. Having staff from all three units available in the information commons, or having cross-trained staff who can answer basic questions in all areas, serves students well. The University of Minnesota opened its information commons following a series of focus groups with students who wanted "one place where students can research and write their papers with librarians, writing tutors, and computer assistants all there."[5]

Teaching and learning centers, another frequent partner in information commons, offer support to faculty who have an interest in developing new curricular materials or entirely new courses. Faculty benefit from having high-end computers and software available in the same facility as library content (which may already be in digital form or can be digitized) and pedagogical experts (instructional technologists or other professionals).

The overall goal of information commons is to improve services to the campus community by offering a seamless environment that supports the way people work

Linking the Information Commons to Learning

Some information commons have vision or mission statements that directly address the relationship between the commons and the learning mission of the university. For example,

> The University of Alberta Libraries' Knowledge Common will become a unique learning hub integrating technology, information, and expertise in order to best strengthen the teaching, research, and learning opportunities that occur within the university community. The Knowledge Common will become a focal point on campus where the elements of meeting, collaboration, and discovery come together (http://www.library.ualberta.ca/kcommon/services/indext.cfm).

Making this linkage operational can be a challenge.

Enabling Student Work

Walking into a busy information commons on a weekday evening, an observer would likely see groups of students clustered around computers, some chatting, others talking on cell phones, some with headphones listening to audio while they work on computers, and some working on their own, perhaps on a laptop, with coffee and snacks, books and notebooks spread out on a table. It would be difficult to tell, without peering over their shoulders, exactly what types of activities the students were engaged in, particularly whether they're recreational or academic. Are they playing computer games? Buying things on the Internet? Sending and receiving instant messages? Or are they involved in more scholarly pursuits, such as accessing journals licensed by the library, using art image collections, writing papers, editing videos for course projects, or accessing assignments through a course management system? The students probably are doing some of each.

Today's students mix academic and social activities. Some see their multitasking as a troublesome lack of ability to concentrate, but it is a logical strategy for students who grew up in a world with media in many formats at their fingertips 24 hours a day. Information commons, with their large numbers of computers, range of software, and spaces configured for groups, provide an ideal environment for students to collaborate with others and multitask. Developing spaces where students can collaborate outside class provides support for an increased emphasis on teamwork, both in and outside higher education.[6]

One satisfied student at the University of Tennessee, where the first phase of its information commons opened in fall 2005, stated,

> Every time I have been in the library after hours, the Commons has been packed full of students. Some students were finishing assignments, some doing group projects, and some just relaxing with friends. The group study areas are of the perfect number and size, and the computers have all the programs I could need on them.[7]

Students spend much of their time learning outside classrooms by reading, exploring, creating, and communicating. The information commons creates an environment that nurtures these activities by providing content in a variety of formats, technologies that might not be affordable to individual students, and spaces built to encourage collaboration and interaction. Outside the classroom, students extend their understanding of the basic course concepts and make the learning their own by investigating a topic and producing a product that integrates it with the content of the course.[8] Doing this type of work engages students in their coursework and the discipline.[9]

A key purpose of an information commons is to leverage the intersection of content, technology, and services in a physical facility to support student learning. For example, a student in a 20th-century film course might develop a paper, primarily text, that embeds film clips and related images from other sources (perhaps illustrating events or costumes from the era of the film) and draws on film criticism from books and journals, or a student in a marketing course might create a Power Point presentation using data from the U.S. Census, statistical software, images to illustrate points, and materials from business journals to develop the presentation. Then, the student can rehearse the presentation in a specially designed "practice presentation" room set up with a podium, computer projector and screen, and chairs for an audience of friends who can critique the presentation. For projects like these, students need access to hardware, software, print and digital content, assistance from individuals with a broad range of expertise; and a place in which all these things are available. (See Figure 2.)

Advertising Available Services

For students initially walking into an information commons, the first impression is that a lot of technology is available, but it is not clear for what purpose. To advertise the range of activities possible in the commons, libraries can provide visual cues to inform students of the rich information resources, the range of software,

Figure 2. Georgia Tech Information Commons Practice Presentation Room

Photo courtesy of Joanne Henning

and the services offered. Some information commons have used colorful banners to promote services. The computer default screens and mouse pads in the information commons can promote the content, software, and services students can access. Libraries can display digital resources on large screens to illustrate the rich content available for use in course projects. The information commons can exhibit student products developed as a result of work in the commons. Staff can collaborate with student focus groups to refine the language of signs that indicate services available. For example, merely adding the word "research" to a sign designating reference services seemed to greatly improve student understanding of what types of questions they might ask at that service point at one information commons.[10]

Students exploring college choices as well as students new to campus may initially explore the library through its Web site. In many cases, it is difficult, if not impossible, to find information about the library's information commons on the library's Web pages. The information commons Web pages could foster the close connection of its resources to learning by emphasizing how the content, hardware, software, and space that it provides are useful for course projects.

Linking to Courses

Librarians can seek out likely courses and work with the faculty to forge a closer relationship between the resources available in the information commons and course assignments. For example, in a course where students do oral history projects, the librarian could work with faculty to develop a guide to sources of context (newspapers, books, image collections, diaries) that would assist students in shaping their projects, and then offer a class or online tutorial to help them use equipment and software to record and edit oral histories that they capture themselves, providing the tools they need to develop a narrative presentation.

Information on the hardware, software, and services offered in the information commons that would be useful for course projects could be embedded into a course management system as well.

Often learning can be strengthened by integrated services. Physical colocation can lead staff to reconfigure services. For example, at Dartmouth College the library reference staff, information technology service staff, and writing center are located on one floor of the library. They have developed a program in which they jointly provide intensive training to a group of students who serve as peer tutors for locating information (library) resources, using technology, and improving writing for course assignments. Normally, these three functions are separate, but students' needs often cross administrative boundaries. The students advertise their services by making brief presentations in writing-intensive classes and scheduling appointments in a library tutoring center.[11]

Leveraging Technology

Providing new types of technology can help the information commons en hance learning. A new option called TeamSpot is currently available in libraries at Stanford University, which calls its implementation GroupSpace (http://academiccomputing.stanford.edu/groupspace/teamspot.html, ch. 35), and the University of Washington (http://depts.washington.edu/sacg/facilities/advtech/teamspot.shtml), among others. The set-up allows a small group of students to connect their laptops to a large display screen that participants can individually control from their desktops (or using a digital pen or remote control), facilitating collaborative work.

Classrooms

Many information commons incorporate classrooms equipped with a variety of technologies, including computers and projectors, smartboards, video editing equipment, and videoconferencing capabilities. Often one or two classrooms are set aside for the library's information literacy instruction program. Classrooms available for general use are either assigned by the registrar or scheduled by the library. On many campuses, concerns have arisen that some faculty request the technology-enabled classrooms because of their location or newness rather than a need to incorporate technology into the learning process. Given the limited number of these classrooms, it would be to the institution's advantage to verify that the classes using these spaces genuinely use the technology. The information commons staff can also make a special effort to develop tools and services for the courses held in their facility. (See Figure 3.)

Information Commons Development

Given their inherent connection to technology, information commons will need to continually change as hardware, software, and networking configurations evolve. Also, as more faculty incorporate technology into the curriculum, and particularly as they encourage student use of technology in their academic work, the use of

Figure 3. Flexible Furniture in Emory University Classrooms

information commons will increase and change. This section identifies some significant issues and trends likely to influence the evolution of information commons.

Mission

Institutions should have a clear purpose for their information commons and yet understand that flexibility will be needed as it evolves. Some institutions try to communicate the mission by renaming a renovated facility, as in the case of libraries or computer labs that have evolved into learning commons. In the learning commons students can perform a wide range of technology and information-related activities in space conducive to group work.[12] The types of facilities described in this chapter are variously called an information commons, learning commons, knowledge commons, or simply commons. In some cases, the traditional term library is used, with no special designation for the area in which these new configurations and services can be found. Some institutions refer to an area of the library as an information or learning commons despite no discernable differences from a traditional reference area. While the name of the facility can be important in conveying its functions to potential users, it is far more important to develop a clear mission for the space and to configure it to support learning.

Assessment

Librarian Joanne Henning visited 25 information commons during a study leave. She asked personnel at each site about the type of assessment conducted there. She found that "few libraries have done formal assessments of their ICs [information commons]; even fewer did a formal information gathering of potential users before implementing the IC" (http://jhenning.law.uvic.ca/final_report.html). Planners of information commons should talk with users to develop an understanding of their needs and priorities. Developing a vision and/or mission statement to guide planning decisions for the information commons will likely be an iterative process. This mission and associated goals should guide the development of a coordinated assessment program for the information commons. Such a program could combine statistical data (gate counts, use of equipment and software, information requests) and qualitative data (interviews with student and faculty users). Ideally, results can be compared with data gathered prior to construction of the information commons. This data can reveal needed changes (satisfaction with services, need for additional equipment or software), justify additional funding, and demonstrate the commons' contribution to teaching and learning.

Services and Staff

While the planning of an information commons frequently begins with the development of a floor plan and consideration of equipment and furniture, a better first step is to understand what types of activities users will engage in and what services will be needed to support those activities. This will have implications for the campus partners involved in the facility, the resources needed, the location of service areas, and the types of support staff. For example, the need to create multimedia products has implications for hardware, software, network infrastructure, furniture, and staff expertise. Or, if the information commons is to provide formal learning that incorporates technology, then classroom space will be required. Institutions that want to draw faculty into the facility sometimes move the campus teaching and learning center into the information commons.

Developing services that have a virtual and physical component is one of the opportunities and challenges of information commons. At the University of Tennessee, Donna Braquet, life sciences librarian, developed a Web site called bioLIBlog: Explore, Share, Grow (http:www.lib.utk.edu/news/biology/archives/biology_nights_the_library/)

> ...as a place for biology students to network and communicate about biological information. This site serves as a one-stop location to ask questions and read responses, post comments about the Biology Night film series, and share science-related blogs, Web sites, books, journals, and magazines with your peers.

The in-person component is a biology-related film series and discussion, held in the library auditorium. The University of Minnesota library hosts a blog service called UThink: Blogs at the University Libraries (http://blog.lib.umn.edu/) for the campus; their Web pages offer advice to faculty on how to use blogs in teaching and provide guidelines to students and faculty for developing blogs. The library also hosts occasional in-person events related to blogging.

Information commons staff typically are located at service desks. Some information commons have a service desk jointly staffed by library and IT staff; others have separate desks for library services, IT services, and those other services housed in the information commons (such as a career center or writing center). Staff of the various units often offer the same types of services they offered prior to the information commons; they do not take advantage of the new configuration to rethink their services or staffing patterns. Two innovative facilities—Dartmouth and Georgia Tech—have altered staffing by hiring students and giving them intensive training by partner units. Dartmouth consolidated its library, IT services, and writing center in one facility. At Georgia Tech, the library and IT units provide intensive multimedia creation training to graduate students who then assist other students in a heavily used service. An increasing number of institutions probably will draw on the talents of their students to deliver services in the information commons. The types of services developed by Dartmouth and Georgia Tech accomplish a number of things:

▶ They leverage the colocation of various units by providing new services that take advantage of the combined talents and expertise of each professional group.

▶ They use peers whom students are more likely to approach with questions.

▶ Services can be offered during more hours of the day due to the willingness of students to work later hours than most staff.

One area for additional collaboration is for information technologists and librarians to work more closely with teaching and learning center staff housed in the information commons. The opportunity for enhancing the curriculum through the combined knowledge of these groups is great.

Furniture

Flexibility is the key consideration in choosing furniture for an information commons. As technology-oriented facilities, they need to change as student use patterns change. For example, the need for fixed workstations rather than tables where students can plug in their own laptops is shifting on many campuses. Soon students may adopt smaller devices such as notebook computers and cell phones, with implications for furniture configuration. Most information commons furniture has wheels for easy mobility. Generally, a mix of desk-style furniture and soft, comfortable seating is desirable. Some information commons include diner-style booths for small groups or areas with beanbag chairs for informal seating. Furniture that allows privacy for small groups while providing a means for people to see above barriers is desirable. Portable whiteboards, used in only a few information commons, might be more widely adopted for sharing information and defining group space in an open area. (See Figure 4.)

Figure 4. Diner-Style Seating at University of Nevada Las Vegas Library

Photo courtesy of Joanne Henning

Technology

Users of the information commons will continue to want wireless network connections for convenience. Sometimes they will need wired Internet connections for specific applications or when wireless connectivity becomes saturated. In addition, power outlets should be ubiquitous so that students can plug in their multiple devices.

Hardware and software choices should be left until the last possible moment before opening an information commons in order to ensure purchase of the latest versions. Will hardware be standardized? Will the same software be loaded onto each machine, or will some have unique software, such as GIS? Many information commons have lending services for laptops, digital and video cameras, and other devices.

In the future, information commons may provide 3D visualization labs, where streams of data are combined to illustrate research concepts. Having a shared institutional resource in the library increases its value to the organization,[13] as not every department can support this type of high-end facility or provide trained staff to operate it. Visualization is becoming increasingly important in many of the sciences as well as in business and the humanities.

Model for More than the Library

Historically, computer labs were designed to hold the most hardware possible in a limited space, loaded with a wide range of software. Configured for individual use, user desk space is limited. Frequently, the labs are staffed by student assistants who primarily provide security for the equipment and check student IDs. In contrast, information commons are configured, at least in part, for group use and have varying furniture configurations to support different modes of use. As campuses rethink the purpose and utility of their computer labs, they may look to the information commons as a replicable model for computer labs, as does the University of Tennessee.[14] The reconfiguration would require new furniture and a new model of staffing, with more highly trained staff available to assist with student needs. The Computing Center at Cox Hall at Emory University (http://www.cet.emory.edu/cox/index.cfm, ch. 8) provides an example of a new-style computer lab, with many group areas, comfortable and moveable furniture configurations, and small classrooms.

College or departmental libraries may transform all or part of their facilities into information commons, as has occurred at the Vanderbilt University Peabody Library (http://www.library.vanderbilt.edu/peabody/commons/index.html), which serves the College of Education, and the University of Iowa Hardin Library for the Health Sciences (http://www.lib.uiowa.edu/commons/). In the future, these facilities may integrate with the college or department computer lab. In large universities with multiple libraries, the undergraduate library (or part of it) may transform into an information commons, as happened at The University of Texas at Austin.[15] Information commons may be part of new buildings that combine library and technology resources with a large number of technology-enabled classrooms, such as the University of Georgia Student Learning Center (http://www.slc.uga.edu/, ch. 41).

Some information commons will develop specialized areas or features. At the Dartmouth College Library, a News Center (http://www.dartmouth.edu/~newscenter/) offers comfortable seating, current print and electronic newspapers, Web access to many electronic news resources, and a large display screen featuring news from around the world. (See Figure 5.) Other organizations might develop group study rooms for graduate students, incorporating electronic thesis and dissertation (ETD) software, guidelines, and other resources. Indiana University Bloomington has created a quiet information commons on a floor above the bustling main information commons (http://ic.indiana.edu/). Information commons will encompass new models and variations, with a wide variety of names, but all will support learning by integrating technology, content, and services in physical space.

Figure 5. Dartmouth Baker/Berry Library News Center

Photo courtesy of Joanne Henning

Transforming the entire library into the information commons model may be particularly suitable for institutions serving primarily undergraduates. In addition, individual components of the information commons model may be adopted in college or department classroom buildings, such as at Georgia Tech, where some departments have replicated the practice presentation room pioneered in the library's information commons.[16]

Aesthetics

While successful information commons have a palpable buzz as students collaborate and interact, the spaces themselves often have a rather austere, even dull, appearance. Information commons generally do not sparkle. Often decorated with neutral colors and utilitarian furniture, they are dominated by computers. The one colorful place may be the café. In the future, planners may pay more attention to aesthetics. Some institutions are involving students in their design process and are seeking ideas from business and retail as they plan new spaces.[17] The use of lively colors, interesting patterns and textures, and natural light can enhance the aesthetic appeal of the information commons. If at all possible, the budget for renovating space for an information commons should include funds for architects and designers.

One facility that has great aesthetic appeal is Emory University's Computing Center at Cox Hall (http://www.cet.emory.edu/cox/index.cfm), a computer facility and not, strictly speaking, an information commons. The facility uses a mix of attractive colors, small but brightly colored lamps, and fanciful furniture to convey a welcoming, informal atmosphere. Several areas provide coffee-table-height surfaces that hold a computer, surrounded by floor cushion seating. The eye-catching combination appeals to many students. This generally informal facility also houses two small classrooms and a more formal conference room, with rich wood surfaces.

The information commons can also build community on campus. Cafés, art display areas, and spaces for films or concerts can all foster campus community. The library can develop Web links and virtual displays to connect in-person events to resources available in the library and on the Web. This type of programming can provide informal learning opportunities for students and others on campus.

Conclusion

With careful planning (see the sidebars), an information commons can be a collaborative learning space, not just a glorified computing lab; it can be a place to access, use, and create information, not just a reference area with rows of computers; and it can provide transparent user services, not fiefdoms of service points. Information commons can enhance learning, provide an environment for students that is both academic and social, and foster a sense of community on campus. Information commons require a large commitment of campus resources to develop and maintain. Clearly articulating the information commons' link to learning and then developing the requisite services and environment can help justify that investment and create a popular and mission-critical space on campus.

Planning an Information Commons

▷ Develop a vision related to learning.
▷ Conduct a needs assessment.
▷ Develop goals.
▷ Design an assessment plan.
▷ Determine appropriate partners.
▷ Define and gain resources.
▷ Determine the location
▷ Define what you want users to be able to do.
▷ Define services to offer.
▷ Determine staff needs.
  (and then...)
▷ Develop the floor plan.
▷ Plan the technology (network, hardware, software).
▷ Choose furniture.

Key Questions for Planners

▷ What is the purpose of the information commons?
▷ What faculty and student needs will be addressed?
▷ What programs will we put into place that will emphasize a link to learning?
▷ Which campus units will be involved, and how will they work together?
▷ What kinds of hardware, software, and seating configurations are needed?
▷ What kinds of staff are needed?
▷ How will we promote the link of the information commons to learning?
▷ How will we measure success?

Endnotes

1. Among others, exceptions include the James and Anne Duderstadt Center at the University of Michigan (http://www.dc.umich.edu/) and the Johnson Center at George Mason University (http://ulcweb.gmu.edu/concept/mission_statement.htm).

2. Suzanne Thorin, "Models of Successful Information Commons," presentation at Academic Libraries 2005: The Information Commons, Saratoga Springs, New York, November 10–11, 2005, <http://www.ny3rs.org/al2005.html>.

3. Dan Gjelten, posting on the EDUCAUSE LIBIT listserv, October 31, 2005.

4. I use the terms *information commons* and *learning commons* interchangeably in this chapter. Although in principle they could describe facilities with different missions, in practice I have found no direct correlation between what the facility offers and its name. Another variation is to name the area simply the Commons. Some sources that provide good background on information commons include D. Russell Bailey, "Information Commons Services for Learners and Researchers: Evolution in Patron Needs, Digital Resources and Scholarly Publishing," INFORUM 2005: 11th Conference on Professional Information Resources (in Czech), Prague, May 24–26, 2005, <http://www.inforum.cz/inforum2005/prispevek.php-prispevek=32.htm>; Donald Beagle, "Conceptualizing an Information Commons," *Journal of Academic Librarianship*, vol. 25, no. 2 (1999), pp. 82–89; and Leslie Haas and Jan Robertson, *The Information Commons*, SPEC Kit 281 (Washington, D.C.: Association of Research Libraries, July 2004).

5. Caroline Crouse and Kristianne Buechler, "Starting with Assessment: The Development of an Information Commons from User's Needs," poster presented at the ACRL National Conference, Minneapolis, April 9, 2005, <http://www.tc.umn.edu/~crous018/acrl-poster/>.

6. Alma Clayton-Pedersen with Nancy O'Neill, "Curricula Designed to Meet 21st-Century Expectations," in *Educating the Net Generation*, Diana G. Oblinger and James L. Oblinger, eds. (Boulder, Colo.: EDUCAUSE, 2005), <http://www.educause.edu/educatingthenetgen/>.

7. Quoted by Barbara Dewey and Brice Bible, "Relationships and Campus Politics in Building the Information Commons," presentation at Academic Libraries 2005: The Information Commons, Saratoga Springs, New York, November 10–11, 2005, <http://www.ny3rs.org/al2005.html>.

8. Colleen Carmean and Jeremy Haefner, "Mind Over Matter," *EDUCAUSE Review*, vol. 37, no. 6 (November/December 2002), pp. 26–34, <http://www.educause.edu/ir/library/pdf/erm0261.pdf>.

9. George D. Kuh and Robert M. Gonyea, "The Role of the Academic Library in Promoting Engagement in Student Learning," *College & Research Libraries*, vol. 64, no. 4 (July 2003), <http://www.ala.org/ala/acrl/acrlpubs/crljournal/backissues2003b/julymonth/candrljuly2003abstracts.htm>.

10. This was a finding at the University of Massachusetts Amherst Learning Commons.

11. Dartmouth College, RWIT: The Student Center for Research, Writing, and Information Technology, <http://www.dartmouth.edu/~rwit/>; Dartmouth does not use the term "information commons" to describe its facility.

12. Malcolm Brown, "Learning Spaces," in *Educating the Net Generation*, Diana G. Oblinger and James L. Oblinger, eds. (Boulder, Colo.: EDUCAUSE, 2005), <http://www.educause.edu/educatingthenetgen/>.

13. Bernard Frischer, "The Ultimate Internet Café: Reflections of a Practicing Digital Humanist About Designing a Future for the Research Library in the Digital Age," *Library as Place: Rethinking Roles, Rethinking Space* (Washington, D.C.: Council on Library and Information Resources, 2005).

14. Dewey and Bible, op. cit.

15. Katherine S. Mangan, "Packing Up the Books," *Chronicle of Higher Education,* July 1, 2005, <http://chronicle.com/free/v51/i43/43a02701.htm>.

16. Linda Cabot and Crit Stewart, "The Evolution of Collaborative Learning Spaces: What We've Learned," presented as part of a general session at the 2005 EDUCAUSE Southeast Regional Conference. The PowerPoint slides from their presentation are available on the Web at <http://www.educause.edu/upload/presentations/SERC05/GS02/EDUCAUSE%20SE%202005%20cabot%20stuart2.ppt>.

17 Chad Kainz, "Thinking Space," presentation at the ACRL Preconference, American Library Association, 2005, <http://hwaet.typepad.com/thinking_space/>.

About the Author

Joan K. Lippincott is the associate executive director of the Coalition for Networked Information (CNI), a joint project of the Association of Research Libraries (ARL) and EDUCAUSE. She held positions at Cornell University, Georgetown University, George Washington University, and SUNY Brockport and has worked in the Research and Policy Analysis Division of the American Council on Education (ACE) and at the National Center for Postsecondary Governance and Finance (NCPGF). Lippincott has written articles and made presentations on Net Gen students, learning spaces, collaboration among professional groups, assessment, and digital information. She received her PhD in higher education policy, planning, and administration from the University of Maryland.

CHAPTER 8

Navigating Toward the Next-Generation Computer Lab

Alan R. Cattier
Emory University

What should Emory University do with its decade-old computer lab? That question hung in the air for the design team in 2002 as they considered a slate of options for the space that had been the primary undergraduate computing facility on campus. What about an update, provisioning it with newer hardware? How about rearranging it, outfitting the space with different furniture? Maybe they should staff it differently, orienting the facility around a changed support approach? As the design team looked at the facility, these questions and their answers seemed too simple and superficial. The Computing Center at Cox Hall was in crisis.

A once state-of-the-art facility had slowly slipped into disuse, losing the centrality of purpose that prompted its creation in 1991. Increasingly, students arrived on campus with their own personal computers, and a new computing area called the InfoCommons provided well over 200 new workstations to support students and their work. The Computing Center at Cox Hall (see Figure 1) had become a hideout for a certain type of computer user—gamers who holed up in the walled-off cubes that defined the space, playing into the wee hours. Gaming was not the reason the university supported the facility with round-the-clock staffing, nor did it require prime real estate at the center of the campus.

Against this backdrop the project team began a different line of inquiry, a different approach to renovation, that reoriented the computing lab. A description of the players and the thinking that effected that reorientation follows, as well as four principles that informed the team's work. This chapter tells the story of Emory's effort to build a collaborative computing lab, relying on team members who might not always participate in a traditional computing lab design team. Finally, it reflects

Figure 1. Original Cox Hall with Many Cubicles

on the importance of informal learning spaces on today's college and university campuses, bridging the bricks-and-mortar and digital worlds that today's faculty and students both live in.

Informal Learning Spaces

What are informal learning spaces? In *Educating the Net Generation,*[1] Malcolm Brown defined them as "those outside the classrooms." He observed that in a world where wireless connectivity is increasingly ubiquitous, and with wireless devices that enable navigating a proverbial sea of digital resources, practically anywhere but the classroom is an informal learning space. The majority of space on any wirelessly networked college or university campus is informal learning space. On campuses not fully wirelessly enabled, the preponderance of informal learning spaces still exists, but the potential for them to be recognized and "activated" depends on the disposition of the digital learners and the tasks they wish to accomplish.

More abstractly, informal learning spaces are those in which learners live and learn at their discretion. They choose the time and the place to address the work that flows from formal learning spaces and into their lives as homework, projects, ideas to mull over, and conversations to have. That the relationship between formal and informal learning spaces has not received the deliberate attention of campus planners underscores the largely uncoordinated nature of the digital campus's emergence on the brick-and-mortar campus. In this environment, learners choose the locations where they feel most empowered—and most comfortable—to complete the work at hand. In places they see the best support for their way of working, they feel safe and so return frequently, knowing they can move through material and concepts on their terms. In places where they feel discomfort, a lack of connection to space and infrastructure, they leave.

The Case for Change

In late 2001, the Computing Center at Cox Hall—a prime informal learning space—did not complement the formal learning spaces of the university. It seemed unconnected to either the digital world or to the brick-and-mortar world that surrounded and informed it. Our first step was to recognize that a simple redesign would not suffice—we had to acknowledge that the very concept of a general-purpose computing lab was in question. Before the project team even formed, we communicated to the student community that the lab would not receive routine upgrades and maintenance while the university considered fundamental changes. This initial communication, however slight it may sound, was actually quite critical because it paved the way for the lab's audience to understand the seriousness of the effort to rethink the facility. This, in turn, prompted a much more responsive and interested user community when end-user surveys asked questions about the lab's future and desired use. A small, simple public commitment to dialogue and reassessment laid the foundation for broad community input.

Within Emory's Information Technology Division, we had known this day of reckoning for the Computing Center at Cox Hall was looming. In preparation, we had begun talking about those things the facility was not doing: supporting academic work, group work, or faculty and students. What the lab was doing, and with a good degree of success, was supporting the cocurricular lives of students who saw online gaming and chatting with far-away friends as key functions of the facility. As those of us responsible for the lab looked at its function, and what it would take to invigorate the facility with new academic purpose, we investigated facilities on other campuses that spoke to the idea of a next-generation computing lab. The one facility we heard about repeatedly was the USITE/Crerar Computing Center and Cybercafé at the University of Chicago (see chapter 40).

The computing lab support group, who would later form the core of the technical members of the project team, joined our vice provost on a trip to Crerar in December 2001. The trip was significant for a number of reasons. First, Crerar demonstrated the computing lab as a facility that featured different types of spaces—for individual work, group work, class work, and distance work. This hybrid model suggested a degree of flexibility and adaptability missing from Cox. Second, the visit allowed a first-hand view of the impact of food services, in this case a cyber café, on the computing lab's atmosphere. As we sat there and drank our coffee, the facility had less feel of a computing center than Cox, and we saw students sit down to work after fixing the environment to their liking. Finally, Crerar aimed—at least in some locations—to support group work. With the diner-type tables and surrounding banquettes, a group of students could sit and work in the type of space that a cubicle-centric lab like Cox inherently thwarted.

The Team

Soon after this visit the project team formed, in early 2002. Building off the lab manager group, who actually owned the facility and had made the initial trip to Chicago, the team added representation from three other groups: the classroom technologies team, the faculty support team, and the Facilities Management Division's Design Studio. The choice to include classroom technologies representatives was straightforward; those responsible for group viewing and presentation in formal learning spaces would surely have something to contribute to support group work within informal learning spaces. The faculty support team, which brought a perspective from both within the division and directly from the dean's office, could inquire how the facility might increase its role in the academic life of students and faculty. Finally, representatives from the Design Studio initially participated in the selection of an architect; as the project moved from concept to construction, they assisted the architect with the overall look and feel of the space.

Moments arise when, looking back, project planners can identify quasi-unplanned developments that benefited the project (and inevitably, some that did not). The addition of the Design Studio's talented designers was one of those developments whose impact is hard to overemphasize. Their engagement and commitment to the color, texture, and lighting of the space—what many have called the character of the Computing Center at Cox Hall—exceeded the knowledge and abilities of the technologists on the team. To many who have heard the composition of the Cox Hall project team, the question often arises how such a diverse group was assembled in the service of reimagining a lab. From those involved in the project, the real question was, with a facility that had so lost its way, could a strategy be designed that saved a role for the general computing lab on a rapidly changing, space-starved campus?

Grounding Principles

When the project team convened, a number of facts structured our dialogue with the architecture team from Collins, Cooper, and Carusi, our Atlanta-based partners in renovating Cox. Most importantly, the Computing Center at Cox Hall was no longer the only option for students seeking computing resources—they could choose from among their personal desktops and laptops, residential and departmental computing labs, and the InfoCommons. We needed not just a renovation of the facility but a reconceptualization of the lab as one node of computing amongst many spread out across campus.

Design for Uniqueness

This realization gave rise to our first design principle: our renovated facility should be shaped by an awareness of the strengths and weakness of the facilities and capabilities around it. In our particular instance, an installation like the InfoCommons dwarfed the computing resources in Cox Hall and clearly provided general computing space. Should we compete against it? That was never a question for the project team. Should we ask what it does well and what it could do better? This question was central as we looked at the InfoCommons and other computing resources across campus, devising a conceptual map of what spaces supported what types of work.

This principle manifested itself in three architectural requirements. First, the renovation must support group work. As the project team inventoried campus facilities and observed students crowding around individual workstations with inadequate space and infrastructure to support their learning materials and their learning partners, the goal of supporting collaborative work came to the fore. Support for collaboration prompted the second requirement: the facility had to accommodate noise, even encourage it, since conversation is a foundation of collaboration. Third, the facility should address user comfort in ways that none of the inventoried facilities did. This commitment to comfort-oriented furniture and seating selection, as well as allowing food and drink in the facility, was something not permitted at any other institutional computing resource across campus.

Focus on Transparency

Our first design principle, that Cox existed in a physically as well as digitally pro-scribed context, gave rise to our second design principle: since it exists in a context, that context needed to be clear and navigable to every user. As we spoke to our architecture team, this requirement came across as "the need for transparency." What does this mean? For the project team, it meant a number of things. Students needed to understand the purpose and place of the renovated Computing Center at Cox Hall. They needed to understand the relationship between our formal and informal learning spaces and the connections—designed and serendipitous—be-tween our facilities. A successful renovation, the project team thought, should demonstrate awareness of students and faculty moving throughout the campus, using resources and infrastructure optimized for a specific use. In Cox Hall, that use was the space and infrastructure to support group work.

In this sense, transparency became a cue to users that their time and experi-ence navigating a changing campus, amidst ever-changing technologies, was not haphazard and did have intentionality—a map, some deliberateness—that they would feel when they arrived in the lab. Once they started working, the vantage, the view, would underscore their arrival in the right space for the type of work they were doing. They could see others doing the same thing and model a mode of working and engagement never consciously and designedly supported on campus. Transparency was about enabling recognition on multiple levels. (See Figure 2.)

Figure 2. Fishbowl Offers Everyone a View

Invite and Encounter

As we reviewed the lab's previous use, it was easy to corroborate the cocurricular activities supported in the facility. More difficult was isolating the curricular, academic activities supported in Cox. That difficulty was unacceptable to the project team and to those who were determining whether the renovation had sufficient merit to fund. From the outset, then, the project team knew they wanted to raise the lab's academic profile. The question became whether to discourage or even eliminate the informal, gaming-type of use within the facility. On this, the project team agreed: The lab was to be a meeting zone, a crossroads between faculty and students, between the curricular and the cocurricular, between work and play—a place of student life. (See Figure 3.)

The project team recognized early on that classrooms would be integral to a new conception of the same space, along with paths and venues for connection and crossover, from having coffee with friends while talking about class to sitting at a table and reviewing class material with a professor. It should *feel* easy to move from one type of use to another. For example, a student might be making a film for a family reunion or working on a documentary for journalism class. The facility would communicate, in its look and feel, that many types of use are acceptable. To the architects and the campus design team, the third principle was clear—the facility was designed to be accommodating on multiple levels, and it should telegraph a message of comfort and suitability at the same time it invites sociability, curiosity, and creativity.

Figure 3. Large Screens in Lab for Group Work

Be Flexible, Be Adaptable

The project team's final design principle grew from the first three and is, in a sense, more overarching then any of the others. To those on the team, it grew from the recognition that we would make mistakes. We were thinking about a computer lab in a way that had few precedents, with no manual to follow or script to copy that would solve our problems. The project team entered unfamiliar territory as the visioning exercise began, and everyone felt we would make mistakes. This awareness fostered a dynamic of collaboration among the team members that channeled trust in wildly interesting ways. For instance, the campus design team recommended workstations where students could recline on large cushions. Mind you, no one had ever seen workstations like this, but the project team decided to give it a try. From the opposite extreme, the technology players, not ordinarily known for their aesthetic or fashion sense, chose from the recommended colors and textures and styles for the lab. Everyone stepped out of their comfort zones, and the project team members respected, even welcomed, incursions that marked true collaboration. As this self-awareness and collaborative working dynamic played itself out before the architecture team, the conclusions became quite simple: Whatever the architects designed, whatever we built, it had to be adaptable.

For the project team and the architect, this became a search for flexibility in everything that would go into the facility. It started with wheels on chairs and tables and progressed to movable walls and whiteboard spaces that could change, adapt, and reinforce the suitability of a location to the work attempted within it, curricular or cocurricular, faculty or student, individual or group. It continued with choosing furniture styles that could hypothetically be reoriented to meet a changing use or need in the lab. (See Figure 4.) Never, the project team vowed, would we wall ourselves into a design that didn't have some humility in the face of the change rippling through our campus and the technologies it offered.

The Way to a New Approach

What started out as an exercise in designing a computer lab and conceptualizing its role on campus became a way of thinking about learning spaces that completely reoriented our approach to facilities. Even that's not quite right, though. In seeing the campus as a network—where students, faculty, and staff constantly step into and out of physical and often digital spaces, sometimes both concurrently—no one on campus had ever indicated to the community any understanding of the navigational challenge posed by the substantial changes that had coursed through

Figure 4. Flexible Technology, Flexible Seating

the campus in the previous 10 years. The commitment to look at the Computing Center at Cox Hall, and to look at it as deeply, as seriously, as collaboratively as the many players in this renovation did, cleared a path of awareness to exactly this gesture.

In the project's wake, the facility became not only a crossroads on the campus but also a signal in/on the concurrent physical and digital campus that flashed that finding one's way in this changing matrix is navigable if one can see the cues that link the campus together, its buildings to its digital ether. (See Figure 5.) That we realized this navigational approach in an informal learning space—an old, out-of-use lab—as opposed to a formal learning space testifies to the changing place of technology in our culture. For the project team, the lesson was clear: you never know what you'll find unless you begin looking. Sometimes, as with the Computing Center at Cox Hall, you discover a new way of looking.

Figure 5. New Cox Hall: No Cubes, No Walls

Endnote

1. Malcolm Brown, "Learning Spaces," in *Educating the Net Generation*, Diana G. Oblinger and James L. Oblinger, eds. (Boulder, Colo.: EDUCAUSE, 2005), p. 12 8, <http://www.educause.edu/LearningSpaces/6072>.

About the Author

Alan R. Cattier is the director of academic technology services at Emory University. He has managed academic technology services for two years and provides coordination and operational management for faculty and student academic computing across the university. He is an adjunct faculty member in the English and environmental studies departments and teaches on literature and the environment. Cattier holds a BA from Dartmouth College and an MA from Middlebury College.

CHAPTER 9

Trends in Learning Space Design

Malcolm Brown
Dartmouth College

Philip Long
MIT

This chapter examines significant trends in learning space design, both in new construction and in renovation, and relates them to learning theory and technological advances. Three major trends inform current learning space design:

▶ Design based on learning principles, resulting in intentional support for social and active learning strategies.

▶ An emphasis on human-centered design.

▶ Increasing ownership of diverse devices that enrich learning.

These trends have been catalyzed by constructivism, digital technology, and a holistic view of learning.

The emergence of the constructivist learning paradigm has led to a focus on learning rather than teaching. It allows us to reevaluate classrooms and to consider informal learning spaces as loci for learning. If learning is not confined to scheduled classroom spaces and times, the whole campus—anywhere and at any time—is potentially an effective learning space. That holistic view of learning presents challenges, however. First, the demands on student time and attention continue to grow; even residential institutions have over-scheduled students. Second, learning doesn't just happen in classrooms; learning also occurs outside the lecture hall. New strategies for enabling learning and accommodating the multiple demands on student time have led to rethinking the use, design, and location of learning spaces.

The emphasis on learning means that we must also think about the learner. Learning spaces are not mere containers for a few, approved activities; instead, they provide *environments for people*. Factors such as the availability of food and drink, comfortable chairs, and furniture that supports a variety of learning activities are emerging as critical in the design of learning spaces—evidence of the second trend, giving consideration to human factors as integral to learning space design.

The rapidly increasing accessibility of digital technology also has changed learning space design. Digital technology continues to advance at a frenetic pace, offering greater capability while simultaneously becoming more mobile and more affordable. Five years ago, most students purchased desktop computers; two years later, most purchased laptops. The implications are significant: more affordable and mobile technology facilitates greater access to content and resources. This enhanced access, in turn, has made it possible to implement a learning paradigm that emphasizes active learning, formative assessment, social engagement, mobility, and multiple paths through content. Although specific technologies may come and go, the enduring trend is technology becoming more capable, affordable, and mobile.

Trend 1: Active and Social Learning Strategies

Today, facilities that encourage learner participation are increasingly important in learning space design. Active learning, interaction, and social engagement will be significant in the future.

Review of Learning Principles

Over the past two decades, a great deal of research has focused on how people learn. Previously, teaching was most often a kind of "broadcast" of course content at regularly scheduled intervals, from an expert to student "receivers." The learning literature agrees that learning can be enhanced, deepened, and made more meaningful if the curriculum makes the learners active participants through interactivity, multiple roles (such as listener, critic, mentor, presenter), and social engagement (such as group work, discussion boards, wikis). Hence, it is no surprise that learning spaces—classrooms as well as informal spaces—have an increasingly important role in catalyzing this type of learning.

Learning Space Design Genealogy

The unrelenting pace of technology change can make IT decisions rapidly obsolete. While platforms and applications come and go, the psychology of how people learn does not. Constructivist learning principles, specifically activities identified as encouraging learning, can be translated into design principles that guide tactical decisions, ensuring that the designs we build and the technology we deploy serve a clear educational purpose. This suggests a design methodology with a clear "genealogy" having constructivist principles as the "parent" of design principles leading to specific tactics that support and enhance learning.

Social interactions such as debate, discussion, and teamwork, for example, encourage learning, prompting a design requirement for rooms that can be reconfigured quickly for small discussion groups. If accepted, this principle leads to decisions such as selecting lightweight, wheeled chairs that permit easy reconfiguration of the room's seating.

Or, consider *metacognition*—the learner's active assessment of his or her own learning. Such a learning principle might lead to the creation of explicit points or locations that will encourage and enable this self-assessment with the instructor's assistance. Locating faculty offices in the learning commons might facilitate this, giving students ready access to mentors for guidance and assessment.

Active and Social Engagement

The traditional layout of auditoria and lecture halls has rarely provided for social engagement among students. No doubt we all have many classrooms whose floor plans look essentially the same. This arrangement is not conducive to discussion among students; the design optimizes instructor transmission. In the traditional classroom floor plan, students receive content, packaged and presented with a "one size fits all" approach, regardless of the learners' unique needs or styles.

There is an increased emphasis on alternatives to a simple transmission model of pedagogy. Personal response systems, videoconferencing capabilities, floor plans that foster face-to-face contact among students, technology that supports the sharing of computer screens, and virtual whiteboards indicate a shift in learning spaces to support how people learn.

Many signs herald a move toward active and social learning spaces. Interest in informal learning spaces stems from the realization that informal spaces are particularly conducive to working spontaneously and deliberately in small or medium-sized groups. "Rethinking" informal space is characterized by coordinating architecture and technology to create powerful learning environments based on floor plans, furniture, and technology. This rethinking embraces services and products such as wireless networks and plasma screens supported by partnerships among units, such as the library and IT.

Trend 2: Human-Centered Design

The trend toward human-centered design is embodied in the shift from the *information commons* to the *learning commons*. The term "commons" means "land or resources belonging to or affecting the whole of a community," according to the *Oxford American Dictionary*, which seems particularly pertinent to the trend of human-centered approaches in learning space design. The notion of the commons is evolving, with an increasing emphasis on users and the range of services learners require; the learning commons illustrates human-centered design.

A quick glance at past practice helps us appreciate the significance of current directions. Through the 1990s, accessing digital resources was a challenge, requiring the use of a computer beyond the financial reach of many students; a minority of students owned laptops. The challenge for most institutions was simply giving students access to computers to do their work. The cost of computers and scarcity of space meant providing clusters of computers in specified areas for student access, echoing the design of transmission-style classrooms. This approach implicitly assumed that access, by itself, was sufficient. With access established and basic operational questions resolved, the students and faculty presumably were empowered to accomplish their academic tasks. Students in particular were assumed—then as now—to know everything about computers. Moreover, the assistance provided was scattered across multiple offices and delivery points, which might have served the support units but not the students and faculty.

Today, given the increasing proliferation of information technology, the need for basic access is not as acute as a decade ago, allowing the focus to shift from the provision of basic access to that of integrated services to aid learning. This shift has given us the leeway to evolve our notion of what the commons is and does. Increasingly, the commons is a locus of integrated support services, including assistance for research, computing, writing, media preparation and production, academic skills, and English-as-a-second-language training. Now explicitly designed into the commons are spaces for both individual and group work. In some cases colocated offices for faculty encourage more direct work with student teams. Food and drink have made a significant comeback—an important factor in humanizing the space.

The learning commons is human-centered. The term *learning* signals a significant change: the focus is not just finding information but applying that information in productive ways to deepen and strengthen learning as well as to construct knowledge. Learning, not information, is increasingly the focus. The move away from transmission to constructivist learning and developments in technology has enabled this redefinition of the commons. If the constructivist model reflects how people learn, a more human-centered design of learning space is a positive change. (See Table 1.)

Table 1. Repositioning the Commons

Previously	Currently
Information downloaded	Information created, integrated
Individual workstations	Social work setting
Isolated support delivery	Integrated support
Students only	Faculty too
7 × 12 access	7 × 20 access
"No talking!"	Whiteboards abound
No food	Cybercafé

The increasing integration of computing technology into the mainstream of daily activity enables this transition. One size may be *adequate* for all, but it's not particularly good for any given learning activity. Learning spaces in the 21st century need to foster discovery, innovation, and scholarship, not simply contain them.

Building spaces for learning has always involved collaboration among a variety of campus groups, including students and departmental faculty. As the emphasis on supporting learning activities rises, more ownership shifts to faculty and students. They are assisted, rather than led, by architects, builders, and facilities professionals. Learning environments should be developed by those who will use them.[1] Faculty and students are the product experts, while the architect is the space development expert. Shifting the focus to users of the space links the process to the human-centered design outcome. It also emphasizes learning activities rather than resources as the driving factor: people and learning, not managing capital goods, must take precedence.

The critical difference in the design processes lies in:

▶ Creation of a systems design requirements document with input from a wide variety of faculty, students, teaching and learning professional staff, facilities staff, and security and maintenance professionals.

▶ Formation of an integrated product team whose job it is to respond in real time during construction to issues, questions, or problems that inevitably arise so that the resulting learning space carries through with the intention of the requirements document.

Systems Design Requirements

An initial prerequisite to building a space that increases learning effectiveness is understanding what kinds of teaching and learning activities the space should enable. This entails identifying the demands for curriculum, learning, laboratory, and workshop activities that the space must meet.

With a clear definition of the learning goals, space design becomes grounded. Critically important is identification of the clients who will use the space, a process made easier when the space is designed for a specific department's needs. When the college or university claims the space, an analysis of the pattern of use of becomes essential. In many cases a small number of departments habitually use the same classrooms simply because of common seating requirements for their courses, without regard to the amenities or technology available in the rooms. Building classroom spaces without a defined client base results in a design that meets no one's needs optimally.

Learning Activity Analysis

Determining what activities the space must support is perhaps key to distinguishing a well-designed learning space from a room in which activity happens. Learning mode analysis (LMA) characterizes learning activities in terms that affect space design. For example, prior to engaging in the renovation of MIT's Guggenheim Laboratory, home of the Department of Aeronautics and Astronautics, university representatives articulated learning activities considered critical for students to master.[2] Knowing what students should learn permits defining the learning activities necessary to achieve mastery of critical subjects; this generates an LMA description. Once the activities and their consequences for space design are known and prioritized, architects can design spaces for these activities.

Integrated Product Team

Inevitably in any construction project, discrepancies emerge between the ideal and the reality. A process for responding to this gap is a normal part of the construction process. Learning-centered design differs in that the group responsible for addressing these gaps includes the original clients—faculty and students. The trend toward a more human-centered design requires that the people who teach and learn in the built space remain engaged throughout the process, ensuring that effective teaching and learning remains the focus.

Trend 3: Devices That Enrich Learning

The pace of technology change makes it increasingly difficult for colleges and universities to provide a robust, contemporary technology infrastructure. Students are entering college with a variety of personal technologies, from MP3 players to computers. With the burden to provide access to technology shifted, technology to support learning moves into focus.

Colleges and universities have the opportunity to redirect resources previously dedicated to computer labs to leverage the technology students bring to campus. This requires a focus on software implementation and interoperability rather than buying and deploying standard technology. The shift represents a significant change, but the resources that students carry with them are potentially powerful academic tools whose capabilities go well beyond their value for recreation and entertainment.

Podcasting

With the explosion of MP3 players, a tool for distributing audio content already is in student backpacks. Duke University's iPod experiment[3] provides an example of how a consumer music player can provide portable digital audio and other types of content (iPods function as a portable hard disk as well). Duke identified five major use categories:

▶ **Course content dissemination:** dissemination of prepared audio content such as lectures, songs, historical speeches, and foreign language content
▶ **Classroom recording:** personal lecture/discussion capture
▶ **Field recording:** field notes, interviews, and so on
▶ **Study support:** replaying audio content, whatever the source, for studying
▶ **File storage and transfer:** simple file transfer and backup, especially for media files.

Institutions participating in these types of experiments have found a close connection between the distribution infrastructure for audio content and the user experience. iTunes and the iTunes Music Store (iTMS) make distribution of music or any other type of content simple. iTMS is, after all, just another digital repository "tuned" for music, podcasts, and now video.

Software Deployment

As students arrive on campus with laptops or other computing devices, they will need applications to support their coursework. Resources once spent buying hardware are being redirected to applications. Software deployment options range from an application server environment that works with many different client computers to building installer packages to load institutionally licensed applications on student-owned machines.

Tools such as Citrix Presentation Server (http://www.citrix.com/) virtualize the delivery of Windows and Linux applications.[4] Only the student's PC needs to run the virtualization client that connects to the presentation server on which the application runs.

Most institutions have already deployed software for students to install on their personal machines. Unfortunately, the technology for installation is not matched by the business models of software vendors who presume a one-to-one relationship between a software purchase and the student's machine. Custom delivery of software requires more flexible and effective licensing models.

Thumb Drive Virtual Environments

As the capacity of USB flash memory drives (UFDs) increases (up to 8 gigabytes at the time of this writing),[5] these raw data storage devices can also serve as self-contained portable application environments. While campuses would still provide keyboards and screens, UFDs could be connected to a basic PC. Students would carry their digital computing environments on their UFDs, equipped with bootable operating systems, a suite of applications, security tools, and even a biometric identification feature so that a lost UFD could not be accessed easily by someone other than its owner.

Companies like U3 or NCD Systems assemble applications on UFDs and also provide build-your-own developer kits. Moving from an enterprise-central infrastructure to personal silicon may cause us to reconsider the economics, scalability, and functions that support student learning.

Cell Phones

Device convergence rouses speculation about the future of cell phones, PDAs, MP3 players, and computers. Using cell phones to better support teaching and learning has largely focused on extending the short message service (SMS) communications function to support interactive personal response services (PRS). Students in Japan use cell-phone messaging to take quizzes in class. Student book purchases, now enabled by Internet textbook stores, are automated in redesigned self-service bookstores through the e-wallet cell phone (Sony's FeliCa Contactless IC technology combined with NTT DoCoMo's Internet services iMode; see <http://www.nttdocomo.com/services>).

Controlling Lab Experiments from a Browser

The Internet promises to extend student access to resources that are in short supply, expensive, dangerous, or otherwise inaccessible to them. Browsers have made astronomy observatories, scanning probe microscopes, and scanning electron microscopes available to researchers around the world.[6] These applications are moving individual, unique implementations to a services-based architecture, grounded in Web standards that will allow access by large numbers of students.

Both technical and economic challenges affect access to scientific devices. The technical issues revolve around establishing a common infrastructure for a range of experiment types using Web services. The economic challenge entails developing a mechanism that allows faculty to share experimental devices without taking on the extra work associated with additional users. A priority scheduling system ensures that researchers' needs are served while sharing extra capacity with students.

A scalable software architecture for offering real experiments to students opens otherwise inaccessible opportunities to distance learners. On residential campuses, experiments brought into the classroom can give students more control over their "lab work."

Conclusion

With the right approach, the entire campus can become a learning space.[7] The three trends highlighted in this chapter underlie this emerging reality: design based on learning principles, human-centered design, and personal devices that enrich learning.

Our growing understanding of how people learn affects the configuration of learning spaces and the technologies supporting them. The constructivist paradigm supplants knowledge transmission as the guide for learning spaces, encouraging more thoughtful space planning. It also necessitates a proactive process to ensure that these learning spaces deliver value.

Human-centered design helps us keep people—not the latest technology—in the forefront of design decisions. With access no longer driving technology deployments, a focus on the "why" rather than the "how" of learning space design becomes possible. You can't build effective spaces for learning without clearly understanding the learning activities intended for them.

Our focus on enabling learning spaces has also shifted to a much more personal view. The technologies that students bring to campus are eclipsing the technologies colleges and universities can supply, broadening our concept of learning spaces to anywhere, anytime learning on residential, commuter, or virtual campuses. The shift from teaching to learning pervades the future design of learning spaces, with learning theory guiding technology implementation.

Further Reading

John D. Bransford, Ann L. Brown, and Rodney R. Cocking, eds., *How People Learn: Brain, Mind, Experience, and School: Expanded Edition* (Washington, D.C.: National Academies Press, 2000); online edition available at <http://www.nap.edu/books/0309070368/html/>.

Arthur W. Chickering and Zelda F. Gamson, "Seven Principles for Good Practice in Undergraduate Education," *AAHE Bulletin*, vol. 39, no. 7 (March 1987), pp. 3–7, available at <http://learningcommons.evergreen.edu/pdf/fall1987.pdf>.

M. Suzanne Donovan, John D. Bransford, and James W. Pellegrino, eds., *How People Learn: Bridging Research and Practice* (Washington, D.C.: National Academies Press, 1999); online edition available at <http://www.nap.edu/openbook/0309065364/html/>.

Endnotes

1. Edward F. Crawley and Steve Imrich, "Process for Designing Learning Spaces, Case Study: The MIT Learning Lab for Complex Systems," presented at the 2004 NLII Fall Focus Session, September 10, 2004, Cambridge, Mass.; available as a PowerPoint presentation from <http://www.educause.edu/LibraryDetailPage/666?ID=NLI0442>.

2. Edward F. Crawley, "Creating the CDIO Syllabus, A Universal Template for Engineering Education," presented at the 32nd ASEE/IEEE Frontiers in Education Conference, Boston, Mass., November 6–9, 2002, <http://www.cdio.org/papers/creating_syll_fie.doc>.

3. Yvonne Belanger, "Duke University iPod First Year Experience Final Evaluation Report," June 2005, <http://cit.duke.edu/pdf/ipod_initiative_04_05.pdf>.

4. Other software providing application virtualization includes Softricity, <http://www.softricity.com/products/index.asp>; Trigence, <http://www.trigence.com/>; and Meiosys, acquired by IBM as announced by an IBM press release, <http://www-03.ibm.com/press/us/en/pressrelease/7755.wss>.

5. Described in an M-Systems press release, "M-Systems Celebrates Five Years of Disk-OnKey USB Flash Drives with the Introduction of a New Whopping 8 Gigabyte Density," <http://www.m-sys.com/site/en-US/Corporate/PressRoom/PressReleases/2006/NR060104-3.htm>; and Edward Mendelson, "The Ultimate USB Key," *PC Magazine* (August 17, 2005), <http://www.pcmag.com/article2/0,1895,1849710,00.asp>.

6. See the Internet2 Web site, Remote Instrumentation, <http://science.internet2.edu/remote.html>; Electron Microprobe Laboratory, University of Minnesota–Twin Cities, Department of Geology and Geophysics, Remote Access, <http://probelab.geo.umn.edu/remote.html>; and the Web site for California State University Channel Islands (CSUCI), Academic Programs, Virtual Instrumentation Access at CSUCI (VIA-CI), <http://viaci.csuci.edu/>.

7. William J. Mitchell, "Rethinking Campus and Classroom Design," PowerPoint presentation at the 2004 NLII Fall Focus Session, September 9, 2004, Cambridge, Mass., <http://www.educause.edu/ir/library/powerpoint/NLI0438A.pps>.

About the Authors

Malcolm Brown is the director of academic computing at Dartmouth College. In this capacity he oversees IT support for teaching, learning, research computing, classroom technology, and media production. An area of particular interest is learning theory and its application in the classroom. He has presented on these topics at the EDUCAUSE conferences and seminars and has participated in EDUCAUSE Learning Initiative (ELI) focus sessions on learning spaces, as well as in Project Kaleidoscope's learning space design workshops for liberal arts colleges. A practitioner as well, he has taught courses on topics in intellectual history in the Jewish Studies program at Dartmouth.

Philip Long is a senior strategist for the academic computing enterprise at MIT and director of learning outreach for MIT iCampus. He provides direction in applying MIT Information Services and Technology resources to support the integration of technology into the curriculum. He leads the MIT iCampus dissemination effort, freely sharing MIT-developed educational technology tools to support active learning and scalable Web services for undergraduate instruction. He publishes regularly in educational technology magazines.

CHAPTER 10

Human-Centered Design Guidelines

Lori Gee
Herman Miller, Inc.

College and university space is for people—for learning, meeting, exploring, thinking, or relaxing. Campus spaces, particularly classrooms, influence our attitudes about education. We all have memories—good and bad—about such campus places. Although too little thought has typically gone into the significance of space in the learning process, we have an opportunity to change that by adopting human-centered design. Human-centered guidelines begin by considering the needs of students and educators, making it possible for space to support the transformation of learning.

Human-centered guidelines aren't just a tool for architects or designers. Faculty want teaching and work environments to support—not hinder—their work. Human-centered guidelines can help. Administrators trying to bring to life a vision of the campus as an engaging place for learning and teaching can use human-centered guidelines. Architects and designers play an important role in helping clients formulate and realize their visions for changing the status quo and realizing the potential of place; they, too, can use human-centered guidelines. No matter your position, if you influence the design of learning spaces, human-centered guidelines can help make you a catalyst for enriching learning.

Guidelines are not just another word for design standards. Current design standards begin with the premise that learning happens in a limited set of ways, thus a finite set of space configurations support them. This industrial, instruction-focused approach arose from the necessity of accommodating large groups of students at the lowest cost.

Human-centered design guidelines build on the premise that learning happens in many ways and that the design possibilities supporting learning are equally numerous. Despite multiple design possibilities, however, there is just one desired outcome: to enrich learning and teaching. As a result, human-centered guidelines are predicated on universal human needs and learning principles.

Human-centered design concerns process as much as results. Traditional processes are often linear, meaning that with funding approved, the learning space development gets turned over to an architectural and design firm and/or facilities team, with little continued representation from educators.

Collaboration—an effective learning style—should be considered an effective design tool. A collaborative and committed team can create a stimulating process and produce innovative results. The best learning space designs come from diverse project teams committed to transforming learning and composed of people who challenge and strengthen each other's ideas. Because design is an iterative process, the design team should stay involved throughout the project.

These human-centered guidelines arose from my professional experience and collaborations with a number of colleges and universities. You can use these guidelines

▶ to clarify the important enablers of learning and teaching;
▶ as a common language to help your team articulate its criteria for success; or
▶ to direct decisions when constraints arise.

Foundations of the Guidelines

People are at the center of learning, so their needs should be at the heart of a human-centered design process. These beliefs formed the foundation of the guidelines.

The First Priority: Basic Human Needs

Humans seek both physical and psychological comfort. Judith Heerwagen talked about a person's sense of well-being and how it influences productivity, creativity, and engagement. Her research has focused on four elements that must coexist to create positive and productive places: cognitive effectiveness, social support, emotional functioning, and physical function.[1]

If people aren't comfortable and don't have a sense of well-being, they become distracted. We must first consider what will make people feel comfortable, freeing their brains and bodies for learning.

Diverse Learning and Teaching Styles

Diversity abounds; individuals learn in different ways. Bob Barr and Jon Tagg recognized this when they wrote, "Our mission is not instruction but rather that of producing learning with every student by whatever means work best."[2] Each brain is uniquely organized, so space should offer variety, both for faculty and for learners. Space should be fluid so that it can accommodate different learning and teaching styles effortlessly.

Guiding Principles

The 12 brain/mind learning principles articulated by Renatta Caine help us understand how humans function and learn. A few of these principles suggest direct connections among stimulation, learning, and physical space.[3]

▶ **The brain/mind is social.** We change in response to engagement with others. Space has a role in determining the quantity and quality of engagement as well as its potential as an effective learning experience.

▶ **Learning involves both focused attention and peripheral perception.** Good space design is visually stimulating. While space should not distract from the ability to focus, it can provide sensory stimulation that influences the experience and thus learning. Space can also be the "silent curriculum"[4] that complements and increases engagement.

▶ **Each brain is uniquely organized.** We all perceive the world in different ways and act accordingly. People do not experience an environment in the same way. The best opportunity for success comes from variety.

Articulating these fundamentals can keep design ideas and processes focused on the most important characteristics of a human-centered learning environment.

Characteristics of Human-Centered Guidelines

These guidelines, although more than a checklist, are not prescriptive. They invite an exploration of learning environments for their capacity to transform learning. While the guidelines can apply to large-scale construction projects or single-classroom renovations, this chapter primarily focuses on the places where teacher/student exchange happens, typically the classroom. Classrooms are a core element of the campus, yet their potential is often overlooked.

Regardless of the unique functional requirements of your project, these guidelines can help direct discussions with anyone involved, whether associated with the institution or a design firm. When used to set direction, these ideas facilitate purposeful choices without adding cost.

This approach is holistic. Although I address each characteristic individually here, it is their interplay that creates human-centered learning spaces.

Healthful

Healthful spaces incorporate ergonomic and environmental principles and sustain physical well-being.

▶ **Lighting.** Tuning the mood and stimulation levels of students can be achieved through a mixture of lighting types, including natural light, augmented with controls. Typically, indirect lighting is the best dominant lighting source in learning areas. A variety of lighting is the most important way to maximize the effect on learning; it can be achieved with different types of lighting or with dimmers.

Quantifiable data does not exist on the impact of daylight on productivity, however, we do know that it has psychological impact, such as reducing stress and elevating mood.[5] The Heschong Mahone Group 1999 study of more than 2,000 classrooms concluded that students in classrooms with daylight improved 20 percent faster in math scores and 26 percent in reading scores over one year compared to students in classrooms without daylight.[6] The follow-up study confirmed favorable benefits for teachers as well.[7]

▶ **Ergonomic considerations.** Ergonomics is about more than a comfortable, adjustable chair. Ergonomic thinking considers the entire environment and how it supports and interacts with the human body. Well-planned pathways, open access to equipment and supplies, and ease of moving furniture are all ergonomic considerations.

Because of the diversity of human sizes, tables and chairs should be adjustable. Instructors and students should feel encouraged to get up and move around. Two principles of sound ergonomic thinking are worth remembering: it shouldn't hurt, and it should prevent injury. At Emory University's Cox Hall, the comfort of individuals is supported through a choice of seating options, from pillows on the floor to adjustable task seating (see chapter 8). See Figure 1.

Stimulating

Stimulating spaces attract people and spark creative thinking. They have the ability to motivate and engage students and educators.

▶ **Sensory cues.** Multisensory experiences engage and stimulate people. Visual, tactile, auditory, and kinesthetic experiences all influence memory and the intake of information.[8] Diverse stimulation raises mental awareness and allows people to absorb the information and ideas that the environment facilitates.[9] Very little of our learning experience or the design of learning environments

Figure 1. Cox Hall at Emory University Provides (a) Pillow Chairs and (b) Movable Chairs

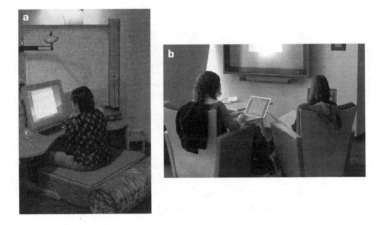

considers this. Yet certain learning experiences can be tied to a particular place, sound, or smell, which provide cues that help the brain build memory and process information. Humans associate what they learn with where they learned it. The key here is that spaces must have variety to stimulate, sometimes accomplished simply by painting rooms different colors.

▶ **Elements of surprise.** Mystery and surprise stimulate the human mind and senses and invite discovery. Consider the potential of hallways and pathways that provide unexpected spaces for group work, casual conversations, or hiding away for quiet work. According to Herman Miller research, "New ideas often emerge during social interactions. Relaxed, informal, and friendly interactions help creative people share openly with others and spark new connections."[10] Consider areas that support chance encounters or lingering after a class. The space design should include opportunities for serendipity and unplanned activities.[11]

▶ **Transparency, visual access.** Connecting visually lets people feel a part of something bigger. To see others engaged in learning can energize learners. Consider adjacent areas and how you can connect formal and informal learning spaces, such as classrooms and lobbies. Corridors, too, become part of the learning experience when they invite activity and have interesting views, as opposed to long, stark, and linear places. Vistas into and out of learning spaces need not cause distraction, instead enhancing cognitive activities. Students and faculty spend much of the day indoors, so providing architectural and design elements that expand and open interior views and provide lines of sight proves engaging.[12] As an example, see Figure 2, which shows the Auburn Career Center. Glass walls visually connect informal learning in the open spaces to the structured activities happening beyond the translucent surfaces. The ceiling changes color throughout the day, mimicking the movement of the sky.

Figure 2. Glass Walls at Auburn Career Center

Copyright Brad Feinknopf; image courtesy of Burgess and Niple

▶ **Connection to nature.** Nature continually stimulates us because of its always changing elements. The human response is positive, though typically subconscious. Environments that simulate nature provide a sense of security and pleasure.[13] Features found in a natural habitat can be associated with a created environment. Consider, for example, reflective surfaces or glass associated with water. Fire, the provider of warmth, food, and light, can be replicated in dining areas—the types of places where people instinctively gather. Varied ceiling heights can represent the safety and comfort of a tree canopy. Meandering halls or pathways mimic nature's patterns. This connection to nature is represented in a Learning Studios space at Estrella Mountain Community College (see chapter 19). See Figure 3.

Figure 3. Learning Studio at Estrella Mountain Community College

▶ **Color and texture.** Textures, colors, and shapes can reinforce association and retention. The key is to think of the total environment, considering ways to achieve interest and variety. Let the timeless and stimulating colors and textures of nature guide the human-made applications you apply.[14]

▶ **Diverse shapes.** Create spaces that offer visual choices of shape and form. A rectangular box is not the only answer; subtle adjustments to the geometry of space can balance hard and soft forms, asymmetrical and symmetrical patterns, creating visual and tactile interest. Consider the influence of geometry on the activities within the classroom. A circle, for example, suggests collaboration and communication, much like a campfire did for early generations.[15] Consider the visual interest possible with architectural shapes and patterns. Off-grid walls and a mixture of curves and corners give life to the Learning Teaching Center at the University of Dayton in Ohio (see chapters 3 and 4). See Figure 4.

Balancing Community and Solitude

Learning spaces need to balance the dual and opposite human needs for community and solitude. Because learning happens both in quiet, private moments and in lively, social settings, environments need to offer a spectrum of private and interactive places.

▶ **Social, community space.** Learning is a social activity. Community and social space connects individuals with other people and other activities. Students and faculty participate in a mutual endeavor—learning—and forge connections that reinforce learning and create a sense of belonging.

▶ **Opportunities and spaces for socialization.** Use classrooms during unscheduled hours for group projects, for example, or target halls and lobbies for informal meeting areas. Provide places to join the community of students. (See Figure 5 for an example of an informal learning area that supports collaborative and individual work with a mixture of relaxed settings.)

Figure 4. Learning Teaching Center, University of Dayton

Copyright Brad Feinknopf; image courtesy of Burgess and Niple

Figure 5. Spaces for Socialization

▶ **Refuges, private spaces.** It is important to create individual, private spaces. These don't have to be compartmentalized—even turning a chair can signal a desire for privacy. A Herman Miller, Inc., research report on patterns of creative work discussed the importance of spaces for quiet, focused thinking: "The quiet moment allows one to finally have a chance to sort out the stimuli and make the connection click."[16] In creating opportunities and spaces for private, thinking time, consider ways to modulate the level of privacy, such as seated-height panels, rolling screens, and plants. This conceptual approach provides private spaces in a variety of degrees of enclosure, shapes, and forms.

Adaptable

Adaptable spaces support people, activities, and change. Learning spaces need to keep pace with a variety of learning and teaching styles.

▶ **Flexibility.** Areas within a space should flex for various types of learning and teaching. Plan the ways in which you can take a single area and transform it from a lecture space to a small group space to a large-group discussion space. (See Figure 6.)

Figure 6. Alternate Floor Plans for the Same Space

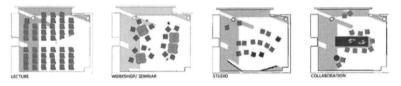

LECTURE   WORKSHOP/ SEMINAR   STUDIO   COLLABORATION

▶ **Adequate space.** Movement of people and furniture to different learning settings requires adequate space. Current space allocations for classrooms discourage movement and circulation areas deter people from lingering and interacting. If the space allocation doesn't support movement, then diversity in teaching and learning methods will be impossible.

▶ **Welcoming and familiar.** Humans have a tendency to seek out familiar places or create places with familiar attributes. Think about the ways you arrange your home. You create the place, the condition, the situation—you arrange furniture and artifacts in a certain way to suit your purpose or preference. Similarly, learning environments should allow students and educators to personalize them. The space should look comfortable in a variety of arrangements and for a variety of people.

▶ **User ownership.** Consider the ways a space can "give" permission for ownership—and not just to faculty. Users must know that all occupants have a say in defining the place. Educating users about how to use the space to its fullest potential and how the various tools and furnishings can support occupants' needs is a prerequisite. Providing furniture that people can rearrange and tools they can manipulate gives them the feeling that they have permission to claim ownership.

▶ **Changeable focal points.** Why establish a fixed front of the room? Without a set orientation, the room's occupants can move and group furnishings, technology, and activity in multiple ways and in many places within a space. Lecture and presentation areas need not be restricted to the front of the room.

▶ **Mobile displays.** Consider how you move flipcharts or computer displays throughout a space, to wherever students and faculty need the tools. For example, a small group may develop information and then reconnect with a larger group to share their work. Tools need to accommodate mobility of people and of information. Design that assumes all information exists in the faculty's PowerPoint slides or overheads limits learning opportunities. The Media Space Classroom project, for example, was developed to address changes in design education at Harvard's Graduate School of Design due to the increasing popularity of digital design methods. This space (see Figure 7) supports remote collaboration, teaching with digital media, and digital design presentations while anticipating future needs.

Figure 7. Media Space Classroom

▶ **Diverse information communication.** Display information in various ways—on the chalkboard, whiteboard, or digitally. Consider how the tools that deliver information can be shared and controlled. Control can rest with the lecturer or with the class during an active dialogue. Well-designed space and technology allow the pace and style of information delivery to change and support multiple learning/teaching styles and people. Maximizing the amount and type of display was a key goal for Estrella Mountain Community College's Learning Studios prototypes (see Figure 8).

▶ **Technology tools.** Technology (projectors, personal computers, and so on) will change more quickly than other elements in the furnished environment. Technology should be integrated into the space to fluidly support learning, but recognize that it will not match the lifespan of the room. Technology tools should support human interaction; they should not become the centerpiece of the space.

▶ **Power/data access.** Mobility of students, faculty, and technology is a given. As a result, you should make power and data access as mobile as possible. Anticipate the locations where users will want access and the range of activity needing support.

Figure 8. Estrella Mountain Community College Learning Studios
(a) Maximize Display and (b) Support Small Group Work

Conclusion

We will know we have succeeded in human-centered design when spaces support learning and create a positive experience. Like technology changes, physical space changes are only as good as the learning they enable. The true test of learning transformation will be measured by the National Survey of Student Engagement (NSSE) and other tools. The NSSE looks for improvements in areas such as active and collaborative learning, student and faculty interaction, and support for learners.[17] All these dimensions are affected by the interior space. Colleges and universities already seeing results from new learning environments include the 20 institutions of the Documenting Effective Educational Practice (DEEP) program. One of the success factors discovered by DEEP is that institutions "adapt environments for educational advantage" and "create engaging spaces for learning."[18]

Human-centered guidelines will help institutions create space that can transform learning. Remember that every decision you make or influence regarding interior spaces will affect the experience of the people learning and teaching in that space. Become a catalyst for change. Imagine how much richer and more effective learning will be when the physical environment is developed as a powerful learning tool.

Endnotes

1. Judith H. Heerwagen, "Design, Productivity, and Well-Being: What Are the Links?" paper presented at the American Institute of Architects Conference on Highly Effective Facilities, March 1998, Cincinnati, Ohio.

2. Robert B. Barr and Jon Tagg, "From Learning to Teaching: A New Paradigm for Undergraduate Education," *Change*, vol. 27, no. 6 (November/December 1995), pp. 13–25.

3. Renatta N. Caine et al., *12 Brain/Mind Learning Principles in Action* (Thousand Oaks, Calif.: Corwin Press, 2005), pp. 2–10.

4. Anne Taylor, "Silent Curriculum: Learning Through Creative Design," paper presented at the American Architectural Foundation's National Summit on School Design, October 2005, Washington, D.C.

5. Ibid.

6. Mark Schneider, *Do School Facilities Affect Academic Outcomes?* (Washington, D.C.: National Clearinghouse for Educational Facilities, 2002), p. 6.

7. Ibid.

8. Barbara Prashing, *The Power of Diversity* (Stafford, U.K.: Network Educational Press Ltd., 2005), pp. 129–133, <http://www.networkpress.co.uk>.

9. Herman Miller, Inc., *Patterns of Creative Work,* internal research report, 2004, p. 31.

10. Ibid., p. 27.

11. Ibid.

12. Prakash Nair and Randall Fielding, *The Language of School Design: Design Patterns for 21st Century Schools* (Minneapolis, Minn.: DesignShare, 2005).

13. Communicated in a phone call January 3, 2006, between Betty Hase, a workplace specialist at Herman Miller Inc., and the author.

14. Janine M. Benyus, *Biomimicry: Innovation Inspired by Nature* (New York: HarperCollins, 2002).

15. David D. Thornburg, "Campfires in Cyberspace: Primordial Metaphors for Learning in the 21st Century," from the Thornburg Center for Professional Development in San Carlos, Calif., <http://www.tcpd.org/Thornburg/Handouts/Campfires.pdf>.

16. Herman Miller, Inc., op. cit., p. 32.

17. "Engagement by Design," 2004 Findings, Community College Survey of Student Engagement, <http://www.ccsse.org>.

18. George D. Kuh et al., *Student Success in College: Creating Conditions That Matter* (San Francisco: Jossey-Bass, 2005).

About the Author

Lori Gee leads Herman Miller's Education Solutions Team and the company's focus on learning trends and higher education environments. This work guides the company's overall development of unique solutions for learning environments. As a design practitioner with 20 years of experience in using space as a strategic tool, she has helped many organizations and institutions set meaningfully different directions for improved results. Her work is a whole-systems approach to planning and creating learning spaces, considering the relationships of all aspects of space.

CHAPTER 11

Designing Blended Learning Space to the Student Experience

Andrew J. Milne
Tidebreak, Inc.

The Emerging Student Experience

What we think of as cutting-edge learning technologies today differ significantly from just a decade ago. Students themselves are changing, too, as their practices are shaped by the technological environment.[1] A majority of today's college students would probably not first associate cut-and-paste with scissors and glue; for them technologies like digital cameras have always existed.[2] And yet the processes we use to develop technology-enhanced learning spaces have not changed significantly in the past several decades. This chapter explores the space design process in the context of today's technological landscape and suggests ways the process can change to become more effective.

Student Characteristics

Developing a realistic, detailed sense of the student experience is an important starting point to the design process. A former director of the Open University in Scotland once observed, "It has taken me 20 years as an educator to realize what was obvious to me as a student."[3] His comment underscores the fact that needs-finding activities are important in understanding the student experience at any particular campus. A few trends are worth considering here.

▸ **Classrooms are not the only form of learning space.** While the classroom is assumed to be a primary location of learning, data suggest that a majority of student learning activity takes place outside the classroom.[4]

▸ **Social interaction is a growing part of learning.** Evaluation methods and performance metrics emphasize individual effort and achievement, but students increasingly are motivated by social interaction with their peers.[5] Pedagogy is shifting to emphasize team activities and collaborative learning.

▶ **Technology is natural.** Computer and networking technologies that once might have appeared exotic (pervasive wireless networking, iPods, smart phones) or transformative are now considered mainstream.[6] While "digital immigrant" faculty may perceive these technologies as a new part of the educational landscape, "digital native" students see them as a natural component of their lives.[7]

▶ **Internet resources can bypass peer review.** Traditional publication processes involved vetting and validating information, but the Web enables near-instantaneous distribution of information without formal review. It becomes increasingly important, then, for students to interact with one another and with faculty to analyze and critique online resources.

▶ **Learning can occur out of sequence.** Although lectures, books, articles, and other traditional tools present information in a deliberate, sequential manner, today's students are comfortable with overlapping discussion threads and parallel activities that may span different types of media, devices, and communities.

▶ **Students construct content rather than just consuming it.** Students are active authors of content, including video documents, online blogs, and other forms of digital expression.[8] Whether delivering a final report or going online to converse with members of an online community, today's students have a range of digital devices and software tools that allow them to create and shape content.

These trends emphasize that learning is becoming more social and informal and less structured. In contrast to the character of formal lecture halls and classrooms, modern learning space design seeks to provide freedom of access and interaction with peers. From a physical point of view, these places are increasingly conceived as comfortable, flexible spaces in which groups can interact and collaborate. Successful integration of technology and physical design into these kinds of spaces requires an understanding of emerging technology interfaces and new design approaches.

Current Conceptions of Learning Technology

Even among IT professionals, it is common to refer to technology in a general way, as if it were a specific type of system. In reality, the term "learning technology" encompasses a wide range of devices, software products, and user experiences.

Acknowledging the differences is a first step toward understanding the relationship between learning technologies and physical space design. Learning technologies fall into six categories.

Virtual Technologies

▶ **Online presence.** These technologies support an online presence, either through real-time interaction or asynchronous personal repositories. They include e-mail (often with multiple addresses), Web sites, blogs, wikis, e-portfolios, instant messaging (IM), short message service (SMS), Skype, Flickr, and podcasts.

▶ **Online resources.** Online resources include Google, courseware management systems, electronic databases, digital libraries, and online publications. They provide access to resources that are public, not personal, in nature.

Installed Appliances

▶ **Media presentation systems.** Many classrooms or seminar rooms have devices that allow playback of media of varying formats. Among these are the videocassette recorder, DVD player, document camera, and slide-to-video unit.

▶ **Remote interaction systems.** Recent improvements in broadband and streaming technologies have made real-time interaction possible. Examples include videoconferencing, Web cameras, and application-sharing suites.

▶ **Room-scale peripherals.** A new class of devices has begun to emerge that support group interaction. Interactive displays, whiteboard capture systems, and room schedule displays fall into this category.

Mobile Devices

▶ **Personal information and communication devices.** Mobile technologies such as laptops, cell phones, PDAs, Tablet PCs, iPods, digital cameras, Wi-Fi finders, USB drives, and GPS systems are part of our personal communication culture.

As indicated, these technology categories fall into three clusters: virtual technologies not tied to particular physical hardware; installed technology appliances that include a specific physical instantiation; and mobile devices. We experience all of these technologies in physical contexts. The challenge is to codesign technologies in a way that addresses both the physical and interactive dimensions in a symbiotic way.

The Need to Focus Design on the Student Interface

The recent interest in learning space design among IT professionals reflects a growing realization that the most interesting opportunities lie at the endpoint of computing networks—the interface between students and technologies. The combination of mobile students and mobile technologies highlights virtual spaces, but in truth these technologies are part of a blended environment.[9] Ubiquitous computing embeds technology within the fabric of the physical environment, creating opportunities for nontraditional human-computer interfaces. Figure 1 illustrates the point that physical context shapes the interface to virtual spaces; the experience of using virtual spaces changes depending on the nature of the physical space from which one or more people access it.[10]

Consider, for example, a group of students sitting together in a team study room using Web-based tools. Their physical context will consist either of each student having a personal copy of the tool (for example, a Web-based collaboration

Figure 1. The Varied Nature of Blended Learning Environments

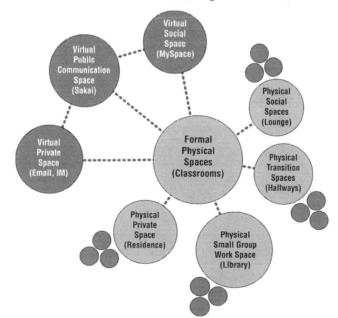

environment) open on a laptop, or all the students crowding around one screen giving verbal commands to one person at the keyboard. The students either work in semi-isolation or all of the group's interactions are filtered through one individual. Neither case represents an ideal interactive group process because the technology forces a particular mode of interaction. For group work, students are using an interface (the laptop) designed for individuals. A new class of group-based technologies is just beginning to be deployed at academic institutions to provide a more appropriate interaction experience (see chapter 35 in this book on GroupSpaces at Stanford University). Such technologies present the potential for new opportunities, but they also fall outside conventional thinking about learning space design.

Creative opportunities lie at the interface between virtual and physical worlds. New physical architectural styles and embedded interactive technologies will support an evolving set of work styles. Institutions will need new human-centered planning, design, and deployment approaches that embrace flexibility and constant change. Learning space development will require iterative design and prototyping methods, a departure from traditional design practices that will require significant process realignment.

The Disconnect Between High-Tech Learning Spaces and Current Design Practice

Learning spaces have traditionally been developed on campuses primarily as part of capital planning projects for new building construction or renovation of existing structures. Building design follows a standard set of phases that has not changed significantly in the past 20 years, even though the nature and prevalence of technology-enabled spaces is dramatically different. Analyzing the way these projects are managed provides insight on how design processes might evolve to accommodate new forms of technology and philosophies of learning space.

Traditional Institutional Spending Practices

Major learning space design projects and their associated technology design efforts can effect significant transformations on a campus. Four major types of learning spaces commonly appear in major projects: classrooms, computer labs, informal learning spaces, and equipment rooms. It is instructive to examine how standard design processes handle these categories of space.

Classrooms

Technology-enabled classrooms are the most identifiable learning space. To date, most of the technologies incorporated into classrooms emphasize a presentation mode of instruction. Videoconferencing and Webcasting systems that have begun to appear in classrooms perpetuate the notion of faculty as presenters and students as audiences. Even advanced classroom concepts such as the "black box theatre"[11] implicitly suggest a performance modality. Recent moves to bring room-scale peripherals into these environments have created silos of technology that don't interoperate or provide a well-integrated experience across devices. Among technology-enabled learning spaces, the truly interactive classroom can be a rarely achieved ideal.

Technology-enabled classroom systems can range in cost from $5,000 to $300,000, depending on the level of sophistication. Classroom technologies often belong to a capital building budget, but they are not necessarily considered basic to a building. A separate allowance typically goes into the furnishings, fixtures, and equipment (FF&E) budget or into a special budget to account for equipment and software costs. The FF&E budget, however, is frequently an early casualty of value engineering (specifically, cost cutting) efforts as a project moves forward and costs escalate. As a result, classroom technology funds are at the mercy of costs in a construction or renovation project. The funding model and their nature—highly customized systems designed as a part of large projects—typically mean no formal mechanism provides for the redesign of classroom systems as they age, despite the fact that pedagogical approaches change and available technologies evolve over time.

Computer Labs

Computer labs originally provided individual computer workstations and expensive or specialized software applications for student use; information commons and multimedia studio facilities are recent variants of this category. The need to provide baseline computing hardware has declined as more students bring their own computers to campus, although the need to provide specialty software remains. At a growing number of institutions, computer labs are being reconceived as places where student teams gather to work on group projects.

Computer labs do not require the customized cabling systems and equipment typically found in classroom technology systems. Hardware changes consist primarily of performance upgrades, with many enhancements implemented through software. As a result, renewal of the technology systems in these spaces is a well-understood process with institutional support. Budgets to fund this renewal recognize it as a recurring expense, with upgrades typically deployed on a three- or four-year cycle.

Informal Learning Spaces

Informal learning spaces are important on campuses today as a result of

▶ Widespread wireless access to the campus network and online resources
▶ Increasing student laptop ownership levels
▶ The realization that a majority of learning activities take place outside formal classroom environments

Informal learning space design is rapidly becoming a primary focus of interest and innovation.

This category suffers a number of challenges relative to others discussed here. Informal spaces are rarely explicitly included in a capital building project, in contrast to classrooms and other formal spaces. Informal spaces are typically not owned by any particular department or constituent group; thus, they often lack technological services, with the exception of wireless. Informal learning spaces also suffer from a lack of precedent—relatively few examples of planned informal spaces exist to use as models, although the number is increasing.

Personal computing devices owned by students (laptops, smartphones, iPods, digital cameras) find their way into formal and informal spaces. If institutions successfully leverage these devices in conjunction with installed technology systems, financial resources used to support traditional computer labs could be repurposed to create new forms of informal learning spaces. (See, for example, chapter 8 on Emory University's Computing Center at Cox Hall.)

Equipment Rooms

The technical infrastructure that supports campus services includes networking hardware, server systems, and software packages. It continues to evolve with the advent of voice over IP (VoIP), wireless networking, and emerging technologies. These spaces are probably the best understood in terms of function and content, yet perhaps not as recognizable as a learning space. This infrastructure, while often invisible to students, is essential to learning spaces, both virtual and physical. Despite its importance, the cost of supplying network infrastructure for learning spaces is not always fully covered under the base building budget.[12] If not built into the initial project, it will draw resources from other line items if added later. Once a building is online, campus or department IT organizations manage these components, and the systems' upkeep becomes that group's responsibility. A variety of models for ongoing support of these systems exist, including per-port service fees to departments or accommodation as part of the overall IT budget.

The Importance of Architecture in Defining Learning Space

A primary focus of architectural design is the macroscopic aspects of a building—the physical form of the building structure itself, including its exterior character, its dimensions, and the adjacencies of its interior spaces. While a design team specifies interior elements such as lighting systems and interior finishes, the selection of furnishings typically occurs at the end of the project, using whatever FF&E funds remain.

Students and faculty, however, experience building design at a personal level. They interact directly with the chairs and tables, look for convenient power outlets to connect their laptops, and view a projected image from a particular location in a classroom. Yet while these personal elements significantly influence the users' experience of the space, they are not a major focus of the design process.

Technology adds even more complexity. In today's world, the character of our workspaces is defined not only by passive elements and patterns of use but also by the nature of dynamic digital content with which we interact in these spaces. The character of space is defined by a total experience; it is the combination of physical design and behavioral norms—and, more recently, technology interfaces—that define place.[13] Learning space design processes have not yet caught up with the implications of these new technologies.

The Nature of Facilities Design at Academic Institutions

Campus building design and construction is often managed by a facilities planning group. The design and construction process follows standard phases sanctioned by the American Institute of Architects, specifically, schematic design, design development, construction documents, bidding and negotiation, and construction contract administration.[14] In some projects, key members of an institution's building committee visit other campuses to explore best practices, but these visits usually take place outside the formal design process.

The fee structure for design services has evolved to conform to this process even though information technology considerations have added complexity to the design. Since capital project spending typically requires board approval or is managed by state construction offices,[15] budget guidelines leave little room for changes to the project scope. In addition, most capital building projects are subject to external schedule pressures that compress timelines to their shortest possible duration, leaving little time to spend developing an understanding of user needs. The needs discovery process is usually limited to a few meetings where future building occupants share their perceived needs and respond to questions from the design team.

In this process, questions about learning technology requirements are often posed in meetings that simultaneously attempt to cover a range of physical design topics. Most data about technology needs is self-reported, making information about daily activity and future practices prone to error. The stakeholders participating in these sessions are primarily faculty and staff; student involvement is minimal. As a result, the design team receives limited information about how learning spaces are used.

The technology systems design work lags the construction process to account for rapidly changing technology. System design work can start several years before implementation, however, since systems design is integrated with the early project planning. While there may be a refresh effort during the project, an opportunity to completely revisit the design rarely arises. Clearly, new processes are needed, more attuned to evolving technology and contemporary design challenges.

The Role of Technology Consultants

The technology consultant can play a critical role in space design by interpreting the institution's needs and specifying systems that will address them. A consulting firm might have specialties in data networking, communications, cabling design, and audio-video systems.

Audio-video is the technology most often considered in learning spaces, yet the palette of audio-video products is limited in that it emphasizes presentation. Even the most sophisticated systems primarily tend to let faculty select audio-video signals from a variety of media playback devices. This reinforces a lecture paradigm rather than enabling students to interact directly with digital content in an ad hoc manner.

New technologies that are beginning to emerge move information between devices across standardized network infrastructures. Ultimately, learning space technology systems will consist of integrated software modules that run on an array of component hardware devices, in contrast to today's systems of highly specialized devices and customized cabling. A new class of technology design services will be needed, delivered by consultants who are well versed in "user experience" design and observant of evolving student work patterns. As learning space systems evolve toward all-digital interactive media tools, these consultants and the academic constituencies they serve will codevelop opportunities for new forms of interactive learning experience.

Moving Forward: A "Design Thinking" Approach

Design outcomes reflect the process by which they are derived. Just as the nature of technology integration in physical learning environments is changing, space design processes need to change to achieve innovative, blended learning places as the end result. These outcomes will grow from a culture of sustained design thinking that embraces the notion that flexible learning spaces remain permanently unfinished[16] in their physical design as well as their technological fit-out. Some first steps in that direction are presented here.

Augment Self-Reported Design Requirements with Direct Data Collection

Effective design processes start with a needs-finding phase that crafts the vision for the final design. Research data that relies on self-reporting from subjects rather than direct observation is inherently biased. A first step in designing improved learning space is to augment the interviews with information collected about students' daily activities.

Ethnographic-style observational studies, although a desirable approach, can be time-consuming and costly. Alternative techniques that leverage student involvement include student photo surveys coupled with journal entries[17] or multi-media blogging that encourages students to discuss their daily activities and record snippets of their experiences over a period of time. Another technique involves the development of surrogate student profiles, in which workshop participants define a collection of detailed student profiles that represent a cross-section of the student demographic, and then use these as a basis for imagining the specific needs of each fictitious student. Ultimately, learning space technologies may include integrated instrumentation that will automatically collect and deliver anonymous usage statistics that institutions can use in conjunction with observational methods to assess the impact of new environments on an ongoing basis.[18]

Initiate Active Prototyping Programs

Existing design practice has an unfortunate byproduct: learning space technologies typically are purchased and deployed in a single linear process. Building committees often make decisions about what technologies to deploy throughout a new building without having an opportunity to try them on a more limited scale. A better approach would establish an ongoing program of structured prototyping and evaluation that iteratively tests new ideas and technologies in a series of experimental and then operational settings. Prototypes provide tacit knowledge not available in a theoretical design. In the near term, prototyping might take the form of *critical function prototypes*, in which a particular capability or subsystem is deployed and tested early in the design process or while the building is under construction. Feedback from this trial would then influence the system design work later in the project life cycle.

In the long term, more substantial changes are needed. Sustainable prototyping programs funded through augmentation of operating budgets will permit explorations not limited to specific building projects. This will enable the creation of permanently unfinished spaces that would become test beds for new technologies and approaches. Institutions can begin by designating a small portion of the building technology budget for prototyping while the structure is being erected. Over time, this kind of activity could be leveraged across collaborating institutions, so that costs and best practice results could be shared. Successful design approaches will integrate ongoing needs analysis and prototyping activities. (See Figure 2.)

Figure 2. A Revised Design Process

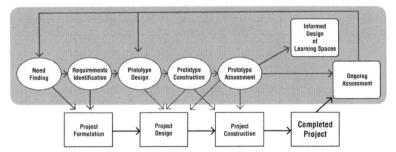

Practice Truly Participatory Design

The lack of long-term, meaningful student involvement in building design projects is common. Although a student or two may be invited to join a committee to represent the interests of the entire student population, this seriously underrepresents a group that constitutes the majority of those who use learning spaces on a daily basis. Because of the lack of student representation, groups typically responsible for learning space design risk making decisions with a limited perspective on the total life of learning spaces.

To promote a more participatory design process, students, faculty, staff, and design professionals should be engaged in the kinds of needs-finding and prototyping efforts described earlier. Design teams could also facilitate design workshops, or charrettes, that provide a focused opportunity to explore ideas and develop a sense of design priorities, both in terms of specific design requirements and the more ephemeral aspects of the design intent.

In the future, design teams will evolve to include individuals with expertise in blended environments that address human interaction issues in terms of physical design and technology interfaces. These teams will not only design physical environments, they will be involved in designing the interaction technologies embedded within these spaces.

Employ Innovative Funding Strategies for Ongoing Support

An important, if not necessary, prerequisite to these process changes will be changes to funding structures. Long-term systemic changes that improve the quality and flexibility of learning spaces will require investment of financial resources as well as staff effort. The real costs of an effective design process should be factored into budget and fundraising goals. As an example, consider the impact of spending 5 percent of a project's technology budget in the early stages of the design process to support technology explorations or adding a technology renewal endowment fund to the fundraising efforts associated with a new building. Money alone will not solve design issues, but additional resources coupled with innovative thinking about the design process would be a positive step.

Conclusion

Current design practices will need to change to meet student expectations and support evolving pedagogical approaches. Learning technologies are just one component of a complex ecosystem in which learning takes place. With the onward advance of technology, materials, and architectural concepts, academic institutions that hope to successfully leverage their facilities and technology assets will evolve their approach to learning space design. They will adopt flexible prototyping methodologies, take steps to modernize funding approaches, and embrace student-centered participatory design practices in the same way that they have student-centered learning pedagogies.

It is important to realize that, especially in the case of learning spaces, design is both a noun and a verb; design outcomes and processes intertwine. New forms of blended learning space will evolve over time as technologies change, people adapt, and new practices emerge. Academic institutions that reconsider how campuses are designed, in both a physical and technological sense, will position themselves to exploit future technologies. Among the most successful institutions will be those that find ways to infuse student ideas into the design process, harnessing the energy and talents of the Net Generation.

Endnotes

1. For a detailed discussion by various authors of student preferences and attitudes, and the implications for academic institutions, see *Educating the Net Generation*, Diana G. Oblinger and James L. Oblinger, eds. (Boulder, Colo.: EDUCAUSE, 2005), <http://www.educause.edu/LibraryDetailPage/666?ID=PUB7101>.

2. See Beloit College's *Mindset List* at <http://www.beloit.edu/~pubaff/mindset/> for more discussion of the world view of students entering college.

3. Communicated in an interview between Dr. John Cowan and the author in February 1990.

4. See slide #28 in the presentation "Process for Designing Learning Spaces" by Ed Crawley and Steve Imrich at the 2004 NLII Fall Focus Session, Cambridge, Massachusetts, September 10, 2004; available at <http://www.educause.edu/LibraryDetailPage/666?ID=NLI0442>.

5. Diana G. Oblinger, "Is It Age or IT: First Steps Toward Understanding the Net Generation," in *Educating the Net Generation*, Diana G. Oblinger and James L. Oblinger, eds. (Boulder, Colo.: EDUCAUSE, 2005), <http://www.educause.edu/LibraryDetailPage/666?ID=PUB7101>.

6. Gregory Roberts, "Technology and Learning Expectations of the Net Generation," in *Educating the Net Generation*, Diana G. Oblinger and James L. Oblinger, eds. (Boulder, Colo.: EDUCAUSE, 2005), <http://www.educause.edu/LibraryDetailPage/666?ID=PUB7101>.

7. See Marc Prensky, "Digital Natives, Digital Immigrants, Part 1," *On the Horizon*, vol. 9, no. 5 (October 2001); available from <http://www.marcprensky.com/writing/>.

8. Amanda Lenhart and Mary Madden, *Teen Content Creators and Consumers* (Washington, D.C.: Pew Internet & American Life Project, 2005), <http://www.pewinternet.org/pdfs/PIP_Teens_Content_Creation.pdf>.

9. Andrew J. Milne, "An Information-Theoretic Approach to the Study of Ubiquitous Computing Workspaces Supporting Geographically Distributed Engineering Design Teams as Group-Users," PhD dissertation (Palo Alto, Calif.: Stanford University, Department of Mechanical Engineering, 2005), pp. 28–34, <http://www-cdr.stanford.edu/~amilne/Publish/AJM-thesis-SUBMITTED_17mar05.pdf>.

10. Ibid. See chapter 2 for a detailed discussion of the design relationship between virtual and physical spaces.

11. Mark Valenti, "The Black Box Theater and AV/IT Convergence: Creating the Classroom of the Future," *EDUCAUSE Review*, vol. 37, no. 5 (September/October 2002), pp. 52–62, <http://www.educause.edu/LibraryDetailPage/666?ID=ERM0254>.

12. Communicated in a meeting between Michael Leiboff and the author in January 2006.

13. Steve Harrison and Paul Douris, "Re-Placing Space: The Roles of Place and Space in Collaborative Systems," in conference proceedings for the ACM Conference on Computer Supported Cooperative Work (CSCW-96), Cambridge, Massachusetts, 1996, pp. 67–76.

14. Standard process phases for building design and construction services are discussed in chapters 17 and 18 of *The Architects Handbook of Professional Practice*, American Institute of Architects (New York: John Wiley & Sons, 2001).

15. For example, state agencies manage fee negotiations for state university projects in Maryland, Idaho, Pennsylvania, and New York.

16. The term "permanently unfinished building" was coined by Larry Friedlander of Stanford University in connection with the Wallenberg Hall facility; see <http://wallenberg.stanford.edu/>.

17. For an example, see EDUCAUSE Learning Initiative (ELI) tools for student photo surveys, <http://www.educause.edu/LibraryDetailPage/666?IE=ELI8001>; available to ELI members only.

18. For a discussion and example of workspace "instrumentation," see Andrew J. Milne and Terry Winograd, "The iLoft Project: A Technologically Advanced Collaborative Design Workspace as Research Instrument," Proceedings of the International Conference on Engineering Design (ICED'03), Stockholm, Sweden, 2003. For the paper see <http://www-cdr.stanford.edu/~amilne/Publish/ICED03_iLoft_Paper.PDF> and for the slides <http://www-cdr.stanford.edu/~amilne/Publish/ICED03-Pres-Milne.pdf>.

About the Author

Andrew J. Milne is CEO and cofounder of Tidebreak, Inc., a global leader for interactive workspace technologies serving academic institutions and enterprises. Tidebreak is deploying its advanced digital infrastructure in libraries, computer labs, study rooms, and classrooms to create "walk-up" team collaboration zones for Millennial students. Milne has spent more than a decade innovating in higher education as a technology consultant for capital projects, a board member at Penn State's Leonhard Center for Enhancing Engineering Education, and an Envisioneer. He earned his PhD in engineering at Stanford University's Center for Design Research, where he focused on supporting distributed engineering design teams with collaboration technology.

CHAPTER 12

Sustaining and Supporting Learning Spaces

Christopher Johnson
Consultant

Formal and informal learning spaces aren't just created—they must be sustained and supported to bring lasting value. As a result, institutions must commit funds, expertise, and technology to the ongoing operation of spaces. But institutions might also need to negotiate how different groups (for example, faculty and information technology staff) see their roles. Along with some general guidelines, this chapter provides examples of how some institutions have approached sustaining and supporting their learning spaces.

Funding

Almost all institutions face the challenge of how to fund the deployment, support, maintenance, and refresh costs for learning spaces. The expenses go beyond the physical infrastructure of hardware, software, networking, furniture, and physical plant to include "intangible assets"[1] such as human expertise and digitized information. Further complicating the challenge, space is often the responsibility of multiple functional units or, in the case of informal space, it might not be perceived as anyone's responsibility.

First-Year Adjustments

When planning for a new space, consider the adjustments often needed in the first one or two years following construction. In the renovation of the Aero-Astro building at MIT, for example, approximately 15 percent of the total renovation costs were allocated to space changes after the renovation was complete.[2]

Replacement Cycle

As a space becomes more heavily used, it is necessary to monitor its use and support. Resources may need to be shifted or new resources added. And, technology will change. What new technologies will need to be incorporated? At what point in their maturation? What new support will they need?

Beyond initial funding and ongoing operations, a replacement cycle should be established for the different components (hardware, software, wiring, physical plant, and personnel). Although some items may have been purchased using "budget dust" (serendipitous, temporary budget surpluses), their ongoing staff costs and downstream, life-of-the-technology costs must still be considered.[3] Beyond the technology, support staff are critical in ensuring learning spaces achieve their potential. It is all too easy to underestimate the cost of staff to support technology.[4]

Cost Model

How much should be budgeted? Metrics or service level agreements can be established for IT services and costs benchmarked. Knowing costs helps in the evaluation of their relative value.

Bill Lewis, chief information officer and vice provost for information technology at Arizona State University (ASU), has developed a model for this type of funding support.[5] Lewis and his staff continually collect data on support costs and refine their cost models for technology-enabled classrooms. These models include both construction and long-term support for new spaces. Based on this model, ASU's senior administration has allocated funds to the central IT budget to ensure adequate support, maintenance, and refresh of the new Lattie F. Coor Hall (http://www.asu.edu/tour/main/coor.html) on the main campus of ASU.[6]

Cost Containment

One way to manage costs is to standardize institutional hardware, software, and support (where possible) to achieve economies of scale. While potentially difficult to do for experimental or discipline-specific spaces, standardization for common baseline services (such as networking) should help. For example, ASU is standardizing technologies across centrally scheduled classrooms. This helps with maintenance and replacement costs. However, it has also helped with other, less tangible costs, such as training and scheduling.

Efficiency

Location may play a role in the efficiency of support. For example, ASU has located staff at service locations close to the classrooms they support. A variety of software tools let staff diagnose, and sometimes fix, problems without leaving their offices. In addition, the University Technology Office works with other units on campus such as facilities, campus architects, and, most importantly, the individual support units located in the colleges to coordinate support of campus learning spaces.

Instructional or Information Technology?

In learning spaces, two ITs are involved: instructional technology and information technology. Information technology professionals—applications and network support specialists—often focus on operations. With the goal of providing secure, reliable technology, systems are often "locked down"; users have minimal control over their computers. Instructors and instructional technology professionals—instructional designers and professional development specialists—tend to explore new ways to use technology to enhance learning. Their mind-set is more experimental, exploratory, and nonstandard than operational, sometimes conflicting with the approach of information technologists.

Both groups have legitimate approaches. Instructors need to experiment with their instructional systems. In today's hacker and virus-infested world, however, systems need to be safe and secure. The concerns of both information technology and instructional technology professionals must balance through all stages of a learning space's life cycle. For example, at the University of Arizona's Manuel Pacheco Integrated Learning Center (see chapter 37), a management team with representation from the library, student services, professional development, information technology, and instructional technology units makes operational decisions.

Awareness building is important. Instructional support staff can help instructors and students appreciate issues facing the information technology staff. Ensuring network security must be seen as a prerequisite to a dependable work environment, not as an unnecessary inconvenience—even if the environment is experimental. Similarly, technology support staff must find ways to allow instructors to deviate from the standard environment and experiment.

Coordination is an ongoing task. Instructors must be willing and able to talk to support staff in order to avoid potential conflicts, for example, by not scheduling a major assignment on the same evening as an upgrade of the campus course management system. Forging lines of communication and understanding between these two cultures ensures that space functions in a smooth and efficient manner.

Policies and Procedures

Space changes may impact existing written or implied policies and procedures such as network access or food service. Current polices should be reviewed to determine if they are still relevant or if more appropriate polices might be implemented.

One example is the campus network access policy. For security purposes, many campuses restrict access solely to students and staff. If the learning space is used to encourage community interaction, such as an information commons, such a policy blocks off-campus users who wish to use their own devices. To resolve this issue, network personnel might develop a process where patrons, working with commons staff, register their devices to obtain network access.

As more attention shifts to informal learning spaces, institutions must rethink policies that interfere with human interaction. For example, when Bertrand Library at Bucknell University remodeled space to create an information commons, they loosened their food policy. According to Gene Spencer of Bucknell, "Our food policy was roughly 'We know you are drinking and eating. Please don't bring in pizza or soup, and if you have a drink, cover it.'"[7] Three years later, a new café located at the front of the library was integrated with the reference, circulation, and technical support desks. The library and food services entered "an informal joint covenant for success," explained Spencer, that "'You can't succeed if we don't succeed.'" Through this agreement, the library has input on the types of food served, so the café now offers only premade sandwiches, salads, muffins, and cookies; they refrain from selling "messy" food items such as pizza or soup. The café also displays signs asking students and instructors to please cover their drinks.

The addition of food services created a need for somewhere to eat. In response to student demand, Bertrand's staff took an area with built-in seating and installed café-style chairs and tables. This space has become the most popular study area in the library. This change lead to another policy revision, as students using the new area often work in groups. Because of this, volume levels have steadily risen. "Basically, we had to let go of the noise volume on the first floor," Spencer said. "We still have spaces dedicated to silent study, but students want social spaces to study."

When determining policies and procedures, planners must find the balance between the sometimes conflicting needs of users and support staff. Kim Braxton of Emory University has found that "rules constrain you.... It's easy to run a place with lots of rules because you don't have to think much; the rules set the precedent.

When you're flexible, you've got to pay attention; everything's a case-by-case basis. You've got to be on your toes. It's harder to be flexible, but I think in the end there is a much higher level of satisfaction; creativity certainly spikes."[8]

Supporting People

Professional development and support of instructors using new learning spaces are key components of making space successful.

Faculty Support

When developing support strategies, it is important to have a rough idea of people's experience with new teaching methodologies. Are users early adopters or the early majority?[9] Some faculty simply need to be pointed in the right direction and given the resources to try out their ideas.[10] Others need quick fixes when problems arise, along with consistent help.

Helping instructors share ideas is also important. For example, in the initial stages of the Integrated Learning Center at the University of Arizona, a specific space was set aside where instructors from diverse disciplines could prepare for or relax after class—the Meeting Place. A member of the University Teaching Center had her office in the Meeting Place, which allowed her to help instructors, see what others were doing, and share ideas about what worked and what didn't.

While most support efforts target instructors, it is also important to understand what types of students will use the space. Although some students are heavy technology users, others have little experience. Nontraditional students may have difficulty accessing and using new technologies. Assessing the skills and comfort level of all users will allow an institution to provide the support needed.

Classroom Support

Classroom support is usually a distributed function on campus. Instructional questions are handled by a faculty development center or center for teaching and learning. Classroom equipment is supported by A/V services. Technology issues (networking, desktop, and laptop support) belong to the help desk. Often multiple help desks exist: one for networking, one for desktop support, one for the course management system, and so on. Instructors and students don't care where support comes from—they simply want assistance. "If faculty get burned once they won't come back; they'll revert to talking heads."[11] Ensuring learning spaces are well utilized requires a coordinated support strategy.

To create a support environment that "focuses on the individual and makes technology less of a barrier to faculty use,"[12] ASU studied its support practices and instituted several changes. Technicians have relocated to offices where they can easily reach technology-enabled classrooms. Phones placed in classrooms let instructors contact support personnel with problems.

ASU intends to "make sure that the rooms are somewhere where faculty want to teach."[13] To ensure this, A/V technicians visit each technology-enabled classroom once a day to verify that the equipment is working. They also clean the boards, put chairs back into position, and scan the room for any problems, then report problems to facilities for resolution. In an effort to decrease interference if an instructor has a problem, ASU is standardizing equipment in centrally scheduled classrooms to allow for hot-swappable replacements. Said Bill Lewis, "Our goal is to have any problem fixed within 10 minutes of receiving a call."[14] ASU has also invested in remote diagnostics that allows technicians to solve some problems without entering the classroom.

Perhaps the most unique change at the ASU main campus is moving room scheduling to the office of the CIO through the Office of Classroom Management, allowing them to maintain a complete inventory of rooms and equipment. Instructors can be assigned to rooms based on pedagogical needs. This arrangement also permits moving an instructor from one room to another similarly equipped room if a problem cannot be fixed quickly. At the beginning of the year, faculty are informed of the classroom they have been assigned and the equipment available, ensuring that instructors are placed in rooms with the desired equipment.[15] The shift has made it possible to target professional development and provide more individualized help to instructors.

At the Integrated Learning Center at the University of Arizona, support is embedded within the facility itself. One A/V technician is permanently assigned to the building, and support staff from the Learning Technologies Center (http://www.ltc .arizona.edu/) and the University Teaching Center (http://www.utc.arizona.edu/) are available to assist with instructional questions. The Office of Student Computing Resources (http://www.oscr.arizona.edu/) is located in the building, providing technology support to students. The support helps instructors and students use the technology tools provided to improve teaching and learning.

It is important for support staff to remember that the goal is to create a welcoming space that encourages users to actively participate in their own learning. Alan Cattier, director of Emory University's Cox Hall Computing Center (see chapter 8), observed, "The old computing lab was a facility. The new computing lab is a relationship.... What ends up happening is that students do the work that they want to do. They go in and they feel empowered; they feel creative because the space is empowering and creative."

Conclusion

Learning spaces require ongoing, coordinated, and institutionalized funding, support, and maintenance. Neither instructors nor students care whose responsibility it is to support the space—they simply want it to work. "If you're not going to support the technology, then don't put it in the classroom. It's worse than not having it," claimed Bill Lewis.[16]

What works today might not work tomorrow, though. New technologies emerge and existing ones become obsolete. New technology availability must be balanced with instructors' and students' acceptance of a given innovation. Constant evaluation and assessment will ensure that support goes where it is needed the most. Well-used and well-supported spaces will help institutions meet the learning needs of our Net Generation students.

Endnotes

1. Kathy Harris, Maurene C. Grey, and Carol Rozwell, *Changing the View of ROI to COI—Value on Investment*, Gartner, Inc., ID no. SPA-14-7350 (November 14, 2001).

2. Philip Long in an e-mail message to the author, December 27, 2005.

3. EDUCAUSE and the National Association of College and University Business Officers (NACUBO), *Funding Information Technology*, EDUCAUSE Executive Briefing (Boulder, Colo.: EDUCAUSE, December 2003), p. 3, <http://www.educause.edu/LibraryDetailPage/666?ID=PUB4002>.

4. Ibid., p. 2.

5. Phone interview January 4, 2006, with Bill Lewis, chief information officer and vice provost for information technology for Arizona State University.

6. For more information on ASU's funding model, please contact the CIO through the Web site at <http://www.asu.edu/it/cio/>.

7. Phone interview with Gene Spencer, associate vice president for information services and resources at Bucknell University, March 15, 2006.

8. Kim Braxton of Emory University speaking in a Web seminar with Alan R. Cattier, *Adventures in Space Design: Building and Supporting a Collaborative Computing Lab*, ELI Web Seminar, April 10, 2006, <http://www.educause.edu/eliweb064>.

9. See Everett M. Rogers's *Diffusion of Innovations, 4th ed.* (New York: The Free Press, 1995) for a more detailed explanation of the various types of adopters.

10. Judi Harris, *Design Tools for the Internet Supported Classroom* (Alexandria, Va.: Association for Supervision and Curriculum Development, 1998), pp. 16–17.

11. Lewis, op. cit.

12. Interview March 13, 2006, with Sarah Hughes, assistant vice provost, Office of Classroom Management, Arizona State University.

13. Phone interview with Sarah Hughes, January 4, 2006.

14. Lewis, op. cit.

15. Hughes, Jan. 4, 2006, op. cit.

16. Lewis, op. cit.

About the Author

Christopher Johnson is a consultant on 21st century learning and an adjunct assistant professor at the University of Arizona South. In 2005, he retired from the University of Arizona, where he served as a senior consultant in the Learning Technologies Center. As facilitator of the Consulting and Enrichment Activities group, his primary focus was assisting faculty in exploring and implementing new teaching methodologies supported by technology. He also served as the director of humanities computing and technology and the Digital Media Resource Center in the Manuel Pacheco Integrated Learning Center. He serves on a variety of technology committees and has shared his knowledge and expertise at a number of conferences. Johnson received his PhD in secondary education from the University of Arizona.

CHAPTER 13

Assessing Learning Spaces

Sawyer Hunley and Molly Schaller
University of Dayton

An eloquent case can be made to explain the relationship between learning spaces and learning. But how do we know when a learning space enhances learning? We need assessment data to answer this question. The answer, in turn, provides guidance for developing learning spaces and for monitoring their impact on learning.

We cannot assess the impact of learning spaces without addressing instructional and programmatic issues, which requires a multifactor, multimethod analysis. The analysis determines the learning space characteristics that enhance student learning and support the faculty's pedagogical strategies. Data can then be used to establish a set of principles or guidelines to inform learning space development, while a monitoring system evaluates space effectiveness. This system should take into account learning outcomes and space utilization and should be sensitive to change over time.

Assessment Framework
Three issues must be addressed in the assessment design:
▶ First, it must be clear whether assessment focuses on teaching or learning.
▶ Second, the audience(s) for the assessment information must be identified to ensure the assessment blends with existing requirements, such as accreditation.
▶ Third, assessment of learning space must take into account the fact that learning and instruction are no longer confined to the classroom.

This chapter provides a framework for assessing the impact of learning spaces on learning. Assessment targets and methods will be identified and then contextualized with an example of one university's approach.

Focus of Assessment
While the goal of higher education is to help the students learn and develop, there is a difference between a learning focus and a teaching focus. An institution with an emphasis on learning measures its success through assessment of student

learning outcomes. While the assessment of teaching might include evaluation of student learning outcomes, it is often limited to the assessment of student satisfaction with courses or peer observation of teaching performance, neither of which directly addresses learning. Assessment should integrate the evaluation of instruction and learning. Learning is facilitated through the pedagogical efforts of the faculty; both faculty and learners are supported by learning space. Therefore, appropriate assessment targets are learning outcomes, teaching methods, and use of learning space.

Accountability

Traditional accountability methods include reports on quality to federal, regional, or state agencies and accreditation bodies. The audience for systematic assessment of institutional quality lies outside the institution. Quality indicators generally are based on indirect measures of academic performance such as selectivity, academic expenditures, faculty-student ratios, and Carnegie classification. Because these measures do not adequately represent the net effects or value added from higher education, alternatives must be sought.

Full accountability is not limited to external audiences. Internal examination of effectiveness is important for institutional growth and development. Pascarella and Terenzini[1] found that educationally effective institutions are differentiated by

▸ student involvement in the academic and nonacademic systems;
▸ the nature and frequency of student contact with peers and faculty members;
▸ interdisciplinary or integrated curricula;
▸ pedagogies that facilitate learning engagement and application;
▸ campus environments that emphasize scholarship and provide opportunities for encounters with diverse individuals and ideas; and
▸ environments that support exploration.

These factors are linked to student learning and can be measured in terms of engagement in learning activities and use of space. The assessment of the relationship between learning spaces and academic engagement aligns closely with accountability and can be included in the overall assessment plan for the institution.

Informal Learning

Informal learning, which occurs outside the formal instructor-facilitated setting, is now recognized as an important part of the overall learning environment. Informal settings include libraries and physical spaces that facilitate group and individual academic activities and computer-assisted learning. Technology has redefined the meaning of learning space by changing our notions of place and time:

▶ Place is defined by both physical and virtual settings.
▶ Learning time has become more flexible and can be formally scheduled or individually selected by the learner.
▶ The structure and content of learning can be formally structured and facilitated within a program or course or it can be self-directed.

Assessment Structure

The assessment structure is extended with the inclusion of informal learning activities. Thus, a comprehensive assessment of learning space addresses the use of physical space that accommodates formal as well as informal and technologically based learning. (See Table 1.)

Table 1. Assessment Structure		
Characteristic	**Formal Learning**	**Informal Learning**
Environment	Physical and virtual	Physical and virtual
Time	Scheduled, self-selected, and flexible	Scheduled, self-selected, and flexible
Structure	Facilitated	Self-directed
Content	Program-directed	Self-directed

Assessment Targets

Institutions should determine assessment targets based on their own missions, goals, and culture. Models, theories, and research suggest relevant targets:

▶ In their general model for assessing change in college students, Pascarella and Terenzini[2] suggested using university-wide targets to determine student growth.
▶ Strange and Banning[3] pointed to the importance of the person-environment interaction.
▶ Huba and Freed[4] emphasized learning outcomes as a direct measure of learning.
▶ Astin's theory of involvement[5] makes the case for measuring student engagement as an indicator for student learning.

General Model for Assessing Change

Pascarella and Terenzini's[6] model approaches growth and development as a function of student background and precollege traits, structural and organizational features of the institution, interaction with agents of socialization, and quality of the study effort. Precollege traits and background can be addressed through the process of selectivity, but are less relevant to the discussion of how students develop once they enter the academy.

For the purpose of measuring the impact of learning space, organizational and structural features are translated into programmatic, pedagogical, and environmental factors. Student growth and development are affected by their level of engagement and quality of study efforts. Thus, learning space assessment targets the facilitation or inhibition of student interactions with faculty and peers within formal and informal environments. The academic and cocurricular program, pedagogical approaches used by faculty, and environment become critical elements affecting engagement and are targets for assessment.

Person-Environment Interaction

Person-environment interaction models can help focus learning space assessment. Strange and Banning[7] identified four person-environment themes:

▶ Physical surroundings encourage or constrain behavior.

▶ The collective socialization by individuals creates or defines environments.

▶ Organizational goals, complexity, centralization, formalization, stratification, production, and efficiency influence environments.

▶ Environmental pressure, social climate, and campus cultures influence perceptions of settings.

Measures that target frequency and type of space use identify factors of the physical environment that encourage or constrain engagement. Focus groups, interviews, and surveys provide descriptive information regarding interactions between individuals, instructional characteristics, institutional climate, and other relevant structures. Quantitative and qualitative assessment methods reveal multiple aspects of the relationship between physical space and learning.

Learning Outcomes

Learning outcomes are observable and measurable indicators of student learning. Huba and Freed[8] suggested that statements of learning outcomes usually begin with the phrase, "Students will be able to...." Maki[9] classified four levels of learning outcomes.

▶ *Institutional outcomes* are general and reflect students' entire educational experience.
▶ *Program outcomes* reflect work within a specific program.
▶ *Course outcomes* reflect the type of work within a particular course.
▶ *Individual outcomes* come from data collected on the same individual over time.

Direct measures of learning outcomes are the most valid and reliable indicators of academic gains. But direct measures to determine the impact of learning spaces on learning are fraught with complexity. For example, students generally participate in courses and learning activities not confined to one type of learning environment. Individual courses may be taught by multiple instructors using a variety of methods. Institution-wide learning goals measured at discrete points during students' matriculation cannot fully account for the impact of their various experiences. Measures of learning specific to courses probably are not sensitive enough to detect differences due to instruction or the setting of variables. Individual measures collected over time would be costly and differ across individuals, making the data difficult to interpret. One alternative measure for student learning is student engagement.

Engagement

Astin's theory of involvement[10] asserts that "students learn by becoming involved." A general consensus in the literature finds student engagement to be a valid indicator of educational effectiveness and a good indicator of learning. Research based on the National Survey of Student Engagement (http://nsse.iub.edu/index.cfm) validates this assessment target.

The flexibility of the concept of engagement makes it useful for investigating the relationship between learning space and learning for several reasons:

▶ The relationship between the learning environment and the individuals occupying that environment can be determined.
▶ The involvement of students in learning activities within formal and informal learning environments can be measured.
▶ Engagement can be measured through direct (observation) and indirect (survey, focus groups) methods.
▶ Measures of engagement are sensitive to changes over time.

Assessment Methods

We have identified three general targets for assessing the impact of learning spaces on learning:

▶ Academic engagement
▶ Teaching methods
▶ Use of learning spaces

Issues such as validity and reliability would be problematic if the assessment system relied on a single method; however, a multifactor, multimethod assessment approach allows for the aggregation and verification of outcomes across measures. Qualitative measures provide insight and a depth of understanding into how individuals respond to space, as well as into their needs and if those needs are being met. Quantitative measures reveal statistical relationships between specific types of space and their uses. Consistent patterns from the analyses demonstrate the impact of the space on learning. Three of the most useful methods are briefly described here.

Focus Groups and Interviews

Focus groups and interviews explore the users' experience of spaces. They provide insight into how faculty and students respond to a particular space, how their views of each other change in different spaces, and how their views of learning are related to a specific space. While this approach relies on individual memory and interpretation, it also allows for a deeper understanding of individual reactions to spaces.

Surveys

While focus groups and interviews produce a rich understanding of users' experience of space, surveys can tap the perspectives of a larger number of students and validate findings from other measures. The National Survey of Student Engagement (http://nsse.iub.edu/index.cfm), for example, assesses engagement of students across multiple institutions; annually developed norms can be used to compare institutions. Surveys administered repeatedly within a single institution can target specific questions and monitor changes in perceptions over time. Well-designed surveys generate both quantitative and qualitative information.

Photographic Studies

Photography, as a direct observational method, can determine usage patterns in learning spaces. Photographic studies capture observational data across time and in multiple settings with minimal intrusiveness and using modest resources. This approach quantifies students' use of space, including their interactions with the physical and human environment. Direct observation offers a validity check for interpretations from other measures.

An Example of Assessment

Over the past decade, the University of Dayton has worked to improve the overall campus environment through planning, renovation, and construction. The multiyear Learning Living Assessment Project examines the relationship of the built environment, academic programs, and learning/engagement involving three innovative campus learning spaces and the library. A two-stage model first identifies the characteristics of learning spaces and academic programming that positively impact learning, then incorporates the findings to develop space and programs while monitoring their effectiveness. The project was launched in fall 2004.

Two unique living/learning spaces that opened on campus in fall 2004 were included in the study. Conceived and developed over a three-year period, ArtStreet includes student townhouses, music practice rooms, classrooms, and studios. The Marianist Hall learning/living space (attached to a residence hall) was designed with a specific integrated learning community in mind. This space has two large classrooms, two smaller meeting rooms, many smaller spaces for faculty and students, and a rotunda for large group meetings. The Learning Teaching Center (LTC)—the third space included in the study—is an established space holding an experimental classroom, one large and one small meeting room, a coffee shop, meeting space, and personal study spaces. The study included the campus library study spaces to encompass a wider range of informal learning spaces on campus.

Methods

The first year of the project focused on determining the relationship among learning, academic programs, and physical learning space. Multiple methods and multiple sources were used in developing a streamlined and user-friendly assessment system. In most cases the measures were administered in the fall and in the spring to identify response patterns over time. Both qualitative and quantitative approaches were used.

Engagement served to represent learning outcomes, as measured through the National Survey of Student Engagement (http://nsse.iub.edu/index.cfm), focus groups, surveys, and photographic studies of both formal and informal learning spaces. Data identified programmatic and pedagogical characteristics that increased both student and faculty engagement in the learning process. These data were also used to generate quantitative information about space usage and qualitative information clarifying why certain spaces were preferred.

The National Survey of Student Engagement data were obtained from the spring 2004 administration of the survey to first-year students and seniors. These data suggested an overall pattern of student engagement for the university. Surveys were administered in the fall and spring to students who lived or took courses in the three innovative living/learning spaces and to a nonparticipant control group. The surveys provided both quantitative and qualitative data regarding perceptions of physical spaces on campus and academic programs. Focus groups recorded the in depth perceptions of students and faculty who participated in the innovative spaces or programs.

Photographic studies were conducted in the three innovative spaces and the library, with a layout of the space used to select photo spots. Still pictures taken on a digital camera were stored on a computer hard drive and then transferred to compact discs for ArtStreet, Marianist Hall, and the LTC. Photographers took a picture at each designated spot, chosen according to the arrangement of furniture and the configuration of the environment. Photos taken on the library's six floors using a video camera were converted to DVDs. Photographers began on the top floor and followed a designated path throughout the building. Floors were designated with "zones" determined by a change in furniture. Photographs were taken by the primary researchers, volunteer students, student staff, or professional staff every hour beginning at approximately a quarter after the hour for one week.

The library space, LTC, and Marianist Hall were each photographed in the fall of 2004. ArtStreet was not photographed at that time due to a delay in construction and opening of the facility until late in the fall term. Marianist Hall and ArtStreet were each photographed in spring 2005. The photographic study will continue to record changes in space use for the next two years.

Insights

Based on our first year of data collection and analysis, we have discovered relationships among learning space, instructional practices, and learning. Academic engagement was encouraged by learning spaces that were comfortable, open, flexible, and appealing. For example, students described classes in one of the innovative spaces as requiring more accountability on their part because there were few physical barriers between themselves and faculty. Students were most engaged in settings and in academic activities that encouraged interpersonal interaction and were supported by technology. In comparison, in more traditional classrooms with seats arranged in rows and the instructor at the front of the room, they felt they had less responsibility for participation. Engagement was discouraged by poor air circulation, uncomfortable temperatures, distractions, and noninteractive pedagogical practices. In addition, our photographic studies showed students using our newest and perhaps most innovative spaces late into the night for individual and group study. Students reported that they felt at home in the space and also that they could stay focused on academics while there.

The results also revealed that no one physical structure accommodated all types of learning needs. A balanced environment facilitates both group and individual activities, with features that support computer access and spaces that allow for a break from focused academic work.

The learning space often limits the faculty's pedagogical repertoire. Faculty discussions or communities of practice expand their awareness of pedagogical options. Faculty who are comfortable leading case studies, discussions, or small group activities in flexible spaces do not believe they can accomplish these same activities in traditional spaces. They prefer flexible space with movable furniture and seamless technology. Faculty who were not comfortable with a range of pedagogical approaches tended to alter our most innovative spaces to obtain a lecture-room feel. In one classroom with no tables, just comfortable chairs in a circle, one faculty member consistently pulled a table in front of her seat and lectured from that position. In order to expand faculty pedagogy, we cannot simply build or design new spaces—faculty need to discuss exploring new approaches for engaging students.

A key to academic engagement is to minimize the separation between living and learning. Learning takes place in all environments, so a complete assessment of the impact of learning environments must include informal as well as formal academic settings. Formal settings are most engaging when they encourage learning through social interaction and are relevant to students' lives. Informal settings must be flexible and comfortable and accommodate a variety of learning activities. This understanding of the relationship between living and learning led our research team to adopt the motto "Bring life to learning; bring learning to life."

Practical Implications

Higher education has significant investments in learning spaces with the expectation of making a positive impact on learning. Well-designed assessments will provide the information needed to confirm the impact of learning spaces on learning. The process must account for the complex interaction among learning spaces, pedagogical practices, and student outcomes. Problems in interpreting the results can be mediated through a system that incorporates data gathered over time from multiple factors, multiple methods, and multiple sources.

A two-stage model for assessment provides

▶ a set of criteria useful in guiding space development that also assists in iden- tifying measurable targets; and

▶ a process for monitoring the impact of space on key learning and engagement targets over time.

While concepts about the impact of learning space on learning are certainly generalizable, assessment procedures should be conducted by each institution to account for individual differences. Higher education must assess its own perfor- mance, address its weaknesses, build on its strengths, and promote high-quality experiences. The main advantage of an assessment strategy is the enhancement of student learning—the goal of every college and university.

Endnotes

1. Ernest T. Pascarella and Patrick T. Terenzini, *How College Affects Students: A Third Decade of Research*, vol. 2 (San Francisco: Jossey-Bass, 2005).

2. Ibid.

3. C. Carney Strange and James H. Banning, *Educating by Design: Creating Campus Learn- ing Environments That Work* (San Francisco: Jossey-Bass, 2001).

4. Mary E. Huba and Jann E. Freed, *Learner Centered Assessment on College Campuses: Shifting the Focus from Teaching to Learning* (Needham Heights, Mass.: Allyn & Bacon, 2000).

5. Alexander W. Astin, "Involvement: The Cornerstone of Excellence," *Change*, vol. 17, no. 4 (1985), pp. 35–39.

6. Pascarella and Terenzini, op. cit.

7. Strange and Banning, op. cit.

8. Huba and Freed, op. cit.

9. Peggy L. Maki, *Assessing for Learning: Building A Sustainable Commitment Across the Institution* (Sterling, Va.: Stylus Publishing, 2004).

10. Astin, op. cit.

About the Authors

Sawyer Hunley is coordinator of the School Psychology Program and a learning/teaching fellow at the University of Dayton in Ohio. As program coordinator, she has advanced the concept of learning and behavioral assessment in a prevention and response to intervention model. In her role as chair for the National Association of School Psychologists Certification Board, she has integrated this model into the requirements for national credentialing. Hunley is currently investigating the impact of learning space on learning at the University of Dayton.

Molly Schaller is an assistant professor and coordinator of the College Student Personnel Program and a fellow in the Learning Teaching Center at the University of Dayton. She and Hunley are engaged in a multiyear, comprehensive study of the relationship between space and learning. She holds a master's degree from Miami University in college student personnel and a PhD in higher education administration from Ohio University. Her research focuses on college student development with a special emphasis on sophomore students.

CHAPTER 14

Learning How to See

Diana G. Oblinger
EDUCAUSE

"We spend a lot of time trying to change people. The thing to do is to change the environment and people will change themselves."[1]

When thinking about colleges and universities, what do you see? First and foremost, you see learners—students, faculty, and staff. You see learning—active, experiential, reflective, and collaborative. You see places—classrooms, laboratories, libraries, cafés, and virtual spaces. And, you see technology—computers, wireless networks, digital learning resources, search engines, and analytical tools. Yet, when asked to describe a learning space, we often revert to a mental image of the classroom—technology enhanced, perhaps—with all seats facing the lectern. If we are committed to transforming learning, perhaps we should practice Da Vinci's *saper vedere*—knowing how to see.

What should we see?

We should see that space is important. Colleges and universities care about learning spaces, not just because of their function but because they embody the institution's philosophy toward teaching and learning as well as people. Space can attract potential students or dampen their interest. Two-thirds of the respondents to a 2005 national survey indicated that the overall quality of the campus facilities was "essential" or "very important" in their choice of a college.[2]

You probably see construction on campus. We are in the largest building boom higher education has ever seen. In the United States, spending on new or renovated facilities is estimated to exceed $18 billion in 2007; approximately 70 million square feet of space will be added to colleges and universities each year between 2005 and 2010.[3] You also see renovation. Buildings outlast all the components inside them. Estimated lifetimes are:

- ▶ 3 years for software systems
- ▶ 5 years for computer hardware and communications systems
- ▶ 10 years for cabling
- ▶ 15 years for furniture
- ▶ 25 years for mechanical and electrical systems
- ▶ 75+ years for building structures[4]

You might also see the impact of technology. The Internet has changed notions of place, time, and space. Historically, the place where faculty and students came together for formal learning was the classroom. Space is no longer just physical, however; it includes the virtual. Wireless networks, virtual worlds, mobile devices, and digital learning resources have become part of the environment "Technologies used in learning are altering the experiences and aspirations of learners."[5] Driven largely by technology, the notion of a classroom has expanded and evolved; the space need no longer be defined by "the class" but by "learning" unconstrained by scheduled class hours or specific room locations. As a result, the notion is emerging of the entire campus—not just classrooms—as a learning space.

Design is a way of seeing things.[6] How you think about a subject depends, in part, on your culture, your experiences, and your expectations—how you see things. When most of us think of a "learning space," we think of a classroom with a professor at the front of the room and maybe blackboards, projectors, or interactive whiteboards. The presumption is of information delivered in a lecture format.

What if you "saw" something different? What if you saw learners rather than lecturers? What if you saw chatter rather than silence and action rather than stillness? What if you saw learning as something social rather than something cerebral? What would be different? Expectations? Learning spaces? Learning?

In the collection that follows you will find many examples of learning spaces that began with seeing things differently. The assumptions were different—there is no front to the room, and learning doesn't happen at fixed times. The focus was different—often on groups rather than individuals. And the desired outcome was different—successful learning rather than teaching.

This content collection is offered to help others "know how to see." As you review the examples, it will quickly become apparent that these learning spaces have a positive impact on people. Words such as *learning, engagement, interaction,* and *excitement* come to mind, but you will see patterns as well:

▶ Space shaped by learning rather than by instruction
▶ Socially catalytic space
▶ A shift from classrooms to learning complexes
▶ Service philosophy
▶ Technology integration
▶ Experimentation and innovation
▶ User involvement

Space Shaped by Learning

Historically, learning spaces were designed around teaching or maximizing the number of students in a room. The presumption was that good teaching results in learning—a presumption that focuses on the instructor. What if the focus shifts to the learner and learning? Student-led sessions result in greater discussion and more complex learning outcomes, for example.[7] Group problem solving works better than individual problem solving.[8] And students develop technical skills more efficiently and use them more readily when they have learned them as needed during ongoing projects.[9]

We are learning to put pedagogy first. Ask what learning activities will lead to the desired learning outcomes, not which projection system to install. Many of those effective learning activities are experiential and collaborative—and often IT-enabled. Using digital archives, databases, and the tools of a profession allows students to engage in first-person learning. Rather than being told the conclusions, students build their own understanding. Spaces that encourage first-person learning may involve project rooms, network access, or videoconferencing.

Classroom designs are moving away from a focus on the front of the room (and the instructor). In some cases students sit closer to the instructor or at small tables such as star clusters or circular tables. Small group conversations are encouraged, which improve learning.[10] SCALE-UP at North Carolina State University (see chapter 29) is an example of a space reconfigured for group activity using round tables and multiple focal points. Even lecture halls can be designed to accommodate interaction, as LeBaron Hall Auditorium at Iowa State University (see chapter 22) illustrates.

Spaces that facilitate peer-to-peer and group learning such as information commons, learning resource centers, or cybercafés are valuable.[11] The Information Commons at Northwestern University (see chapter 30) or the USITE/Crerar Computing Cluster and Cybercafé at the University of Chicago (see chapter 40) are examples. Small group spaces, such as Flyspace at North Carolina State University (see chapter 28), encourage learning as well.

Movable furniture and space that can be reconfigured for different learning modes is increasingly common. For example, many of the spaces at the University of Dayton (see chapters 3 and 4) are reconfigurable thanks to movable furniture. This is true in classrooms as well as in informal spaces.

Emerging patterns include:

▶ Creating multiple focal points in classrooms, not just a single focal point at the front of the room
▶ Grouping or clustering students rather than seating them in rows
▶ Establishing informal group work spaces
▶ Providing movable furniture
▶ Building reconfigurable space

Catalyzing Social Encounters

People learn from other people. If the environment limits random encounters, discourages conversation, or provides no comfortable place to sit, learning opportunities are lost. Many campuses have designed "socially catalytic" spaces.[12] According to a Joint Information Systems Committee (JISC) guide to designing learning spaces, "Well-designed social spaces are likely to increase students' motivation and may even have an impact on their ability to learn."[13]

Information commons (see chapter 7) provide spaces for interaction and exchange; silence is not required. Atria or cafés, such as MIT's Steam Café (see chapter 27), promote visibility and accessibility so that casual conversations can occur. Other institutions, such as Indiana University-Purdue University Indianapolis (see chapter 21) or the University of Dayton (see chapters 3 and 4), have found ways of creating social space in hallways. External spaces equipped with tables, chairs, and wireless can become informal learning spaces used by individuals or groups. Not only do these types of spaces make interaction possible, they also provide students with space to work or relax between classes.

"If catering facilities, common rooms, even corridor space, are reconsidered as social meeting and group learning environments, institutions could...make a statement about their vision for learning as a pervasive and inclusive activity based on social interaction," advised JISC.[14] When wireless enabled, these spaces are not "set apart from learning."[15]

Emerging patterns include:

▶ Making people visible to each other using atria, cafés, or windows
▶ Providing movable furniture so that small groups can form spontaneously
▶ Offering wireless access
▶ Displaying artwork, artifacts, or research

Shifting to Learning Complexes

Learning is continuous; it can occur in any place at any time. There are different ways of learning, although most learning styles can be categorized as doing, conversing, or reflecting. Different types of spaces are conducive to specific types of learning.[16] (See Table 1.)

Table 1. Type of Learning Space			
Type of Space	**Doing**	**Conversing**	**Reflecting**
Group teaching/ learning	XXX	XX	XXX
Simulated environment	XXX	X	
Immersive environment	X	X	X
Peer-to-peer and social learning		XXX	X
Learning cluster	X	X	X
Individual learning spaces	X		XXX
External spaces		X	X

With no single learning time, style, or space to guide planning, many institutions are shifting from classrooms to learning complexes where learning ebbs and flows depending on the need and circumstance. In learning complexes, informal spaces are adjacent to classrooms. Eating spaces and atria serve as gathering spots. Group spaces are interspersed with areas for individual reflection. Faculty offices and support desks are often nearby. Technology is a ubiquitous enabler.

Buildings like Torgersen Hall at Virginia Tech (see chapter 43) link a three-story atrium, an electronic study court, classrooms, and informal spaces—making it a learning complex. Information commons are self-contained learning complexes. Multiple types of work spaces are integrated in the Information Commons at Northwestern University (see chapter 30), the University of

Chicago's USITE/Crerar Computing Cluster and Cybercafé (see chapter 40), Duke University's Perkins Library (see chapter 17), and the Peter H. Armacost Library at Eckerd College (see chapter 18). Students move from one space to another, depending on the need. In its Center for Integrated Learning and Information Technology, Michigan Technological University (see chapter 25) is linking its formal and informal learning spaces, not only to provide a seamless learning environment but also to protect students from harsh weather. The Smeal College of Business at The Pennsylvania State University (see chapter 33) and Sir John Cass Business School, City of London (see chapter 15), integrate classrooms, study areas, trading floors, and faculty offices in a complex designed to bring people together. At the University of Dayton (see chapters 3 and 4), a learning center called Marianist Hall adjoins a residence hall.

Emerging patterns include.

▶ Interconnecting multiple types of spaces, such as individual and group space, or formal and informal spaces

▶ Clustering formal and informal spaces, such as computer labs or cybercafés near classrooms

▶ Locating faculty offices near student spaces

▶ Paying attention to passageways that link people, not just hallways

Developing a Service Philosophy

Learning involves researching, writing, thinking, critiquing, and conversing. Learners are pressured and time-constrained. Institutions that have reconceptualized spaces and services from a user perspective are developing a service philosophy manifest in an integrated support structure. Having all the tools—and people—readily accessible enables learner success.

Information commons (see chapter 7) and places such as the Cox Hall Computing Center at Emory University (see chapter 8) have integrated space, service, technology, and support. Whether users need assistance with research, writing, or a new application, help is readily accessible.

Faculty are critical to student support. Many institutions have made faculty offices more easily accessible, ensuring that answers to questions about courses or careers—or just casual conversations—are never far away.

Support also is being designed into classroom buildings. If a faculty member encounters technical difficulty during class, a quick solution is vital. Institutions such as Arizona State University (see chapter 12) have relocated support personnel to classroom buildings to ensure readily accessible support. Stanford University (see chapter 36), for example, takes service a step farther, training support staff in pedagogy and technology.

Emerging patterns include:

▶ Integrating service centers
▶ Locating faculty offices near student areas
▶ Offering in-house IT support
▶ Training staff in pedagogy and technology

Integrating Technology

Technology has become part of the higher education landscape. Ubiquitous wireless access is increasingly common—and expected. Classroom technologies range from projectors to audio and video capture. Tools such as student response systems or wireless keyboards and mice allow students to become active participants and presenters.

Virtually all disciplines rely on technology tools. These tools are finding their way into learning spaces. For example, the Smeal College of Business (see chapter 33) and the Sir John Cass Business School (see chapter 15) have trading rooms.

Technology is integrated in the operation of the buildings as well. Hamilton College's Science Center (see chapter 20) features a display that not only explains many of the green features of the Science Center but also allows learners to monitor internal and external environmental conditions, as well as the operation of the geothermal and heat-recovery systems.

Outside class, wireless networks allow almost any space to become a learning space. Whether in a hallway, an outdoor courtyard, or a café, students sit with their laptops, working and socializing.

New types of applications may promote greater student learning. Stanford's GroupSpaces (see chapter 35), for example, make it possible for members of a group to share control of large displays, enhancing their ability to collaborate.

Emerging patterns include:

▶ Providing ubiquitous wireless
▶ Using disciplinary tools
▶ Offering group and collaborative tools

Designing for Experimentation and Innovation

Institutions are designing places for experimentation and innovation. Depending on the learning activity, a different combination of pedagogy, space, and technology might be optimal. Learning innovations that have improved student success, such as SCALE-UP (see chapter 29) and the Math Emporium at Virginia Tech (see chapter 42), resulted from experimentation. Others, such as Stanford's Wallenberg Hall (see chapter 36) and the Ohio State University's Digital Union (see chapter 31) set aside space for prototyping and experimentation. The presence of movable furniture, screens, and wireless controls makes it possible to experiment with just about any space.

Locating different disciplines (for example, fine arts and technology) in the same space can catalyze innovation and experimentation, as in the case of Denison University's MIX Lab (see chapter 16). In other cases, such as BOX at the London School of Economics (see chapter 23), the innovation comes from colocating academic and business personnel. Joint projects and problem solving encourage innovative thinking.

It is increasingly common—and necessary—for institutions to integrate experimentation into the overall design process. Years may pass between the time space planning begins and a facility's completion. In that time pedagogy and technology will change. And, with the lifespan of a facility exceeding 50 years and the half-life of many technologies being one to two years, flexibility and renewal must be an ongoing part of the design process.

Emerging patterns include:

▶ Setting aside space for experimentation
▶ Colocating different specialties in the same facility to stimulate innovation
▶ Displaying art work, exhibits, and artifacts to stimulate interest and creativity
▶ Using a portion of the budget for technology experimentation

Involving Users

Increasingly users—students, faculty, and staff—participate in learning space design. User perspectives are critical, as architects or facilities personnel may view space design quite differently. "In fact, 'expert' decisions are not necessarily better than 'lay' decisions," asserted Henry Sanoff. "Given the facts with which to make decisions, users can examine the available alternatives and choose among them."[17] Completing the facility is not the end of the process, however; it must be adapted to changing needs. Sanoff concluded that "Those most directly involved with the product—the users—are best able to assume those tasks."

Users' involvement in ongoing maintenance and management might also be valuable. This involvement could be directly on committees or indirectly through surveys or interviews, such as at the Manuel Pacheco Integrated Learning Center at the University of Arizona (see chapter 37).

Emerging patterns include:

▶ Getting input from students on different types of spaces, such as through photo surveys, rather than through committee appointments

▶ Involving users in creating new designs

▶ Forming user councils that involve facilities, IT, academic affairs, faculty, and students

Conclusion

Learning space is a means to an end. Perhaps the focus on learning space will help us know how to see learners and learning more clearly. If we look carefully, active, social, and experiential learning happens continuously on our campuses and in the virtual spaces surrounding us.

Ultimately, the goal is to improve learner success. As Buckminster Fuller reportedly said, "Reform the environment. They will reform themselves if the environment is right."

Endnotes

1. Les Watson, pro vice-chancellor, Glasgow Caledonian University, quoted in Joint Information Systems Committee (JISC), *Designing Space for Effective Learning: A Guide to 21st Century Learning Space Design* (Bristol, U.K.: Higher Education Funding Council for England, 2006), p. 24, <http://www.jisc.ac.uk/uploaded_documents/JISClearningspaces.pdf>.

2. David Cain and Gary L. Reynolds, "The Impact of Facilities on Recruitment and Retention of Students," *Facilities Manager*, vol. 22, no. 2 (March/April 2006), pp. 54–60.

3. Mark Maves and Martin Sharpless, "When Space Becomes More Than a Place," presentation at the 2005 EDUCAUSE Annual Conference, Orlando, Florida, October 19, 2005, <http://www.educause.edu/ir/LibraryDetailPage/666?ID=EDU05180>.

4. Ibid.

5. JISC, op. cit., p. 2.

6. My thanks to Marvin Malecha, dean of the College of Design at North Carolina State University, for helping me understand this definition of design.

7. Tang (1998), cited in *Spaces for Learning: A Review of Learning Spaces in Further and Higher Education*, Scottish Funding Council, 2006, p. 23, <http://www.sfc.ac.uk/information/information_learning/Spaces_for_Learning_report.pdf>. Tang's study was originally reported in John D. Bransford, Ann L. Brown, and Rodney R. Cocking, eds., *How People Learn: Brain, Mind, Experience, and School: Expanded Edition* (Washington, D.C.: National Academy Press, 2000), <http://fermat.nap.edu/catalog/9853.html>.

8. Evans (1989), cited in *Spaces for Learning: A Review of Learning Spaces in Further and Higher Education*, Scottish Funding Council, 2006, p. 23, <http://www.sfc.ac.uk/information/information_learning/Spaces_for_Learning_report.pdf> Evans's study was originally reported in John D. Bransford, Ann L. Brown, and Rodney R. Cocking, eds., *How People Learn: Brain, Mind, Experience, and School: Expanded Edition* (Washington, D.C.: National Academies Press, 2000), <http://fermat.nap.edu/catalog/9853.html>.

9. Edward Allen, "Second Studio: A Model for Technical Teaching," *Journal of Architectural Education*, vol. 51, no. 2 (November 1997), cited in *Spaces for Learning: A Review of Learning Spaces in Further and Higher Education*, Scottish Funding Council, 2006, p. 23, <http://www.sfc.ac.uk/information/information_learning/Spaces_for_Learning_report.pdf>.

10. *Spaces for Learning: A Review of Learning Spaces in Further and Higher Education*, Scottish Funding Council, 2006, p. 7, <http://www.sfc.ac.uk/information/information_learning/Spaces_for_Learning_report.pdf>.

11. Ibid., p. 8.

12. Kathleen Manning and George D. Kuh, *Student Success in College: Making Place Matter to Student Success*, Occasional Paper #13 (Bloomington, Ind.: Indiana University Center for Postsecondary Research, 2005), <http://nsse.iub.edu/institute/documents/briefs/DEEP%20Practice%20Brief%2013%20Making%20Place%20Matter%20to%20Student%20Success.pdf>.

13. JISC, op. cit., p. 28.

14. Ibid.

15. Ibid.

16. Alexi Marmot, "Spaces for Learning," presented at the Scottish Funding Council Seminar in Glasgow, Scotland, October 28, 2005, <http://www.sfc.ac.uk/information/information_learning/AMA_spaces_for_learning.pdf>.

17. Henry Sanoff, *Community Participation Methods in Design and Planning* (New York: John Wiley & Sons, 2000), pp. 13–14.

About the Author

Diana G. Oblinger is a vice president at EDUCAUSE, where she directs the EDUCAUSE Learning Initiative (ELI). Previously Oblinger served as the vice president for information resources and the chief information officer for the 16-campus University of North Carolina system and as a senior fellow for the EDUCAUSE Center for Applied Research (ECAR). Prior to that she was the executive director of higher education for Microsoft Corporation and led the Institute for Academic Technology for IBM. Oblinger was on the faculty at Michigan State University and the University of Missouri–Columbia, where she also served as an academic dean. Oblinger has authored and edited numerous books and publications, including the award-winning *What Business Wants from Higher Education* and the first EDUCAUSE e-book, *Educating the Net Generation*, with James L. Oblinger.

CHAPTER 15

The Sir John Cass Business School

City of London

Clive Holtham

What Is It?

The Sir John Cass Business School (http://www.cass.city.ac.uk) is a research-intensive international school ranked in the top 50 institutions worldwide for MBA education. The school enrolls some 2,800 overwhelmingly postgraduate students who study exclusively in a new building; undergraduates normally study at the main university campus. The new building, which opened in May 2003, lies in the heart of London's central financial district, The City. The building has seven floors plus a basement. (See Figure 1.) Built in the shape of a letter B, it has two relatively small atriums, one four stories high and the other six stories, designed to provide light and to support the natural ventilation system. (See Figure 2.)

With the benefit of hindsight, one of the major advantages of the design process was the exceedingly long time it took to find both a site and the financial resources for the new building. This time was productively used

Figure 1. Cass Business School (a) Front Entrance and (b) North Side

(a)

(b)

©2006 Clive Holtham

Figure 2. Cass Business School (a) East Atrium and (b) West Atrium

(a)

(b)

in researching the requirements of a flexible 21st-century learning space that would serve the needs of both students and the business communities in and beyond London.

What Happens Here?

The building houses the full, self-contained range of administrative, academic, research, and teaching and learning functions. The lower ground floor houses two 60-seat classrooms with level floors and a 180-seat auditorium with near-perfect acoustics that do not require amplification. The auditorium is used intensively for large classes and, particularly in the evenings, business conferences and events. A reception area outside the auditorium—one of the most flexible multifunction spaces in the building—is used for refreshments and exhibitions. (See Figure 3.) The ground floor contains a raked, or sloping, 80-seat classroom and a high-technology securities-dealing room sponsored by Bloomberg. (See Figure 4.) With its glass wall, the classroom has high visibility from the reception area.

The learning resources center occupies the first floor. The high atrium above it ensures the visibility of scholarship—literally—at the heart of the school. The first floor also has two computer classrooms, a special business information room sponsored by Reuters, and a group decision support and videoconferencing room that users can reserve. The second and third floors house the remaining 8 large classrooms and 16 team rooms. The café (on the ground floor) and restaurant

Figure 3. (a) Auditorium and (b) Milling Area

(a)   (b)

Figure 4. (a) Raked Classroom and (b) Securities Dealing Room

(a)   (b)

(third floor) were always conceived of as part of the learning space of the building. Generous amounts of social space accommodate informal student meetings, supported with extra seats and tables in line with student demand since the building opened. (See Figure 5.)

How Is Technology Used?

The building has 350 km of network wiring with more than 3,500 data points, each capable of taking voice, data, or video. Every raked classroom has power and Internet access at every seat, and power and Internet points are available in virtually all areas used by staff and students. Each classroom has a high-technology lectern, allowing full control over all audiovisual facilities. Overhead projectors have been replaced by electronic visualizers (document cameras) in all classrooms.

Figure 5. (a) Learning Resources Center and (b) Café

(a) (b)

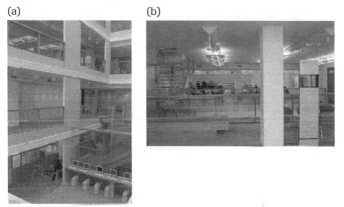

Unusual high-technology features distinguish Room 2001, a 60-seat classroom with a fold-down flat-screen computer beneath every desktop. (See Figure 6.) The desks can be used normally with no computer visible, and then converted in a few seconds into computer workstations simply by lifting the desktop. The lectern in this room uses Tablet PC functionality.

Figure 6. Room 2001, a Computer-Enhanced General Classroom

More than 30 kiosk PCs spread throughout the building enable students to check e-mail quickly. A low priority was put on wireless, since the building is one of the most intensively wired business schools in the world; however, a wireless network is being installed for use by visitors and executive education programs.

What Makes the Space Successful?

The first factor in the building's success is the diversity of the spaces. Creating such diversity was a key result of the research project that preceded the architectural design. The second factor is the close attention paid to design detail. The acoustics and lighting in particular benefited from the expertise of high-quality architects and consultants. In some cases the design uses acoustics to ensure quiet; in others, such as some public spaces, the acoustical properties of the concrete deliberately promote noise, producing a "buzz" in the building through most of the day and evening.

It proved vital that the university rejected the appointment of signature architects who might have imposed an idiosyncratic design on the school. Instead the job went to a London-based firm, Bennetts Associates, with a reputation for understanding the exact needs of the client and converting those creatively into award-winning designs that work on a day-to-day basis.

What Principles Were Behind the Design?

At the design stage, the business school reviewed its pedagogic strategy and decided on a high-tech, high-touch building. This clarified that almost every space would provide staff and students wired access to the Internet and offer opportunities for non-technology-based face-to-face interaction. The earlier research project had shown that knowledge work relies heavily on accidental meetings and discourse; workspace planning can both help and hinder such opportunities. Once this subtlety in the design requirement was clear, the architects went to great lengths to produce a diversity of spaces that would support a range of encounters, both formal and informal. This decision pedagogically to concentrate on the high-tech, high-touch combination narrowed the range of choices available and has continued to inform the updating of the facilities.

At the earliest stages, the dean of the business school mandated that the user requirements for the building be derived from a research study into global best practices to meet his vision of a "world-class temple of knowledge." At this stage—prior to the appointment of architects—visits were made to locations worldwide, including the Agora in Athens, which had successfully linked the worlds of business, government, and academic thinking. Ultimately, the single most powerful influence came from the San Marco Monastery in Florence, since almost every configuration of its space is optimized to support and stimulate knowledge work. (See Figure 7.) The Cass Business School does not look like a monastery, but its design reflects a similar diversity and quality of knowledge space.

Figure 7. Cloister-like Corridor in Learning Resource Centre

Once architects were appointed, the university made no attempt to impose a particular architectural style despite the architects' success in the mainstream modernist tradition rather than the postmodernist or any other tradition. A further round of research was carried out with visits internationally to a wide range of business schools. These visits helped identify what was disliked as much as what to copy. The visits also served as an excellent team-building exercise among the university, the architects, and the business school.

The clarity in advance thinking by the business school meant rejecting two early design schemes because they didn't fully reflect the spirit sought in the building. To the architects' credit, they continued listening. They produced a configuration that met the planning and cost constraints on the one hand and the core need to design world-class learning spaces on the other hand. The resulting building also represents an intellectual hub for the City of London.

What Is Unique or Noteworthy?

A crucial aspect of the design process was the setting up of 13 user groups involving frontline staff who had in-depth understanding of the practical space needs for their own functions. For example, a group for the front desk design (see Figure 8) involved the receptionist team, a group for the lectern design involved academics, and so on.

Figure 8. Cass Business School Lobby

The cautious and protracted research into design options before hiring the architects meant that the school had a very clear idea of the "spirit" wanted for the new building. Once the architects listened to and locked on to what this spirit really meant, they articulated that vision in elegant physical terms. The whole building is based on principles of flexibility and transparency, reflecting the values of the Sir John Cass Business School.

About the Author

Clive Holtham is professor of information management and director of the Cass Learning Laboratory at the Cass Business School, City University, in London.

CHAPTER 16

MIX Lab

Denison University

Scott Siddall

The MIX Lab is a technologically rich space for multimedia supporting the fine and performing arts at Denison University (http://www.denison.edu/), a small liberal arts college of 2,100 students in Granville, Ohio. The lab contains 15 Macintosh workstations, each configured with three dozen basic and advanced multimedia applications; 10 other Macintosh workstations have a basic suite of applications.

The lab, created in 2003 at a cost of $340,000, occupies a former dining hall (44 × 24 feet) in Mulberry House, a satellite residence for students—hence the name, Mulberry Inter-media eXperimental (MIX) Lab. The lab is at once a classroom, a lab, a studio, and a resource for independent work; it is a hub for new media creation and exploration. Virtually all the furnishings and technologies are mobile, allowing for both short- and long-term rearrangement of the space. Figure 1 shows one of many possible floor layouts for the MIX Lab.

Figure 1. A Possible Layout for the MIX Lab

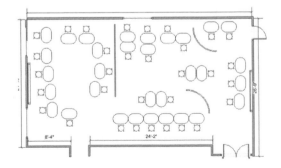

There is far more to the story of Denison's MIX Lab than the facts. From inception and funding through implementation and use, the lab's design has been innovative, collaborative, and transformative, driven by principles of learning space design.

Innovative Vision Yields Innovative Outcomes

At a meeting in 2003, instructional technologists and the chairpersons of Denison's fine and performing arts departments (Studio Art and Art History, Cinema, Dance, Music, and Theatre) focused on digitizing the disciplines. Convinced of the importance of "creative computing" (the analog to research computing for the arts), the chairs and staff developed a proposal[1] with an innovative vision to "blur distinctions among disciplines and build bridges among our departments for both students and faculty." The goal was to create new synergies among the five fine arts departments.

The faculty's innovative vision was for curricular synergy—a focus on a single, technologically-rich space to foster collaboration, learning, and interdisciplinary work for both students and faculty. Our institutional leaders committed space and funds to make the vision a reality. The instructional technologists carefully integrated a large array of hardware and software tools to meet the faculty's interdisciplinary goals. More than 50 applications are accessible in the MIX Lab, making possible a full range of interdisciplinary multimedia work with audio, video, 3D modeling, composition, presentation, and more. Each workstation (see Figure 2) includes all input and output devices to support a broad range of creative work and collaboration.

Figure 2. MIX Lab Workstation

Collaboration in Planning and Use

Collaborative planning involving all five departments was essential for this learning space to succeed. The MIX Lab plan was guided by Denison's "Checklist for Improving Your Learning Spaces" (http://www.denison.edu/learningspaces/checkl.pdf):

▶ Gather all stakeholders
▶ Define precisely how a space should support learning
▶ Review the attributes of the space that will affect learning
▶ Gather resources to implement and sustain the plan

Instructional technology staff provided technical and logistical support for planning and marketing, including public presentations to the campus.

Collaboration among the fine arts faculty and students continues in the daily operation of the MIX Lab. Working from a service level agreement (http://www.denison.edu/computing/academic/sla.html), a faculty management committee manages lab access, student assistants, supplies, and communication with instructional technology staff who provide hardware and software support, training, upgrades, and replacements.

Faculty-directed student teams work together on joint projects and generate new work processes and relationships among the traditionally separated disciplines. Faculty also benefit from each other's experiences, talents, and skills. Throughout the day, faculty members from all five disciplines hold classes in the lab and give students hands-on opportunities to experiment with the new tools and equipment. When the lab is not being used for instruction, students, faculty, and staff from across the university can use the space for their own projects. The open design of the space invites individuals to work together comfortably on joint projects.

Transformed Space That Transforms the Curriculum

Marginal improvements to a space rarely change the teaching and learning practices that take place there. Transformational changes may change practices, but such broad, sweeping changes require a strong, shared vision and an institutional commitment to potentially high-risk projects. We often lower risks by working incrementally toward a shared vision, but incremental improvements (such as better seating or room color) neither alter our teaching practices and learning outcomes nor expand our thinking about what might be possible. Converting a nonacademic space into a learning space provides a unique opportunity to discover authentic learning outcomes that arise from learning space transformations.

The MIX Lab, a transformed space, has in turn transformed the fine arts curriculum. Interest in creative computing runs high, and faculty members have adopted collaboration as a best practice. New courses integrate the visual arts with music in new ways, while dance and theater performances showcase the products and processes derived from the MIX Lab. Ever more ambitious student projects require collaboration for success. Based on the MIX Lab model, the fine arts are planning a "Center for Collaboration in the Arts."

A Learning Space Driven by Design Principles

The design and management of the MIX Lab is driven by eight principles of learning space design (http://www.denison.edu/learningspaces/mission.html) developed in 2002 as part of Denison's Learning Spaces Project (http://www.denison.edu/learningspaces/):

▶ **Learning spaces should support a diversity of learning styles.** The space accommodates lectures and demonstrations, artistic exploration and production, small group projects and individual work.

▶ **Learning spaces must be versatile.** Raised flooring with a very high density network as well as power distribution (one network and electrical outlet every three feet) and wheeled furniture provide on-the-fly flexibility and an impressive array of possible room configurations. (See Figure 3.)

Figure 3. Raised Floor with Network and Electrical Outlets

▶ **Learning spaces must be comfortable and attractive.** Seating, custom-designed ergonomic desks, and appropriate lighting were all important design elements. Solid-oak custom-designed multimedia workstations (see Figure 4) organize the equipment for each student, including a CPU, two monitors, audio and video inputs, switcher, scanner, MIDI keyboard, and more.

Figure 4. Multimedia Workstation

▶ **Learning spaces are technologically rich and supported.** An instructional technologist who is also an accomplished artist supports wireless and high-speed networking and an array of hardware and software options.
▶ **Learning spaces must be maintained continuously.** A capital budget supports a regular replacement cycle for equipment; an operating budget covers student salaries and supplies.
▶ **Leaning spaces should be ubiquitous in space and time.** The MIX Lab is accessible 24 hours a day through "one-card" access for students and faculty. Closed circuit television monitoring ensures security.
▶ **Learning spaces should be used effectively.** The popularity and high functionality of the MIX Lab has resulted in very high use levels and the need for careful scheduling. Outstanding documentation (http://www.denison.edu/computing/academic/news/mixguide.pdf) for the facility ensures effective use.
▶ **Learning spaces must be allocated sufficient resources.** Technologically rich and well-supported learning spaces depend on the allocation of sufficient resources—financial, human, and technical.

The MIX Lab is both the cause and effect of innovation, a transformed space that has transformed the curriculum. More than any other learning space at Denison, it has changed the way students and artists work and learn. The interdepartmental vision of a shared space has produced a successful technological learning space that has spawned greater aspirations for collaboration. The MIX Lab provides a unique example of how technology can break down barriers, promote new approaches to teaching and learning, and foster broad curricular transformation.

Endnote

1. For a copy of the proposal, see <http://www.denison.edu/learningspaces/fa/proposal.html>.

About the Author

Scott Siddall is assistant provost and director of instructional technology at Denison University.

CHAPTER 17

Perkins Library
Duke University

Marilyn M. Lombardi and Thomas B. Wall

What Is It?

In 2003, Duke University broke ground on a multimillion dollar expansion and renovation of the William R. Perkins Library, the university's largest and most centrally located library. The existing Perkins Library, constructed in three phases between 1928 and 1968, had interior spaces that were dim, musty, claustrophobic, and utterly unsuited to the changing nature of intellectual work in the electronic age. Unaltered for nearly 40 years, Perkins had "inadequate infrastructure, outdated mechanical systems, ineffective use of space, inferior study spaces, stacks filled beyond capacity, confusing layout, and poorly coordinated service areas."[1] Yet, the existing library, situated adjacent to Duke Chapel at the heart of the university's main campus, represented the only centralized location where new and emerging technologies might be combined with traditional resources to provide a service-rich and uniquely social environment for learning and research. The renovated and expanded Perkins Library, a space not unlike the ancient marketplace or *agora*, serves students and faculty as an inviting "third place." Neither a formal workplace (scheduled classroom) nor a private realm (dormitory or apartment), the Perkins has become a center for student life as well as intellectual hub and laboratory for learning. (See Figure 1.)

Planning for the reinvigorated Perkins Library began in 2000. The project reached a significant milestone in October 2005 with the opening of two new facilities. The five-story Bostock Library, linked to the original Perkins Library on four floors, and the von der Heyden Pavilion café (see Figure 2), a graceful solarium-like extension designed for informal study, collaboration, and special events, were designed to echo the Collegiate Gothic architecture that distinguishes the main campus of Duke University. Both buildings, along with the soon-to-be-completed Perkins Tower, add a total of 122,275 square feet to the university's main library, translating into 72,996 linear feet of shelving for the library's collection, open seating for 517 people, 96 computer workstations, 87 individual carrels, 9 group study rooms, and 7 reading rooms.

Figure 1. Perkins Library, Exterior View

Figure 2. The von der Heyden Pavilion at Night

The Perkins Renovation Project is far more than an expansion of the library's space—it signals a complete reconsideration of the academic library as a physical place and a qualitative experience. The older Perkins reflected a traditional concept of the library as *gatekeeper*. Its interior spaces were devoted primarily to the processing, preservation, and security of printed collections, and its layout was confusing for all but the most dedicated of scholars. By contrast, the renovated Perkins embodies a 21st-century vision of the library as gateway and commons, a gathering place for learners rather than a warehouse for books.

After consulting with constituencies across campus, the Perkins Library Renovation Committee worked with an architectural firm[2] to design a library for the future, one where public services supporting the entire spectrum of scholarly activity, from idea formation to knowledge production, were brought together at the physical center of an expanded library complex and made absolutely transparent to library patrons. The redesigned first floor of the Perkins Library facilitates this kind of scholarship, making space for a student writing center and a technology support desk. The number of technology-infused group study rooms and project-development spaces has increased substantially to acknowledge that students and faculty have gravitated toward interactive learning and collaboration in the analysis, presentation, and publication of knowledge because of their increasing reliance on electronic databases, digitized formats, and interactive media. While many areas for quiet study remain throughout the library, the sounds of learning are encouraged.

Finally, by embracing the information commons model, Duke librarians understood that they would be moving away from an exclusively location-based notion of service and toward a ubiquitous service concept, one that accepted the full integration of technology into traditional library functions. Duke librarians have taken on an important instructional and consultative role, preparing students who are technologically literate (but not necessarily information literate) to participate in a culture of research governed by general and discipline-specific methods of scholarship, attribution, and dissemination.

What Makes the Space Successful?

Today's students, having grown up in a networked world, arrive on campus with high technology expectations. They regard visual media as their vernacular, multitasking as a way of life, and project-based group work as their preferred mode of learning. They consider technology a vehicle for social interaction that occurs through instant messaging, mobile phones, wikis, blogs, and student-owned laptops. With wireless connectivity and mobile computing, students are moving out from behind their computer monitors to engage with others at any time and anywhere. As a result, the library and all other communal spaces on the traditional campus (corridors, lobbies, adjacencies, gardens, quadrangles) are being rethought. Once augmented with wireless connectivity, whiteboards, and comfortable seating, these public areas take on new purpose and meaning.

The particular value of the Perkins Library as a mixed-use facility rests with its capacity to bring students, faculty, reference librarians, and technology support staff into close proximity with one another, setting the necessary conditions for research-oriented conversation and facilitation. Taking its design cues from the spirit of the modern commercial bookstore and wireless cybercafé, the agile space uses subtle shifts in wall color to distinguish work areas, employs natural light to support mobility and mood, softens harsh right angles with reconfigurable furnishings that offer visual interest and mental stimulation, and provides sheltered spaces within a broader social context for independent or small group work. Comfortable chairs near data ports, electrical outlets, and wireless access points provide refuge for independent study and the opportunity for relaxation. (See Figure 3.)

Figure 3. Comfortable Seating for Study and Relaxation

Functionally and aesthetically, the new Bostock addition to the library complex is a vast improvement over the older Perkins facility. Using extensive input from all sectors of campus, including feedback via LibQual+ and focus groups, planners determined that faculty, students, and staff all wanted large reading rooms, natural lighting, open space design, and the seamless integration of technological services in support of scholarship. (See Figure 4.) The mandate, then, called for inviting spaces equipped with technology and grounded in a robust service program.[3]

Students flocked to the new Bostock Library from the moment it opened in 2005. Now they can use group study spaces, consult with staff, and produce a final project in their chosen medium and format, all without leaving the library. Duke students, 90

Figure 4. Reading Room with Natural Light

percent of whom own laptops or other portable computing devices, are in the habit of bringing them to the library, with its wireless capabilities, and settling in one of the many comfortable study areas to complete their work. The new Bostock addition (see Figure 5) has increased student library usage by 40 percent between spring semester 2005 and spring semester 2006. Reference desk transactions went up from 809 to 1,115 over that same time period. Revealingly, the number of purely directional questions dropped dramatically, indicating that the library's transparent layout is self-explanatory. Content questions (as opposed to directional inquiries) from undergraduates were up 24 percent, while content questions from faculty and graduate students doubled.

Figure 5. Main Floor of the Bostock Addition

How Is Technology Used?

When it comes to reenvisioning the library to meet the needs of students and scholars in a postdigital age, the importance of strategic partnerships cannot be overstated. At Duke, library administrators worked closely with the university's central technology organization to eliminate any technical barriers that stood in the way of providing seamless, convenient, and easy access to support for the full range of scholarly activities, from idea generation to publication in the appropriate medium and format. The first problem to address involved wireless electronic printing in a new era of portable laptops and mobile computing. Prior to the renovation, the Perkins Library and the central technology organization offered separate e-printing services, a distinction that made little sense to students or faculty. The renovation offered both organizations an opportunity to rethink their relationship and combine forces to build a centrally administered, seamless service tailored to patron needs. As a result, the library now makes use of ePrint, Duke's unified public printing technology, allowing students to print using their laptops, library computers, and IT workstations interchangeably. Students simply download one program/driver, send their print jobs to the central print queue, and retrieve their documents from any ePrint device, regardless of whether that device is in the library, computer lab, or student center.

The unified public printing service deployment quickly became a prototype for the kind of cross-organizational cooperation and integration essential to the success of the information commons model. Together, the library and the central technology organization addressed other issues that required a new culture of sharing across functional boundaries. For example, the library had the goal of adding a substantial number of workstations to extend the quick look-up and database/Internet searching capabilities of traditional library computers by adding productivity software, several Web applications, and tools to let users develop their knowledge products. The issue of how best to manage public workstations located in various locations across a highly decentralized campus is challenging for many universities and colleges. The Perkins Library renovation prompted a new culture of sharing and trust between the library and the central IT organization, leading to the development of an efficient management solution that met the library's goal of offering students exemplary service. The central IT organization now deploys a common roster of software applications (or "central image"), ensuring that students find the same applications installed on the new library workstations as on the machines in the public computer labs elsewhere on campus. At the same time, however, the library retains the ability to add software to or cull software from this central image at its discretion. Prompted by the Perkins renovation, the library and the central IT organization have begun to share physical spaces, staff, resources, and ideas, embarking on a partnership that promises to benefit the entire Duke community for years to come.

As a computing experience, the Perkins renovation offers workstations for students and faculty that meet a variety of needs. First, computer kiosks configured for printing with touch-screen capabilities and basic features (browsers, Office reader plugins, Adobe Reader, media players) are located near the library entrance and the elevators on each floor. Representing a mere 10 percent of the available public computers in the renovated library, these kiosks nevertheless continue to serve an important function, enabling library patrons to conduct quick library searches, check e-mail, text message, and send their papers or presentations to their campus network space for storage. The main floors of the library contain a second tier of computers loaded with general-use productivity suites (for example, Microsoft Office suite, Dreamweaver, Adobe Acrobat, EndNote, iTunes, a freeware image editor, Photoshop Elements, some statistical packages, and so forth) and scanners, along with access to Duke's databases and online resources for students and faculty completing research projects and papers. Finally, the library's upper-floor workstations, which contain more specialized applications (language kits/input editors, data-use and analysis packages, higher-end geographic information systems technology and multimedia production tools, and so forth), are located adjacent to library specialists in international studies, area studies, and social science data, increasing the likelihood that students will take advantage of library human resources as they use tools that require more extensive instruction and/or support.

The Bostock Library owes its popularity more than anything else to its abundance of natural light. Students gravitate to the upper floors, where reading rooms offer the warmth of arts and crafts style interiors, soaring ceilings, large windows, and beautiful views of the Duke Chapel. Using LabStats, library personnel concerned that students would steer clear of the lower-level technology spaces because of the lack of natural light have watched as the popularity of these spaces has grown.[4] Students flock to the lower-level resources, which include group study rooms with plasma screens and audio capabilities and a classroom where library personnel instruct students in the effective use of information resources and central IT organization staff train students in specific software applications and multimedia technologies.

In the next phase of the information commons project, Bostock's lower level and that of the renovated Perkins Library will form a continuous technology concourse offering a broad range of classroom spaces and technology production rooms along with an array of multimedia and format integration technologies.

What Principles Were Behind the Design?

The redesign of a campus's central library demands that a college or university revisit its most fundamental goals as an institution. How can the library balance its traditional role as an acquirer and preserver of substantial collections with its emerging role as a user-centered, service-rich space for research, collaboration, and creativity and remain agile enough to respond quickly to the changing work patterns of its patrons? The design principles that underlie the Perkins Library renovation represent a thorough acknowledgment of the ways in which technology, by freeing up space once used to shelve printed collections and making it available for human interactions, has renewed the importance of the library as a physical space for teaching, learning, and research. This rediscovery of the library as *place* is accompanied by a redefinition of the librarian as *facilitator*, helping guide the new undergraduate curriculum while ensuring that Duke's students leave the university with a level of information literacy that equips them for a lifetime of learning and leadership in a post-digital era. Along with a central information commons, the reinvigorated Perkins Library includes project-development rooms and faculty laboratory spaces that can be reconfigured to support experimentation with new learning models and instructional technologies.

Underlying Duke's approach to library renovation is the notion of *built pedagogy*, which recognizes that the design of a physical space will influence how people behave within those spaces, encouraging some activities while constraining others. Educational architects speak of the way in which university planners inevitably embody their current pedagogical philosophies in the design of physical spaces, imposing directions for how a space should be used. The information commons model rests on the conviction that the library's physical space must be flexible to encourage serendipitous and ad hoc learning activities in keeping with changing study patterns and student desires. The information commons approach—a human-centered design—privileges those structural elements that encourage multiple types of learning practices and styles. For example, we have learned that students use different spaces for different activities. Many prefer a more industrial space (rows of computers) when focusing on a product like a term paper; when studying, they like solitude with natural light; and designated and ad hoc group study rooms are always popular. The overall design should convey a sense of flow and connection between spaces (fluidity); signal the fact that rooms may be used for multiple purposes (versatility); build in a degree of adaptability at the structural level so that the spaces can be redesigned by others in later years (convertibility); prepare for the possibility of expansion or contraction (scalability); and invite users to rearrange the room and its furnishings as they see fit (modifiability). The trick, of course, is to come up with a design that is both responsive to current needs and flexible enough to accommodate unforeseeable changes in technology, usage, and policy.[5]

What Is Unique or Noteworthy?

When asked to describe what distinguished the planning process at Duke from those undertaken by other campuses with whom he had collaborated, architect Geoffrey Freeman singled out the very deliberate participation of constituencies from across the university and the clarity they achieved regarding the role of the library in Duke's future.[6] Duke acknowledged as much in 2002 when it recognized the planning process with the university's teamwork award, pointing to the manner in which the goals of faculty, students, library staff, senior administrators, and trustees were reconciled to build a common vision of the library's place in a changing world.[7]

Endnotes

1. From <http://library.duke.edu/about/perkinsproject/>.

2. The architectural firm was Shepley, Bulfinch, Richardson, and Abbott. The committee was chaired by Robert Byrd, associate university librarian and director of the Rare Book, Manuscript, and Special Collections Library.

3. For more details, contact author Thomas Wall.

4. LabStats is an application from Computer Lab Solutions designed to measure public computer lab use by workstation platform, location, and time of day (http://www.computerlabsolutions.com/). Anecdotal evidence suggests that students are staying for longer periods of time in the renovated library than they did in the older facility. The library plans to track the duration of student visits and introduce this metric into future analyses.

5. For a detailed discussion, see Torin Monahan, "Flexible Space & Built Pedagogy: Emerging IT Embodiments," *Inventio*, vol. 4, no. 1 (2002), pp. 1–19, <http://www.torinmonahan.com/papers/Inventio.html>.

6. See the report "University Libraries: Clarity About the Role of the Library," Duke University Development, <http://152.3.224.76/development/finalreport/nine.html>.

7. For further information regarding the Perkins Renovation and Information Commons planning processes, please contact Robert Byrd, associate university librarian and director of the Rare Book, Manuscript, and Special Collections Library, or Thomas Wall, associate university librarian and director of Public Services. For information regarding the library's tiered approach to computing and collaboration with the central IT organization, contact Ed Gomes, head of Library Systems Support; John Little, senior IT analyst; or Kevin Davis, senior manager of Student Technology Services, Office of Information Technology. For contact information, see the Duke University staff directory at <http://library.duke.edu/about/directory/>.

About the Authors

Marilyn M. Lombardi is senior strategist for the Office of Information Technology at Duke University and an EDUCAUSE Learning Initiative (ELI) scholar in residence. **Thomas B. Wall** is associate university librarian and director of public services at Duke University.

CHAPTER 18

Peter H. Armacost Library
Eckerd College

J. Michael Barber

What Is It?

Located on the waterfront of St. Petersburg, Florida, Eckerd College (http://www.eckerd.edu/librarydedication/?f=home) is a private, coeducational college of liberal arts and sciences with an enrollment of 1,800 students. Eckerd College is the only national private liberal arts college in Florida and is one of only 40 liberal arts colleges profiled in Loren Pope's *Colleges That Change Lives.*

The new Peter H. Armacost Library (see Figure 1) at Eckerd College, designed by Ayers/Saint/Gross (http://www.asg-architects.com), presents a vision for the library of the 21st century through the integration of books and information technology as well as by providing unique and inviting spaces that encourage collaborative learning.

Figure 1. Peter H. Armacost Library

©2006 J. Michael Barber

What Happens Here?

The Armacost Library facilitates research, collaborative learning, individual learning, informal gatherings, videoconferencing, multimedia instruction, and computing through a variety of services and technologies.

For research, library users can access 250,000 volumes on site as well as electronic catalogues, databases, subject guides, encyclopedias, dictionaries, and an e-book collection (http://www.eckerd.edu/library/). (See Figure 2.)

Figure 2. Reference Area

Seventeen group study rooms furnished either with tablet-arm lounge seating or tables and chairs create a variety of learning and collaborative environments. (See Figure 3.)

To support individual learning, 72 custom-designed study carrels are wired with power and data connections; 8 have multimedia stations for electronic access to audio and video collections. Several open lounges, including an outdoor lanai (screened patio), provide casual settings for individuals or groups to study.

A 28-seat meeting room permits users to connect with remote sites throughout the world, while a 30-person multimedia instruction lab provides multimedia training to augment instruction, research, and writing. The campus computing center is strategically placed in the facility to let librarians, programmers, and network specialists collaborate in creating state-of-the-art information storage and retrieval systems.

Figure 3. Group Study Area

How Is Technology Used?

Users can access information in any setting, even from the lawn areas outside the building, thanks to the wireless access provided. Wired access points, available throughout the building, provide reliable high-speed network connections. Videoconferencing services support collaboration with people on campus and around the world, and reference materials are easily available digitally using online research tools.

The technology center houses the campus servers and network maintenance facilities. IT staff are colocated, enabling collaboration between IT specialists and librarians.

What Makes the Space Successful?

Books and information technology are everywhere—and they are integrated. The library is wired and wireless, as is the space around it. Integration of the physical and the digital ensures easy access to resources, no matter what the format. (See Figure 4.)

The library responds to and respects the way students like to study, with ubiquitous Internet access, soft furniture, lounges, abundant windows, various sizes of study spaces, and bright, warm, visually inviting colors. The Armacost Library serves as a nexus of student residential life, academic and student life facilities, student programs, and staff offices.

The library's unique location and outdoor spaces take advantage of the surrounding Florida landscape and natural environment.

Figure 4. Books and Technology Are Integrated

What Principles Were Behind the Design?

The Armacost Library design focused on integration with the master plan and encouraged stakeholder input. Goals for the final design included an open plan, variety, accessibility, and sustainability.

A collaborative design effort between master planners and building designers resulted in identifying a building site that best suited the project. The design team then sought feedback from the building users to design custom solutions that met the unique needs of Eckerd College. Sight lines and views were carefully considered, not only to provide natural light and interesting views from all areas of the building but also to allow a flexible approach to library staffing.

Various study environments allow everything from lively collaboration to contemplative study, while the broad concept of accessibility encompasses easy access to the building by the campus community as well as access to information in all its forms. Natural lighting, solar shading, high-performance glazing, energy efficient lighting, and low-flow plumbing fixtures throughout the facility reduce the demand on energy and natural resources.

The library promotes collaborative learning through the provision of small and large study rooms, large tables, and lounge space. Students can choose the space that best meets their needs. (See Figure 5.)

Figure 5. A Variety of Spaces

What Is Unique or Noteworthy?

The Armacost Library is noteworthy for integrating the design with the university's master plan and for taking advantage of the Florida environment. The building was shaped through a unique collaboration between the master planning and design teams. Its orientation, form, materials, and landscape design were developed to seamlessly integrate with the existing context, including the surrounding Florida environment, and future campus projects. Abundant natural light, water views, and a temperate climate were leveraged in this unique design. (See Figure 6.)

As Eckerd College President Donald R. Eastman, III, said during the library's dedication ceremony,[1] "We believe we have built a library that enhances and enriches what Eckerd College has always done—which is provide the finest possible personal environment for learning."

Figure 6. Taking Advantage of the Environment

Endnote

1. Donald R. Eastman, III, president, Eckerd College, Peter H. Armacost Library dedication ceremony, February 18, 2005, <http://eckerd.edu/librarydedication/index.php?f=president>.

About the Author

J. Michael Barber is a senior associate with Ayers/Saint/Gross, Architects + Planners.

CHAPTER 19

Learning Studios Project
Estrella Mountain Community College

Homero Lopez and Lori Gee

What Is It?

Estrella Mountain Community College (EMCC), one of the ten colleges in the Maricopa Community College District of Arizona, recognized that today's college students have very different ideas about how and where learning takes place. To meet these changing needs and expectations, the college aimed to maximize learning opportunities through the design of innovative learning spaces and the integration of technology. In 2005, Estrella Mountain forged partnerships with Herman Miller, Inc., and its local dealership, Goodmans Interior Structures in Arizona. Together they explored more effective approaches to the traditional classroom environment and engaged in discussions that resulted in the unique transformation of two liberal arts classrooms into prototype "Learning Studios."

The new Learning Studios provided faculty and learners with an opportunity to experiment with radical flexibility in space, furnishings, and technology—all targeted at increasing student engagement and success. Based on findings from a student focus group and considerable input from faculty, the prototype studios were designed as dynamic, customizable learning spaces that made the most of the face-to-face class experience. (See Figure 1.) Operating on the principle of radical flexibility, the design set up space, furniture, and technology to be changeable on the fly, not only making the rooms adaptable and more engaging but also enabling experimentation and further refinement by students and faculty using the studios.

The overall goals of the project were:

▸ Streamlining classroom design, technology, furniture, lighting, and electrical access.

▸ Selecting furniture that facilitates learning activities, wireless networking, and quick reconfiguration.

▸ Making technology easy to use and lighting adaptable to facilitate mobile teaching stations and collaborative spaces for group work.

Figure 1. Learning Studios Create Face-to-Face Experiences

Photo: Andrew Nolte © 2005 Estrella Mountain Community College

▸ Learning more about how innovative spatial relationships, ergonomic design, and seamless technology can increase student engagement and success.

Ultimately, each of the two studios was set up to accommodate 32 students in 900-square-foot rooms equipped with:

▸ Laptops
▸ Data projectors
▸ Mobile teaching stations
▸ Wheeled and folding tables that could be easily moved and reconfigured
▸ Ergonomically designed chairs with wheels for easy movement
▸ Adjustable lighting
▸ Combination whiteboards and projection surfaces throughout
▸ A nature-inspired palette of colors and clean, modern design in the furnishings and walls

The design of the two learning studios was similar, but not identical. Differences were driven in part by distinct traits of the physical layout of the two spaces. For example, one of the rooms had no windows. To compensate, panels patterned with images of trees and water were placed in a zigzag arrangement along one of the existing walls to enliven the space. The wall also served to hold multiple whiteboards to encourage group discussions and informal learning within the formal learning environment. (See Figure 2.)

Figure 2. Zigzag Panels and Whiteboards Create Informal Learning Areas

Photo: Ralph Campbell. © 2005 Estrella Mountain Community College

Other differences sprang from experimentation. For example, student desks in one studio consisted of wheeled tables with folding leaves. Depending on how the leaves were set, the tables served as desk space for two students, a group table for four students, or any number of other combinations; collapsing both leaves allowed the compact tables to be pushed aside. The other studio featured tables that when standing alone served as desks for individual students and when wheeled together could serve as large group work spaces.

One of the elements common to both learning studios was the infusion of technology. Both studios provided wireless-enabled laptops for students, giving them easy access to information and creating clearer sight lines than those afforded by desktop computers. Another notable feature of both studios was the use of "teaching stations" rather than fixed podiums for faculty. These mobile tables could be equipped with wireless-enabled laptops and wheeled to any position in the classroom. This broadened the ways faculty could approach their teaching and helped break down barriers between faculty and students.

All these features helped free students and faculty from the regimentation, tacit hierarchies, and institutional feel of traditional classrooms. In addition, the combination of features created a more fluid, collaborative setting, suiting students who are increasingly accustomed to highly interactive, technology-infused environments.

Using extensive feedback from students and faculty about their experiences and perceptions of the Learning Studios prototypes, the Learning Studios project team further improved the model. In 2006, the team applied the revised model to 22 classrooms in the new Ocotillo Hall classroom complex. With the opening of Ocotillo Hall, the college committed to the continued evaluation of existing spaces while creating more prototypes. Faculty and learners are encouraged to visualize, play, experiment, test, and assess prototypes of spaces before the institution makes significant investments in future capital or remodeling projects.

What Happens Here?

Created as alternative learning spaces for traditional liberal arts classes, the prototype Learning Studios are used primarily for classes. The studios depart from tradition, however, in the power they give both students and faculty to actively create environments that suit a range of learning activities. For the faculty, the studios not only enabled but inspired them to experiment with new approaches to teaching. The minimal setup time facilitated the ability to lecture, share a Web site, demonstrate an idea with PowerPoint projections, or even group the furniture at the edge of the room to simulate a theater. Students likewise could customize and adjust the space, from simply adjusting their chairs for greater comfort to setting up impromptu collaborative groups around whiteboards. To fully maximize the new spaces, students use the Learning Studios around scheduled class activities for informal, self-directed learning.

How Is Technology Used?

"Technology is everywhere, but not in the way," observed EMCC's E-Learning Faculty Coordinator Polly Miller in describing the seamless integration of technology in the Learning Studios.

▶ Wireless laptop computers available to every student (see Figure 3)
▶ Data projectors and numerous projection surfaces
▶ Readily available access to electrical power

Students benefited from Internet access in finding quick answers and additional information about topics being discussed. They also appreciated the nonthreatening setting the studios presented for practicing and improving their technology skills. They gained from the guided discovery of computers and the Internet for research, current-affairs awareness, and fact checking.

Figure 3. Wireless Laptops Provide Information Access and Clearer Sight Lines

Photo: Andrew Nolte. © 2005 Estrella Mountain Community College

What Makes the Space Successful?

Following the prototype project, the Learning Studios project team conducted an extensive study of students and faculty to determine the project's successes and shortcomings. Eighty-seven percent of the faculty surveyed indicated a preference for the Learning Studios over traditional learning environments. The salient features can be expressed as: access to technology + interaction + comfort = greater engagement.

▶ **Increased engagement:** Because the studios fostered a direct, conversational relationship between students and faculty and provided easy access to technology, they avoided the passivity and isolation associated with traditional classrooms and instead engendered active student engagement.

▶ **Lowered barriers to participation:** The studios fostered small group discussion and faculty circulation around the room, creating a lively, dynamic, and supportive environment that encouraged participation even among timid students.

▶ **Flexibility:** Faculty could easily customize the Learning Studios to reflect their own teaching styles and employed a wider range of tools and methods to reach their students.

▶ **Support of self-directed learning:** The Learning Studios encouraged greater participation in group activities, broke down the hierarchies that can make students less willing to ask questions, and gave students ready access to the Internet to fulfill their quests for more information.

▶ **Inviting environment:** The studios were perceived as comfortable and modern spaces, with a warm and peaceful feel. They also embodied more fully than traditional classrooms the ideals students and faculty associate with higher education.

What Principles Were Behind the Design?

The Learning Studios team identified three principles critical to the studios' design:

▶ **Leveraging physical space:** The design focused on creating a space for learning that not only supports pedagogical objectives but also enhances the experience of learning.

▶ **Engaging stakeholders:** Actively gathering and using input from all stakeholders—students, faculty, and staff—about what makes a dynamic learning space contributed substantially to the concepts applied in the prototype studios.

▶ **Employing radical flexibility:** Freeing faculty and students from the physical limitations of the traditional classroom by transforming it into a highly adaptable learning space allowed them to rearrange the studios on the fly to support changing pedagogical demands.

What Is Unique or Noteworthy?

Radical flexibility was embraced in the studios' space, furnishings, and technology. This important concept emerged from meetings, focus groups, and surveys on pedagogy and delivery strategies with students, faculty, and staff. It calls for the freeing of faculty and students from the physical limitations of traditional learning environments and from the constraints they can place on innovation and engagement in both teaching and learning. This was accomplished in the Learning Studios by making the rooms' physical elements (furniture, technologies, and so on) customizable on the fly by both faculty and students, so they could easily adapt them to the pedagogical demands of the moment. (See Figure 4.) Through reliance on hands-on manipulation of the learning environment, radical flexibility also fosters a sense of ownership in the learning process. Its application to the Learning Studios project made for a dynamic learning environment that encouraged learning (both formal and informal), research, creativity, and collaboration.

Extensive user involvement and assessment were central to the studios' initial design, evolution, and ultimate success. The Learning Studios prototype designs were informed by faculty and staff input as well as student surveys

Figure 4. Learning Studios Can Be Reconfigured Easily

Photo: Ralph Campbell. © 2005 Estrella Mountain Community College

and focus groups. And before the Learning Studios approach was adopted for 22 classrooms in the new Ocotillo Hall, extensive research determined the outcomes of the Learning Studios prototypes.

For More Information

"Radical Flexibility and the Learning Studios at EMCC": <http://www.estrellamountain.edu/awareness/download/06/HLCfinal.doc>

Herman Miller Case Study on the EMCC Project: <http://www.hermanmiller.com/hm/content/case_studies/pdf_full/CS_EAZ_FULL.pdf>

EMCC Summary of the Learning Studios Project: <http://www.mcli.dist.maricopa.edu/mlx/slip.php?item=1797>

Diana G. Oblinger, "Radical Flexibility and Student Success: An Interview with Homero Lopez," *EDUCAUSE Review*, vol. 41, no. 1 (January/February 2006), <http://www.educause.edu/apps/er/erm06/erm0612.asp>

About the Authors

Homero Lopez is the founding president of Estrella Mountain Community College and since 1987 has served as a consultant-evaluator for the Higher Learning Commission of the North Central Association of Colleges and Schools. **Lori Gee** leads the Education Solutions Team for Herman Miller, Inc., and the company's focus on learning trends and higher education environments.

CHAPTER 20

Science Center
Hamilton College

Nikki Reynolds and Douglas A. Weldon

History

Hamilton College is a small, selective, residential liberal arts college located in central New York State. The college emphasizes the importance of communication, student responsibility, and rigorous study. Personalized education and high levels of faculty and student interaction are considered hallmarks of the Hamilton College experience.

By the 1990s, it became obvious that the science programs at Hamilton suffered from overcrowding and out-of-date facilities. Teaching methods have changed, with an increased focus on hands-on learning. Emphasis on student research and public presentation of the results has increased, as well. Moreover, new interdisciplinary programs at the college require close proximity of the various science departments.

Process

The decision was made to renovate and expand the existing main science building. As part of the programming and design process, teams of faculty traveled to more than 20 institutions that had recently completed science facilities. Campus committees consisting of administrators, faculty, staff, and students met continually with architects and participated in the decision-making processes. The outcome was a building designed around the following principles:

▶ The Science Center celebrates the learning and discovery of science by making the activities that occur inside the building visible. (See Figure 1.)

▶ Classrooms and seminar rooms are distributed throughout the building, so student traffic keeps the building "alive."

▶ Classrooms and laboratories are designed to maximize flexibility and to accommodate different pedagogical approaches.

▶ Teaching labs allow the combination of lecture and hands-on activities in a single class session.

Figure 1. Science Center Stairway

Photo: Bob Handelman

▶ Laboratories are designed to allow students to engage in hands-on research, with student labs and faculty research labs placed near each other. All of Hamilton's seniors are required to complete a research project, and there is also an active summer research program.

▶ Faculty in different departments are located near each other to maximize interdisciplinary connections in the sciences.

▶ Student study spaces are arranged throughout the building in close proximity to faculty offices to support access to faculty during informal or ad hoc study periods.

▶ Up-to-date technology in the building includes network connections made via wireless technology or 1,000 hard ports. Technology is built into all spaces in the building, not just the classrooms and labs.

▶ The Science Center is environmentally friendly, using a heat-recovery system, geothermal technology in the atrium area, and certified wood (i.e., wood from forests maintained in a sustainable manner) in casework and millwork.

The Building

The resulting 208-gross-square-foot Science Center (20 percent renovation and 80 percent new construction) is a pleasing amalgam of traditional and new elements, blending the stone typical of the existing college architecture with new materials. (See Figure 2.)

Figure 2. Science Center Front Façade

Photo: Peter Finger

The front atrium of the Science Center (see Figure 3) is both the aesthetic centerpiece of the building and an instructional area that highlights green architecture. In this area, air cooled and heated via a geothermal loop system powers a

Figure 3. Science Center Main Atrium

Photo: Marianita Amodio

displacement ventilation system integrated with a double-glass façade that serves as the front of the building. A touch screen and flat display explain many green features of the Science Center; sensors provide dynamic information on outside environmental conditions, inside environmental conditions, and operation of the geothermal and heat-recovery systems.

Classrooms

Each classroom has a touch screen to control projection of computer, DVD, or video images. Of the three tiered classrooms, the largest seats 125 students. This main auditorium (see Figure 4) has a full complement of presentation technologies, including three data projectors, a surround-sound system with speaker microphones, and a separate projection booth with a 16mm projector and additional DVD/VHS and sound equipment.

Figure 4. Science Center Main Auditorium

Photo: Marianita Amodio

The remaining two tiered classrooms have two data projectors each without a separate projection booth, but they are fully equipped otherwise. A touch-screen interface controls the rooms' facilities. One of these classrooms is designed with two rows per tier, to make it convenient for students to form discussion groups (see Figure 5) and then return to a lecture format.

Each of the flat-floored classrooms has a single data projector with touch-screen control for all the technologies. To maximize flexibility, classrooms are equipped with standard tables that have wheels at one end so that they can be

Figure 5. Science Center Tiered Classroom

Photo: Bill Denison

moved easily for different pedagogical arrangements (seminar, small groups, or lecture). Each of the eight general seminar rooms is equipped with a data projector and computer with a wireless keyboard and mouse that can be passed around as students make presentations.

Laboratories

Laboratories were designed to facilitate specific pedagogical approaches. For example, the geosciences microscope laboratory contains pods with four microscopes each, networked together. (See Figure 6.) When students locate items of interest, they can present to the entire class, and the instructor can project images from two different microscopes onto two wall screens using ceiling-mounted projectors for the class to make comparisons.

Another specialized teaching laboratory clearly visible through windows in the corridor walls is the electron microscopy lab. In addition to two electron microscopes, this lab has a wall-mounted flat-screen display and desktop computers. (See Figure 7.)

Figure 6. Geosciences Microscope Laboratory

Photo: Bill Denison

Figure 7. Electron Microscopy Laboratory

Photo: Bill Denison

Student Study Areas

To make the building effective as a location for student work, many kinds of study areas were included in the design: private study rooms, departmental common areas, and the main atrium. Each set of two to four faculty offices contains a glass-enclosed tutorial area immediately outside (see Figures 8 and 9), where students can wait to see one of the faculty members or work with them. Common areas

Figure 8. Biology Department Student Study Lounge

Photo: Marianita Amodio

Figure 9. Biology Faculty Office Tutorial Area

Photo: Marianita Amodio

outside faculty offices are furnished to support student study and tutorial sessions. Wireless technology throughout the building lets students use their laptops in any of these spaces. Additionally, many spaces are configured as effective areas for students to study, either alone or in groups. (See Figure 10.)

Figure 10. Student Study Areas

Photo: Bob Handleman

Overall Effect

The combination of aesthetics and effective spaces for learning encourages heavy use of the Hamilton College Science Center by students and faculty from all areas of the campus. The technological support, comfortable areas for individual or group study, and easy access to faculty promote student engagement and learning, contributing to the Hamilton College experience.

About the Authors

Nikki Reynolds is the director of instructional technology services and **Douglas A. Weldon** is Stone Professor of Psychology at Hamilton College.

CHAPTER 21

The ES Corridor Project
Indiana University-Purdue University Indianapolis

Nancy Van Note Chism

What Is It?

An urban research university with more than 29,000 students, Indiana University-Purdue University Indianapolis (IUPUI) supports both a wide range of high-level professional programs and undergraduate programs for a largely commuter student population. Because most of our undergraduate students are struggling to fit their studies within full lives that often include work, family, community service, or some combination of these responsibilities, IUPUI strives to create ways to make the campus "sticky." To help students establish an identity as students and as members of the IUPUI community and feel pride in IUPUI, we need to take every opportunity to create an environment that supports their studies and reinforces their decision to participate in higher education.

One such opportunity came in the form of a wide corridor that serves as a main passageway through the Education and Social Work (ES) building, one of four interconnected core academic buildings through which many people routinely pass. Several classrooms open into one side of this corridor, which is bordered on the remaining side by solid glass windows, allowing a panoramic view of downtown Indianapolis. The original design of the corridor provided for niches outside each classroom, which were furnished with a square built-in platform for seating. (See Figure 1.)

Entrusted with creating a good physical environment for learning, the IUPUI Learning Environments Committee seized on the ES corridor as a perfect place for an experiment in informal learning spaces. Having no funds for this experiment, we envisioned a "parade of learning spaces" competition, modeled on realtors' "parade of homes" competitions. We enlisted community partners—a furniture company and three leading interior design firms—to contribute designs for different kinds of spaces in this corridor and to implement them.

Figure 1. Seating Platform

Photo: Monnica Lewis

The participants created five unique learning spaces that test out different design elements, yet all are united in their intention to serve as a "front porch" to the adjoining classrooms:

▶ The first features a recycling bar at which students can sit and observe corridor traffic, a work table and chairs, and comfortable chairs for relaxing or talking. (See Figure 2.)

Figure 2. Recycling Bar

Photo: Christina Lynn Wrightsman

▶ The second uses cabinetry to divide the space into three distinct sections supporting activities such as project work, quiet study, or informal conversation. (See Figure 3.)

Figure 3. Divided Space

Photo: Christina Lynn Wrightsman

▶ The third contains a "walltalker" whiteboard divider and stools for working with visual information, as well as casual chairs for group discussion. (See Figure 4.)

Figure 4. Whiteboard Divider

Photo: Christina Lynn Wrightsman

▶ The fourth area is built around "the kitchen counter" at which conversations and project work can occur, a sectional sofa for relaxed conversation, and a standee unit. (See Figure 5.)

Figure 5. Kitchen Counter Arrangement

Photo: Christina Lynn Wrightsman

▶ The fifth unit, originally unplanned but installed during the project to use an empty corner where two corridors met, employs more traditional study carrel furniture of an updated variety that lets users move and recombine the parts. (See Figure 6.)

Figure 6. Study Carrels

Photo: Christina Lynn Wrightsman

The corridor project also involved removing a rail between the corridor and windows, adding plants and carpeting, and changing the wall colors and lighting of the niches.

What Happens Here?

The learning spaces were designed to support a variety of activities by providing places for

▶ students to talk and get to know each other;
▶ project teams to do their work before, during, or after class;
▶ faculty and students to meet before or after class; and
▶ commuter students to comfortably study or relax while they wait before, in between, or after class.

Our first series of studies of these spaces show that they are indeed used in a variety of ways.

Study Spaces

Students use these spaces to read, solve problems, review class notes, and carry out other study tasks. They most often use the spaces prior to or following classes in the adjoining rooms, but some prefer these spaces as their normal places to be. One student joked that she was going to bring in a nameplate to label an area as "her office."

Social Spaces

Even though these spaces are connected to a building with a café, many students eat lunch in the spaces and use the area for such activities as playing cards or having casual conversations.

Class Work Spaces

Classes in the adjacent classrooms use the areas for group space or areas that will accommodate special activities. One course that involves clinical interviews used the spaces to simulate practice settings for students to do reciprocal interviews; another used them for students to practice first-aid techniques in groups.

Project/Team Spaces

Commuter students who find it hard to schedule meetings of project teams have taken to holding meetings in the spaces before or after class sessions. At any given time, one can see groups of students huddled around a laptop, diagramming on the whiteboard, or seated around a table with notebooks accomplishing some group activity.

Faculty-Student Contact Spaces

Before or after class, faculty members can stop and chat with students in comfort. They report being relieved of the anxiety they feel when another class is waiting for the room or occupying it while their own students want to talk with them.

How Is Technology Used?

These spaces occupy a wireless environment, and students regularly use laptops in them. One finding of the first studies of the space, however, is that we did not provide enough power outlets for recharging batteries. The spaces also have no capabilities to project images from laptops to the walls or screens or to save information from the whiteboard for students working on a common project. Although the designers had entertained the idea of playing images off some of the surfaces in the corridor as a way to add interest or information (such as news feeds or educational videos), the final design did not include resources to support these ideas. Successive corridor projects will have to consider integrating technologies in a more systematic way.

What Makes the Space Successful?

The renovated ES corridor provides attractive, comfortable surroundings for people passing through or stopping to use the space. It is close to formal learning spaces and offers areas outside classrooms for students to meet and work. The spaces have also contributed to feelings of pride in the campus and the building of relationships among students and faculty.

Attractiveness and Comfort

One of the main reasons for the success of this space is its attractiveness. Design, color, and lighting command the attention of those using the corridor. First impressions recorded in the study underscored the students' excitement with the overall "feel" of the corridor. Students who were interviewed compared it to the commercial spaces in bookstores and coffee shops where they like to linger. They also praised the associated quality of comfort, singling out the comfortable upholstered furniture as desirable over the hard plastic chairs and metal or wooden stools used in the designs.

Proximity

The space also succeeds because of its proximity to formal learning activities. As "front porches" to classrooms, the spaces serve as places where busy students can meet and work without having to spend precious time walking to and from the library or other formal or informal learning spaces. They provide a convenient meeting space for groups or study partners seeking to get together before or after classes scheduled in the adjoining rooms.

The spaces also serve the formal classrooms in providing overflow areas for special activities—group work, practice clinical interviews, tutoring, and other components of the class-based instruction. Instructors who had not ordinarily incorporated active learning components in their course design reported that they now use these spaces routinely for students to discuss, run simulations, plan, or accomplish other learning tasks. The spaces thereby illustrate a teaching development impact.

Effect on Pride

Less tangible, but no less important, is the impact that the spaces have had on campus pride and the building of relationships. The comfortable and attractive ambiance of the spaces has led to lingering, socializing, and group work—all vital to our campus as it struggles with retention and student success. The spaces have also increased pride in IUPUI as a learning space. One faculty member commented, "I think it was one of the wisest uses of space and the best thing I have seen for students in many years."

What Principles Were Behind the Design?

When the project was proposed to the companies that ultimately brought it to fruition, the learning principles behind it were emphasized. The Learning Environments Committee had articulated these early on in two papers[1] and in a slide show prepared to invite the partners to participate in the ES Corridor Project. The learning principles are rooted in current theories of cognition that stress active engagement in the construction of knowledge; on student retention theories that point to the importance of engagement and identification in the campus; in data on the changing composition of the student body that emphasize social learning, multitasking, and technology use; and on principles of space design that focus on flexibility, aesthetics, practicality, and functionality. These and other aspects of the project were emphasized in a presentation at the EDUCAUSE Learning Initiative (ELI) 2005 Fall Focus Session.[2]

What Is Unique or Noteworthy?

Several features stand out in the ES corridor redesign: the community partnership involved in the design and implementation; the regular assessment conducted on its impact; and its replicability.

Community Partnership

One of the most noteworthy aspects of this project is the community partnership involved, which represents a contribution of about $400,000 worth of goods and services to IUPUI from nearly 30 firms including the original furniture company, RJE Business Interiors; the three leading Indianapolis design firms, CSO, Maregatti, and Rowland; and many other contributors ranging from cabinet makers to lighting installers. It is thus a case in philanthropy as well as space construction. Our partners were delighted with the opportunity to do something meaningful that engaged their talents in service to the community. The "parade of learning spaces" idea was replaced with an exercise in collaboration. Designers who had previously only worked in competition found that they derived considerable enjoyment from working together. They found the original design charrette to be exciting and inspiring. The partners became even more invested with IUPUI than previously. The collaboration between the partners continues as they talk about this project and its impact.

Assessment

A second noteworthy aspect of this project is the way in which it has been studied. IUPUI's values on undergraduate research and the existence of its Interior Design Department and School of Education were tremendous assets to call upon in the study of our ES corridor spaces. An interior design faculty member identified two students desiring practicum credit for a postoccupancy study, and an education faculty member pointed a graduate student toward this project for her paper in a capstone course. The study team developed a comprehensive design that involved nonparticipant observation of the spaces and surveys of students, faculty, and maintenance staff involved in the spaces. Study results were reported to each of the firms that contributed to the design and construction of the spaces, as well as in national presentations and publications.[3] The emphasis has been on understanding the impact of the spaces.

Replicable Results

Finally, the project is spawning the design and construction of other informal learning spaces. It has demonstrated that not all learning takes place in classrooms and that the establishment of places for interchange, project work, or socialization directly influences student success and persistence. As a model space, it has inspired others to request similar spaces in their locations. At the time of this writing, five other projects are being developed along with a major request for funding. Results of the impact study will be reflected in the design of these spaces and have also captured attention outside the university.

Endnotes

1. The papers are available at <http://www.opd.iupui.edu/uploads/library/APPD/APPD7971.doc> and <http://www.opd.iupui.edu/uploads/library/APPD/APPD2416.doc>.

2. For the ELI 2005 Fall Focus Session slides, see <http://www.educause.edu/LibraryDetailPage/666?ID=ELI0532>.

3. A slide show of the study results can be found at <http://www.opd.iupui.edu/uploads/library/APPD/APPD8980.ppt>.

About the Author

Nancy Van Note Chism is the associate vice chancellor for academic affairs and associate dean of the faculties at Indiana University-Purdue University Indianapolis and a professor of higher education at Indiana University.

CHAPTER 22

LeBaron Hall Auditorium
Iowa State University

Jim Twetten

What Is It?

Located in Ames, Iowa, Iowa State University (ISU) is a land-grant, research-extensive institution with an enrollment of 26,000 students (http://www.iastate.edu/about/). Iowa State maintains 222 general classrooms, ranging in capacity from 20 to 500 seats. While large lecture auditoriums are not optimum for engaging students, economic realities suggest these large learning spaces are not going away anytime soon. The LeBaron Hall Auditorium is an attempt to make a large auditorium an engaging and interactive learning atmosphere.

The LeBaron Hall Auditorium (see Figure 1) was recently reconstructed as part of a multiyear capital project to upgrade classroom facilities on the Iowa State University campus. The old auditorium was razed to make way for the newly designed space, first used in August 2005. Unlike its predecessor, the new 363-seat LeBaron Hall Auditorium was designed to facilitate instructor-to-student as well as student-to-student contact, collaboration, and active learning.

Figure 1. Entrance to LeBaron Hall Auditorium

©2006 Jim Twetten

Auditorium Layout

The auditorium is laid out in a 75-degree arc. The seating is placed on six tiers, each tier containing two rows running the width of the auditorium This wider design kept the depth of the auditorium to a minimum, only 12 rows deep, so even back-row students feel closer to the instructor. (The original auditorium was more than twice that depth.) Two aisles bisect the auditorium roughly into thirds, allowing the instructor to easily maneuver in and around the students. A walkway between the fourth and fifth row, suitable for wheelchair access, also allows the instructor to work through the room horizontally. In addition, all other rows are wide enough for the instructor to maneuver down each row. The instructor can reach each student in the class, either while lecturing or acting as a facilitator during group activities. This same broad spacing of the rows allows students to move around during group activities, to easily reach the front of the auditorium to share a report with their peers, or to work on the whiteboard at the front of the hall. (See Figure 2.)

Figure 2. Easy Passage Through the Auditorium

Customized Seat Design

A notable feature of the LeBaron Hall Auditorium is the design of some of its seats. To facilitate group interaction, auditorium designers sought chairs that swiveled to allow students to turn to one another during peer-to-peer activities. Classroom chairs were researched; the swivel chairs discovered only allowed a 180-degree turn. This effectively allowed students to turn to their left or directly behind them, but limited all movement to the students' right.

Auditorium designers worked with an educational furniture manufacturer to come up with a chair that provided more flexibility. The manufacturer agreed to modify an existing 180-degree swivel chair to reach 240 degrees. This allows students to turn their chairs to face most adjacent peers. Due to this advanced arc, the chair's "spring back to front" feature had to be disabled. This actually benefits students, who now don't have to subconsciously fight the chair's spring to stay facing a neighbor. It causes minor problems for janitorial staff, however, as they must maneuver around chairs that are left facing all different directions.

While ideally all seats in the auditorium would have this same swivel flexibility, cost constraints did not allow it. Consequently, the seats in the front row of each tier are swivel seats, while the back row of each tier is equipped with a row of fixed seats. (See Figure 3.) Student groups collect themselves for activities with other students adjacent on the same tier. (See Figure 4.)

Figure 3. Swivel Seats in Front of Fixed Seats

Wheelchair Access

In addressing Americans with Disabilities Act (ADA) requirements, designers wanted the auditorium to be as accommodating as possible. Many older auditoriums are retrofitted for wheelchair access with space either in the front or back of the auditorium. The LeBaron Hall Auditorium has six separate wheelchair stations, on the first, third, and sixth tiers, allowing the wheelchair-bound to have a greater selection in seating. An elevator immediately outside the auditorium provides access to all three levels.

Figure 4. Students Face Peers in Work Groups

What Happens Here?

The LeBaron Hall Auditorium is intended primarily for ISU classes. The most frequent auditorium users wanted a space where students could interact in a variety of ways, with their instructor and with their peers. The hope is to populate the auditorium with classes that emphasize activities for student engagement. (See Figure 5.)

Figure 5. LeBaron Supports Student Activities

A secondary purpose of the auditorium is to host guest lectures and to record them via high-quality video systems. A third purpose, not yet enabled, is to electronically view best practices in the auditorium. Once funding is available, the room will be equipped with technology that will allow ISU's Center for Excellence in Learning and Teaching to observe instructors for faculty development purposes.

How Is Technology Used?

The electronic technology available in the room is consistent with the highest level of classroom support provided in ISU's 222 general classrooms. Electronic technology in the LeBaron Hall Auditorium includes:

▶ Dual projection to a single, continuous, double-wide projection surface. The instructor can send any input to either projector. The ceiling height allows projection above the whiteboard, letting the faculty member use both instructional tools simultaneously.

▶ Projector input devices that can be used by the instructor include a laptop computer, digital document camera, and a DVD/VCR combination player. (See Figure 6.)

Figure 6. Video and Media Volume Controls

▸ A simple control system for instructors. (See Figure 7.) The RS-232 control system is the same in all technology equipped classrooms on campus, so instructors can move from classroom to classroom without having to learn a new interface. The system can be remotely monitored for device usage, projector lamp hours, and system status. If an instructor needs assistance, classroom technology support staff can control or switch devices remotely.

Figure 7. Instructor's Control Station

▸ A two-amplifier sound system. One amplifier drives the front-mounted speakers, which are the primary sound source for the audience. The second amplifier drives a distributed speaker system above the audience seating, for sound reinforcement.

▸ A wireless lavalier microphone for the primary speaker and a wireless handheld microphone for passing around to students during any student input session.

▸ Wireless access (802.11g).

▸ A student response system receiver, for faculty who wish to use student clickers.

▸ Independent control of lighting elements for the speaker, the whiteboard, the projection screens, and the remainder of the auditorium.

▸ A yet-to-be-enabled IP video camera system that would allow people external to the class to view instructor best practices, with permission.

▸ Any additional technology, while not standard in each classroom, can be accessed and installed for faculty members on request.

What Makes the Space Successful?

The ability to make the space as interactive as possible is a key success factor in LeBaron Hall Auditorium's design. While several classrooms on campus host the same or similar electronic technology, the seating layout and swivel-seat design allow for student participation and active learning. (See Figure 8.)

Figure 8. Seating Layout Promotes Participation

The design decisions were not arrived at quickly. The design committee included facility planners, space management staff, learning and teaching experts, faculty users, and technology providers. Each constituency was receptive to the needs and concerns of the others—probably the most important factor to success. The facility planners, for instance, under pressures of economy and efficiency, were used to assigning a certain number of classroom seats per square foot. Faculty and student learning experts wanted to promote student interaction and faculty mobility, both of which reduce the number of seats possible in a fixed space. The result is a compromise. A less-collaborative group could not have achieved the same result.[1]

What Principles Were Behind the Design?

The auditorium design and technology selection addressed four of Chickering and Gamson's seven principles for good practice in undergraduate education.[2] The resulting learning space greatly improves contact between the faculty member and students. Active learning is facilitated, in part, through group interaction. Student reciprocity and cooperation are promoted through the social, collaborative atmosphere of the auditorium. The close proximity with the instructor and electronic technology in the room provide ample opportunities for prompt feedback.

The redesigned space has a new, rejuvenated feel. Strategically placed, rich grained wood paneling provides warmth, while cushioned chairs offer comfortable seating.

What Is Unique or Noteworthy?

Faculty and students alike have commented on LeBaron Hall Auditorium's new environment. Corly Brooke of the Center for Excellence in Teaching and Learning stated, "The best thing it does for my students is create community in the classroom—I can see all the students, and I can get them interacting easily." (See Figure 9.) Students who experienced the auditorium commented, "It is my favorite classroom on campus. I felt close to the instructor and ready to learn," and "No matter where I sat In the room, I felt closely connected with the instructor." Another comment illustrates the importance of the swivel seating: "This was so helpful during group discussions and projects. It turned a classroom of 350+ into a small group of four who were able to communicate as though we were the only ones in the room with the instructor."

Figure 9. Faculty-Student Interaction

The design and construction of the new LeBaron Hall Auditorium was a team effort, in the truest sense—and now the students can work in teams too.

Endnotes

1. Champions in the design of the LeBaron Hall Auditorium include Dr. Corly Brooke, professor and director of the Center for Excellence in Learning and Teaching; Dr. Mary Gregoire, professor and chair of apparel, educational studies, and hospitality management; Kathleen Baumgarn, manager of classroom facilities space management; Matthew Darbyshire, manager of classroom services, information technology services; Mark Grief, facilities project manager; architects Baldwin & White of Des Moines, Iowa; and educational furniture manufacturer KI of Green Bay, Wisconsin.

2. A. W. Chickering and Z. F. Gamson, "Seven Principles for Good Practice in Undergraduate Education," *AAHE Bulletin*, vol. 39, no. 7 (1987), pp. 3–7.

About the Author

Jim Twetten is the assistant director of academic technologies, information technology services, at Iowa State University.

CHAPTER 23

BOX

London School of Economics

Andrew Harrison

What Is It?

BOX (http://www.boxexchange.net/) is an innovation lab established in 2004 at the London School of Economics and Political Science (LSE) (http://www .lse.ac.uk/). BOX facilitates the international exchange of innovation-focused research by bringing together people from academia and business to engage in complex problem-solving tasks or to accelerate and improve decision making across large groups.

LSE is a world-class center for teaching and research across the full range of the social, political, and economic sciences. LSE seeks to be a laboratory of the social sciences, a place where ideas are developed, analyzed, evaluated, and disseminated around the globe. The LSE consists of 19 academic departments and 5 interdisciplinary institutes with 7,500 full-time students and around 800 part-time students, 52 percent of whom are postgraduates. LSE has more than 1,700 full-time staff, with 97 percent of them actively engaged in research.

BOX exemplifies a new type of hybrid academic/commercial space that blurs the boundaries between the classroom, the laboratory, the office, and the club. It also reflects the current organizational imperative to create new types of workplaces specifically designed for encouraging creative behaviors and supporting innovation.[1] Innovation laboratories can take various forms but generally blend space, artifacts, and event facilitation. The key purposes of the physical space are to emphasize dislocation from day-to-day activity, eliminate organizational hierarchy, and encourage participation.[2]

The lab itself is 220 square meters of space in the heart of the LSE's central London campus. BOX provides a dynamic learning environment enriched with the latest ambient technology[3] and influenced by the comfort of home and the eclecticism of the Far East. A key feature of the design is the Cabinet of Wonder,

©2006 Andrew Harrison

a wall holding visible and invisible treasures that enable the viewer to see the world in a multitude of ways. The Cabinet of Wonder uses light, sounds, and artifacts to intrigue as well as encourage discussion and original thinking.

For images of BOX, see Figure 1 and <http://www.degw.com/BOX/BOX_images_2005.PDF>.

Figure 1. BOX Main Room

What Happens Here?

BOX is the first node in a wholly new kind of space that provides innovation and knowledge transfer services to a tightly linked, international university-business network. It functions as a laboratory for academics and students from a number of LSE academic departments exploring decision making and collaboration processes. Participants explore these processes through a diverse range of workshops featuring various facilitation tools and techniques such as LEGO Serious Play. (See Figure 2.)

The space is also used by academics linked to the BOX research program as a community club to inhabit, communicate, and explore ideas. (See <http://boxchange.blogspot.com/>.) BOX hosts a significant number of internal LSE seminars and workshops, as well as collaborative policy development events for both governmental and nongovernmental organizations, such as the workshop Creating Pro-Poor Markets for Ecosystem Services, organized by the United Nations Environmental Program in conjunction with the LSE.

Figure 2. A Networking Event at BOX

The more commercially focused BOX services include:

▶ Sophisticated deal-making and venture-building expertise, drawing on the best of business and university capabilities from a network of U.K. and international universities

▶ Decision acceleration and assessment processes

▶ Design and management of customized corporate innovation programs

▶ Design and management of inspirational environments and experiences, from custom-designed facilities for public or corporate clients to out-of-doors engagements that scale workplace barriers to creative collaboration

▶ Program and design support for educational and precommercial ventures

▶ One-to-one coaching to support maximum voice (that is, assertiveness training) and contribution to complex collaborations

▶ World-class innovation events and seminars to support the BOX sponsor community

How Is Technology Used?

When developing the brief for BOX, one of the guiding principles was that the space should not be about technology. The BOX experience is about collaboration, face-to-face communication, and mind-body, physical activity, including play. Initial aspirations to exclude all plasma screens and ban PowerPoint, however, had to be tempered by an understanding of the diverse nature of BOX users and events.

Consequently, a Category 5 structured cable system was installed throughout the space to allow access to LSE and corporate networks, and a plasma screen was built into the Cabinet of Wonder (but hidden behind wood panels).

Most of the technology installed at BOX is designed to take participants out of their normal realm of experience and, through exposing them to objects of wonder, inspire "good play" and deep, collaborative emergence of new ideas:

▶ When visitors arrive, an ambient sound piece created by Milccce, one of the resident artists at BOX during its first year of operation, creates a transition space, signaling clearly that they are not entering conventional academic or office space.

▶ A generative sound piece inside the main space, also by Mileece, delivers continuous bird song throughout the space.

▶ The Cabinet of Wonder—a full-height cabinet 11 meters long—contains 27 display cases of various sizes plus concealed technology and storage space. Category 5 data cable (250 meters) links the case controls to a bank of six computers in the Communications Room that control a range of light and sound experiences using pressure pads under the carpet, infrared sensors, and movement sensors. As a visitor interacts with the artifacts in the cabinet or stands in front of some of the items, hypersonic speakers concealed above the ceiling tiles deliver a series of sound effects.

▶ Four cabinet elements can create an additional soundscape, where up to four participants can simultaneously *play* the cabinet as a musical instrument.

▶ The entire BOX space can be controlled using a wireless touch pad that controls all light and sound effects. The touch pad can be used to trigger the playing of sound files through the ceiling speakers or of video clips on the plasma screen.

What Makes the Space Successful?

BOX is a unique learning environment designed to raise more questions than it answers. The apparently random combination of virtual and physical artifacts contributes to the overall narrative about complexity and emergence. Two-hundred-year-old tables jostle for attention with books on planetary exploration; 150-million-year-old fossils can be held and examined; and LEGOs can be used to explore complex problems. The space encourages interaction with objects—tactile explorations of the past, present, and future.

The goal of the space is to provoke wonder and curiosity. Feedback from both academic and commercial participants has been overwhelmingly positive, despite some initial concerns about the birdsong and Cabinet of Wonder. A workshop or seminar at BOX is something you remember and talk about with colleagues.

The space has been adaptable enough to support small-scale intensive workshops and large-scale interactive sessions for up to 100 where every bit of space is used for seminar and breakout or socializing space. What has worked particularly well is the division of the space into two halves: the highly expressive, idiosyncratic side containing the front of the cabinet and a range of informal seating and work areas, and on the other side of cabinet, an open space with retracting dividing walls and mobile, stacking furniture that can be used to create the appropriate layout for each event. Universities in Europe, Asia, and North America have already shown interest in developing similar blended academic and commercial spaces exploring innovation processes.

What Principles Were Behind the Design?

Innovation and creativity are increasingly seen as critical to the continued success of both individual organizations and economies. BOX is at the forefront of initiatives around the world creating new types of academic and commercial partnerships and exploring the role that buildings and places can play in fostering innovation and creativity.

BOX is one of the LSE's responses to the 2003 Lambert Review of Business-University Collaboration in the United Kingdom.[4] This review explored how U.K. business can sharpen its competitive edge through new types of partnerships with universities: accessing new ideas and expertise, participating in publicly funded research projects, and recruiting new staff direct from the universities. BOX has provided a focus for interaction and research between the LSE, the corporate BOX partners, and the wider group of public and private organizations who participate in BOX events.

In 2005, for example, Sir George Cox, the chairman of the Design Council, was commissioned to examine how U.K. businesses—subject matter experts and modern manufacturers in particular—apply creativity and design to improve their productivity and performance. His report[5] argued that challenges posed by the global knowledge economy mean that the future of the U.K. economy depends on "design, innovation, creativity, exploitation of technology, and speed to market." Data gathered by the Cox Review suggests, however, that 86 percent of senior management lack the skills to lead the U.K. economy in this direction. Two key reasons for this failure are dull physical work environments and a workplace atmosphere and working practices not conducive to the development of creative skills. In short, how people work and where they work need to change in order to meet the challenges identified by the Cox Review.

As the managing director of BOX put it:

> The root of the idea, like all big ideas, can be simply put: the history not just of humankind but of all existence can be seen as the emergence— the necessary emergence—of new patterns, and new structure, out of a maelstrom of complex interactions. Given enough richness of interaction and complexity, innovation will result—and, usually, all at once.
>
> What we do at BOX is intend that sudden emergence of order, right from the heart of what can seem blindingly complex, and then, in the light of behavioural science, look at the emergent properties that develop. And—delightfully—we find that the best tools of this new trade are a cultivated capacity for hands-on, playful fun, built on a child's sense and intuition for wonder and inspiration. At BOX, innova tion, week by week, is the profoundly simple result of playing well.[6]

What Is Unique or Noteworthy?

BOX is a new type of academic space—the physical manifestation of a new type of academic-business collaboration. The LSE has been a fundamental part of its success and remains deeply involved, linking BOX to its ongoing research program and engagement with industry as well as introducing BOX to other institutions the LSE collaborates with in other parts of the world. This is a two-way process; BOX is also committed to introducing its commercial clients to the diverse expertise available at the LSE and to developing opportunities for funded research and development of new business opportunities for the LSE.

The creation of BOX was an intensive and personal process involving a collabo- ration among the client, the academic institution, and the design team at DEGW. The project included creating the name of the space, determining its graphic and visual identity, designing the space, choosing the technology strategy, and selecting and curating the objects in the space. During the 12-week design process, more than 20 different consultants contributed to the concept's successful execution. As BOX expands to become a global network of innovation spaces, the challenge will be to create similarly rich, idiosyncratic, and message-laden spaces that reflect the unique academic cultures in which they are embedded.

Acknowledgment

BOX was initially funded and managed by EDS as part of its ongoing relationship with the London School of Economics. While EDS continues to fund a research program at the LSE, the company no longer has a direct role at BOX. BOX is now an independent entity directed by Lewis Pinault, working with partners to deliver innovation and knowledge transfer services at the LSE.

Endnotes

1. Tore Kristensen, "The Physical Context of Creativity," in *Creativity and Innovation Management*, vol. 13, no. 2 (June 2004), pp. 89–96.

2. Michael Lewis and James Moultrie, "The Organizational Innovation Laboratory," in *Creativity and Innovation Management*, vol. 14, no. 1 (March 2005), pp. 73–83.

3. Ambient technology includes lighting effects triggered by motion or infrared sensors, along with sound installations and effects delivered through hypersonic speakers.

4. "Lambert Review of Business-University Collaboration: Final Report," HM Treasury on behalf of HMSO, London, December 2003, <http://www.hm-treasury.gov.uk/media/DDE/65/lambert_review_final_450.pdf>.

5. Sir George Cox, "Cox Review of Creativity in Business," HM Treasury, December 2, 2005, <http://www.hm-treasury.gov.uk/independent_reviews/cox_review/coxreview_index.cfm>.

6. Lewis Pinault, BOX, information sheet used at launch of 2005 Innovation RCA event at the Royal College of Arts, London, October 2005 (unpublished).

About the Author

Andrew Harrison is director of Learning Environments, DEGW, and was the project lead for BOX.

CHAPTER 24

Boyer Hall
Messiah College

Dennis Lynch

What Is It?

The new Boyer Hall at Messiah College (http://www.messiah.edu/) was designed by Ayers/Saint/Gross (http://www.asg-architects.com/). The largest academic building on the campus, it houses roughly 50 percent of the academic departments and 40 percent of the faculty. (See Figure 1.) As such, the building is central to the academic life on campus. Beyond the essential academic functions of hosting classes and providing open and inviting faculty offices, the building also hosts a variety of events that reach out to the larger community. Some of these include banquets and receptions in the atrium or on the exterior terrace and film festivals in the Parmer Cinema. The building is also used extensively in the summer as an integral part of an active schedule of conferences for outside organizations hosted by the college.

Figure 1. Boyer Hall

©2006 Dennis Lynch

Messiah College is a Christian college of the liberal and applied arts and sciences whose mission is to educate men and women toward maturity of intellect, character, and Christian faith in preparation for lives of service, leadership, and reconciliation in church and society. Messiah College offers a private, coed, undergraduate education for more than 2,900 students in a residential setting. The main campus is located on 485 acres in Grantham, Pennsylvania, approximately 12 miles southwest of Harrisburg. The college also has a satellite campus in Philadelphia that is affiliated with Temple University

What Happens Here?
Boyer Hall provides instruction, research, and outreach in formal and informal settings.

Instruction, Research, Collaboration
Boyer Hall is an academic building designed to house the 11 departments of the School of Humanities and the School of Education and Social Sciences. Its 18 general classrooms range in size from 30 to 60 seats, and a dedicated education classroom is furnished with shelving, cabinets, and a countertop and sink for the hands-on projects that are integral to the education curriculum. The building also has a tiered 70-seat classroom with built-in tables providing power and data connectivity for students, two computer labs, and one language lab furnished with computers at each student station. The language lab is arranged in hexagonal clusters of six seats each to promote interaction among students. (See Figure 2.)

Figure 2. Language Lab

The Boyer Center suite, adjacent to the main lobby, houses the archives of the building's namesake, Messiah College alumnus Ernest L. Boyer, Sr., a prominent educator who served as secretary of education under President Carter (http://www.messiah.edu/boyer_center). The suite also includes offices for visiting faculty. Four interview rooms and a group play area flanked by two observation rooms support the psychology department's research into childhood development.

Group projects and interdisciplinary learning are supported by resource rooms located at the ends of the main corridor. Embedded within the faculty office suites, these light-filled spaces encourage mentoring and interaction between faculty and students.

Special Events

Banquets and receptions are held in the atrium or on the exterior terrace. Film festivals take place in the Parmer Cinema. This 129-seat cinema/auditorium on the ground floor supports the film studies program and doubles as an auditorium for larger lecture classes. (See Figure 3.) The double-height atrium (see Figure 4) and adjacent exterior terrace are the "living room" of this facility. Filled with natural light and views of the adjacent grove of trees, this space provides opportunities for quiet study or student-faculty interaction. The building is also used extensively in the summer as an integral part of an active schedule of conferences for outside organizations hosted by the college.

Figure 3. Parmer Cinema

Figure 4. Atrium

How Is Technology Used?

Boyer Hall provides technology support in the general classrooms, Parmer Cinema, language lab, and interview/observation rooms (http://soundandcommunications .com/applications/2005_05_apps.htm). The building is equipped with a generous number of data outlets both in the classrooms and in corridors near built-in bench alcoves. (See Figure 5.)

Figure 5. Corridor Nook

Each classroom is equipped with an instructor's station housing a PC, DVD player, VCR, and document camera. A Crestron control unit integrates these devices with a ceiling-mounted LCD projector and retractable projection screen. The larger classrooms also allow lighting and motorized shades to be controlled from the instructor's station. (See Figure 6.)

Figure 6. Classroom

A working cinema with two film projectors supporting 16 and 32mm media, the Parmer Cinema facility also includes the same digital technology provided in the general classrooms. For maximum flexibility, the A/V, lighting, and window shades can be controlled from the projection room or the instructor's station at the front of the room.

The language lab uses a low-profile raised floor system to distribute power and data cabling to furniture clusters (http://www.zephyrcomm.com/nexus.htm). Language instruction is facilitated by a special software system installed on the PCs in the space. The room is also equipped with the same A/V and controls as the general classrooms.

Interview rooms are equipped with inconspicuous, ceiling-mounted cameras and microphones connected to two observation rooms.

What Makes the Space Successful?

Several factors contribute to Boyer Hall's success: integrated technology, a variety of classroom sizes and shapes, and the provision of informal gathering spaces.

The integration of the A/V technology with lighting and window shades allows total control of the environment from the instructor's station in each classroom. Ample chalkboard space is available even when the projection screen is in use. The variety and quantity of classrooms bring a dynamic level of activity to the building and encourage interdisciplinary learning. Because the building hosts such a large percentage of classes and faculty on the campus, students and faculty from diverse backgrounds have the opportunity to interact and build the collegial atmosphere so important to Messiah College.

The resource rooms, atrium, and generous corridors with built-in benches and display cases all encourage interaction among students and faculty. Interaction among departments is facilitated as well due to their colocation in Boyer Hall.

What Principles Were Behind the Design?

A collaborative design effort between the master plan and building design resulted in a building well suited to its site and context. The design team met extensively with the building users to ensure that the design would meet the unique needs of Messiah College. Because of the size and complexity of the program, listening to and guiding the various user groups through the design process was essential to the project's success.

Another guiding principle in the design of the building was to encourage openness and communication between faculty and students, among departments, and between interior and exterior spaces. The faculty offices were located in close proximity to the classrooms and designed to be open to the public corridor with no intermediate space separating faculty from students. The principle of openness was also a driving force in the development of the atrium as a two-story space at the heart of the building with a large glass wall linking the atrium to the exterior terrace and grove of trees beyond.

What Is Unique or Noteworthy?

The culture of Messiah College is one of openness, teamwork, and intellectual curiosity. These qualities guided many aspects of the design with the goal of fostering open communication and learning between faculty and students, among academic departments, and between Messiah College and the larger community.

Given the size and location of Boyer Hall on campus, Messiah College gave the design team the opportunity to set a new standard of quality and architectural character to guide the future development of the heart of campus. The design team and the decision makers at the college were committed to quality and value on the project from start to finish, integrating technology and furnishings within the building. This integration was critical to the project's success, as was the freedom granted the design team. Boyer Hall blends traditional masonry construction with contemporary aluminum and glass elements that tie the building to the history of the campus while looking ahead to its future.

About the Author
Dennis Lynch is an associate with Ayers/Saint/Gross, Architects + Planners.

CHAPTER 25

Center for Integrated Learning and Information Technology

Michigan Technological University

Paul Urbanek

What Is It?

Michigan Technological University (http://www.mtu.edu/) in Houghton, Michigan, was founded in 1885 as the Michigan Mining School to support the copper mining industry. Today MTU has 6,500 students, with more than 3,700 enrolled in engineering programs. Certificate, associate, bachelor's, master's, and doctoral degrees are offered. The university also offers programs in the sciences, business, communications, and forestry and environmental sciences.

The Center for Integrated Learning and Information Technology (CILIT) at MTU includes a 44,000-square-foot addition to the existing Van Pelt Library and a new 50,000-square-foot computer science building. (Figure 1 shows the entrance to the computer science building, also known as the Rekhi Computer Science Hall.) The integration of instructional and information systems allows for innovative student engagement through learning and teaching, research, and collaboration. CILIT offers collaborative study areas and social spaces for students, faculty, and staff.

CILIT provides students and faculty with:
▶ A fully integrated learning environment
▶ A highly accessible and visibly inviting gateway into campus
▶ Enclosed pedestrian pathway
▶ Group study rooms
▶ Wireless networking
▶ High-tech instructional classrooms
▶ Flexible labs and research spaces

Figure 1. Computer Science Building Entrance

  Two main components are associated with CILIT: the John and Ruanne Opie Library (the addition to the Van Pelt Library) and the Kanwal and Ann Rekhi Computer Science Hall (the new computer science building).

Opie Library

Through extensive reorganization and renovation, the 50-year-old Van Pelt Library became an all-inclusive academic student center. (See Figure 2.) The library's major collections were relocated to the lower level of the building, on compact shelving. This move accommodates easy access and browsing of the collections while reserving the majority of the upper floors for individual and collaborative student work.

  CILIT adds 44,000 square feet of new library space to 80,000 square feet of renovated space. Features include

▶ A 24-hour, 3,400-square-foot reading room
▶ A high-tech information wall providing the latest news about the weather, the world, the campus, and library activities
▶ 26 small group study rooms that accommodate up to 10 people each
▶ 50 public computers with wireless access

Figure 2. Entrance to Opie Library

▶ A digital studio allowing students and faculty to integrate information from print, the Internet, sound recordings, or film into their work
▶ Two general computer classrooms

At the heart of this academic student center is the reading room (see Figure 3). This grand space is open 24 hours a day, allowing students to study and socialize—an especially welcome feature during winter weather at this northern Michigan campus. The reading room is enclosed by a curved glass curtain wall maximizing the amount of daylight entering the building.

Rekhi Computer Science Hall

The new computer science hall provides the technology needed by the university's fastest-growing undergraduate degree program. It includes computer classrooms, distance education classrooms, and research laboratories.

▶ Four undergraduate general-purpose computer labs
▶ Two graduate study labs and special-purpose labs for:
  ▷ Cluster computing (linking multiple computers together to allow increased speed and memory)

Figure 3. Reading Room

▷ Robotics/artificial intelligence
▷ Computational science and engineering
▷ Distributed computing
▷ Graphics
▷ System administration, networking, and visualization

Occupying the interior of the computer science hall is the two-story student lounge. (See Figure 4.) This space, located along the pedestrian path, is commonly referred to as a "place for techies."

What Happens Here?

CILIT's six classrooms are reserved primarily for computer science education and research. Four are equipped for high-tech instruction, and two support distance education. (See Figure 5.) Students have access to a 24-hour study space, which also houses a high-tech information wall providing the latest news about the weather, the world, and campus and library activities. The center is also equipped with 26 small group study rooms accommodating more intensive learning environments, and the reading room is available 24 hours a day, five days a week.

Figure 4. Student Lounge

Figure 5. CILIT Distance Education Classroom

CILIT facilitates student interaction by providing collaborative study areas and social spaces for students, faculty, and staff. Small and large group study areas encourage formal and informal study gatherings. Both the student lounge and the integrated pedestrian pathway make it easier for students and staff to meet between classes, research, and study sessions.

How Is Technology Used?

The technology at CILIT is used for multimedia applications, distance learning, and student center learning and research projects. A digital studio allows students and faculty to integrate information from print, the Internet, sound recordings, or film into their work.

The center supports wireless and wired high-speed network access (http://www.RoverNet.mtu.edu/). A raised floor system allows for future technological upgrades and changes. Current technology used in the center, primarily in teaching labs in distance education spaces, includes:

▶ Sound systems with wireless microphones
▶ DVD/video tape recorders/players
▶ Touch-screen control system
▶ Video projectors
▶ Video camera and document camera
▶ Overhead projectors
▶ Tablet PCs
▶ Recording/streaming/Webcasting of presentations
▶ Videoconferencing
▶ Digital cameras

What Makes the Space Successful?

The new center is visible from a main highway thoroughfare—a prime location on campus. The oversized, curved-glass, south-facing wall of the library provides a welcoming window into the university.

In a place that can receive up to 100 inches of snow during the month of January alone, students can now work outside their dorm rooms at any hour and enjoy constant access to electronic media and the Internet. All the student spaces along the enclosed campus route are available 24 hours a day, seven days a week, for both group and individual learning.

Today, Phase 1 of an enclosed 100-foot pedestrian pathway unites the Opie Library (the addition to the existing Van Pelt Library) and the Rekhi Computer Science Hall, connecting all three facilities that make up CILIT. When completed as part of a separate physics and math building project, an enclosed pedestrian pathway will integrate *all* of the facilities on campus, including the dormitories. This will enable students to avoid having to venture out into frigid winter conditions.

What Principles Were Behind the Design?

Key principles influenced the design of CILIT, from the concept of supporting self-directed study to a desire to provide an attractive window into the university.

▶ **Self-directed study:** The major design principle was to enable student learning and self-directed study, building an environment for students to use as they see fit. Students can use CILIT at any time, whether 3:00 p.m. or 3:00 a.m.

▶ **Academic learning center:** The design in many ways is a repurposing of the library as the academic learning center for MTU, both for self-directed and group study. This contrasts with the library's former purpose as a center of knowledge.

▶ **Integration:** The center was created with distinct functions—as libraries and a computer science facility—that now function as an integrated learning environment for both formal and informal learning.

▶ **Accessibility:** To make the learning environment more convenient for students, it was important to link the learning environments of the Opie Library and Rekhi Computer Science Hall. Particularly in bad weather, students are disinclined to travel from one location to another. The accessibility of Opie Library and Rekhi Hall via a second-story pedestrian clearspan bridge makes it easy for students to get from one place to another. Future phases will create an enclosed pedestrian pathway throughout campus.

▶ **Visibility:** Opie Library and Rekhi Hall provide a window on the university. Even those just entering campus from the highway see a welcoming image of the university's spaces.

What Is Unique or Noteworthy?

The project is particularly well-aligned with university's four goals:

▶ To create an integrated learning center that allows students to gather knowledge from multiple media and bring it to their desktops.

▶ To create a new image or "front door" for the city side that visually expresses the energy of the university's students. The highway façade of the library addition and the computer science building align to strengthen and define the southern edge of the campus.

▶ To provide a facility tailored to the environment. This is done with the linking of the campus-wide enclosed pedestrian walkway, which started with the linking of the library and new computer science building.

▶ To recognize the project's donors. The project's two major donors—MTU alumni Kanwal Rekhi and John Opie—wanted an integrated learning environment that successfully connected two separate programmatic facilities. At the same time, the donors wanted a facility that encouraged the connection of all students, faculty, and staff.

About the Author

Paul Urbanek is vice president of design for SmithGroup.

CHAPTER 26

The Brain and Cognitive Sciences Complex

MIT

Phillip D. Long

What Is It?

MIT (http://web.mit.edu/) is a private research institution located in Cambridge, Massachusetts. MIT had an enrollment of 4,066 undergraduates and 6,140 graduate students in fall 2005.

The Brain and Cognitive Sciences Complex (BCSC) at MIT is the largest neuroscience center in the world (http://web.mit.edu/evolving/buildings/bcsc/index.html). This interdisciplinary research and teaching facility integrates three pioneering institutions devoted to uncovering the mysteries of the brain: the Department of Brain and Cognitive Sciences, the McGovern Institute for Brain Research, and the Pickower Institute for Learning and Memory.

Completed in October 2005, the 411,000-square-foot facility houses headquarters, research laboratories, animal facilities, faculty offices, and collaborative areas. The eight-story complex, designed to accommodate about 500 people, includes a 90-foot-high, five-story, day-lit atrium, an auditorium, three large seminar rooms, a café, glass-walled reading rooms with spectacular views of the campus, tea rooms, libraries, imaging centers, and 48 state-of-the-art wet and dry research laboratories.

What Happens Here?

The BCSC accommodates learning, meetings, and informal gatherings. Facilities include an imaging center, wet and dry labs, and animal facilities.

The BCSC's classrooms, seminars, teaching labs, and conference events support interdisciplinary work in the neurosciences. State-of-the-art wet and dry labs serve investigators in biology, molecular biology, biochemistry, and electrophysiology, as well as cognitive and behavioral neurosciences. Wet labs have multiple LCD monitors to show laptop signals from the instructor and document camera, to project dissections, or to show other lab material.

The Athinoula A. Martinos Center for Biomedical Imaging at the McGovern Institute houses a 3T Siemens magnetic resonance imaging (MRI) scanner and a 9.4T animal scanner from Bruker, providing one of the few places in the world where researchers can conduct comparative studies of the human brain and the brains of different animal species. A multipart vivarium on the top floor of the facility houses research animals.

Terraces overlook the five-story atrium, which provides room for receptions, performances, and public gatherings. Social gathering spaces are scattered throughout the BCSC: tea rooms provide a place for quiet discussion and reading, and the café invites students and faculty to gather.

What Makes the Space Successful?

The space provides a feeling of being generous and open to many views simultaneously. The detailing gives the impression that the building was carefully considered. It is brightly lit from all directions and gives people the chance to see other colleagues working, moving around, or just relaxing. In this sense it seems like a community facility, unlike a row of offices served by dark, narrow corridors.

All the corridors lead to the monumental atrium in the center, which is the heart of the complex. Subtly sculpted surfaces are illuminated by daylight from the skylight above. Looking up, visitors see the lines of exhaust vents, white against the sky, evoking the sense of being carried on an ocean liner. Flights of stairs, dexterously placed along the periphery, connect the various levels, animating the atrium even when no one is around—a vivid symbol of the human interaction so crucial to cutting-edge scientific research.

What Principles Were Behind the Design?

The space embodies several of the university's goals, including an ongoing commitment to research, giving students the opportunity to participate in primary research, and making the best scientific and technological resources available. The design started with a traditional race-track configuration—a loop of corridors with shared facilities at the center. Instead of providing separate loops for each of the three institutes, the design arranged them in a way that melds all three into one continuous system, thus maximizing the flexibility MIT will need in the decades ahead. The three institutes can grow independently to the south and west.

The three institutes' lobbies vary in scale, form, and entryway. The first transition invites people to move from street to plaza to lobby. Inside the building subtle cues signal transitions from laboratories to faculty tea rooms, to meeting rooms, and to a completely shared atrium. The BCSC is fundamentally an interdisciplinary, collaborative space, using tea rooms at the intersections and corners of the spaces to support informal gatherings and casual dining.

The structural and engineering systems were designed to allow changes in laboratory or other interior spaces. Large glass windows bring light from outside into the laboratories, which are also transparent to passersby in the animal or researchers' corridors. The atrium and its surrounding platforms and steps are open from all sides and from many different heights. The atrium serves many functions: as a pedestrian street for MIT people to pass through en route to other parts of the campus, as a conference center with meeting rooms and auditorium, as a café, as a site for large dinners and performances, and many others.

The building minimizes energy and water consumption, and operational strategies foster a healthy indoor environment. Features include high-performance exterior materials, gray-water recycling for flushing toilets, exhaust air stream heat-recovery, and interior finishes that minimally impact indoor air quality. The building was designed to achieve a Silver LEED rating—a measure of environmental responsibility administered by the U.S. Green Building Council.

How Is Technology Used?

The primary function of the space is to support authentic, leading research in cellular, molecular, behavioral, cognitive, and computational neuroscience. The most visible technologies are the discipline-specific tools of the 21st-century researcher, including a specialized imaging facility to house three fMRI magnets. Building technology is largely transparent, leaving research and teaching to remain center stage.

The auditorium features dual LCD projectors for computers and video sources, program and speech audio systems, and ceiling microphones over seating areas. There are laptop inputs at the podium, and cameras to provide video into two flat-floor overflow rooms. These three rooms can originate or receive presentations from the other rooms via Tandberg videoconferencing codecs for computer, video, and audio. The codecs can deliver content captured in these spaces to the world via IP. Videoconferencing uses robotic tracking cameras and ceiling-mounted audio capture arrays supporting H.323.

The building is wireless (802.11 b/g) throughout, as is the entire MIT campus. In addition, MIT Net provides fixed network ports (100 megabits per second to the 10 gigabyte backbone) and supports a virtual private network (VPN) for sensitive research equipment. Multiple high-performance computing Beowulf clusters are available.

What Is Unique or Noteworthy?

BCSC features several unusual elements, from its transparent architecture to its incorporation of a railroad line. The tea rooms, for example, with their varied design and informal character, contrast with the more formal laboratory spaces. Mostly associated with the public atrium, they can be seen from all around, especially the tea rooms with open terraces.

As it reinforces the street edge, the built form enlivens and activates the life of the street. The complex offers itself to the neighborhood through large expanses of glass—in some cases several stories tall—that give passersby an opportunity to glimpse the life inside.

The transparent architecture provides as many striking vistas for pedestrians as it does for occupants. Public spaces along the outer edges of the envelope house giant palm and bamboo plants that tower over hallways and sidewalks. Depending on the vantage point—inside or outside the building—windows reveal or reflect the urban landscape, the fast-moving clouds over Cambridge, and Frank Gehry's Stata Center directly across Vassar Street.

The crossing of the railroad at a height of about 22 meters through the center of the building site means that passage across the building requires a large movement up and down by stair or elevator. Because of the low-frequency vibration caused by the railway, the building is stabilized by steel pylons to the solid ground below. Sound-proofing has muted the railway noise and sirens from the surrounding streets.

The building, in crossing an active freight rail corridor, was designed to open the way for the campus's expansion to the north. The tall exterior walls were designed to enclose the three streets the building faces, especially Main Street, where it attempts to unify the random blocks of Technology Square. Two plazas add to the interest of the surrounding streets.

For a virtual tour, visit <http://web.mit.edu/mcgovern/html/Who_We_Are/building.shtml>.

About the Author

Phillip D. Long is senior strategist for academic computing and director of learning outreach for iCampus at MIT.

CHAPTER 27

Steam Café
MIT

Scott Francisco

What Is It?

Steam Café at MIT is a spatial experiment, both physical and virtual, that serves up great food and community interaction. The café arose as a collaborative venture of students from the School of Architecture and Planning in partnership with MIT Dining and the Sodexho Corporation. Steam uses "open source" problem solving to bring people together to discuss and improve the venture—an ongoing creation of food and space that reflects and inspires a community.

Steam Café has become a destination for the entire MIT community—a place where food and constant dialogue create an energetic exchange of ideas and a place for informal learning as part of everyday life. Delicious, healthy food from around the world is served here every day, with equal emphasis on nutrition and community interaction. (See Figure 1.)

Figure 1. Interior of Steam Café

©2006 Scott Francisco

The space consists of a 300-square-foot serving area, a series of specially designed booths that flank an intersection along MIT's Infinite Corridor, and a Web site designed to elicit regular input from the community.

What Happens Here?

Steam Café offers a place to eat, socialize, and work, in many combinations. Food is available between 8:00 a.m. and 5:00 p.m., but people use the space 24 hours a day. Visitors to Steam find diverse numbers and types of people using the space in many different ways, depending on the time of day. The most common uses are for:

▶ Small group dining
▶ Small group meetings and discussions
▶ Individual concentrative work (with or without food)
▶ Impromptu meetings and discussions (often five minutes or less)
▶ Evening receptions
▶ Weekend use by visiting school groups

The simple, open source menu makes for mutually supportive nutrition, convenience, and community participation. Based on steamed organic brown rice with various ragouts, stews, and sauces to accompany it, the menu offers both vegetarian and meat-based dishes and changes regularly. Patrons are encouraged to submit recipes on the Steam Café Web site (http://steamcafe.mit.edu/). Café specialties include breakfast offerings of organic Irish steel-cut oats and boiled egg with baby spinach, plus a wide selection of salads, sandwiches, organic snack foods, juices, yogurts, and fresh fruit.

Each booth consists of a table that users can relocate for special functions and open-box benches that allow for many seating configurations. (See Figure 2.) Up to six people can use a booth when the café is busy, or a student can lie down for a nap on a booth bench during quiet times.

Lighting was critical in achieving the desired atmosphere and task-sensitive work environment. A low-voltage system provides warm but bright light and a lower installation cost.

How Is Technology Used?

Steam Café includes
▶ an active Web site,
▶ a plasma monitor in the booth area, and
▶ wireless access.

Figure 2. Steam Booths

The café Web site is an important feature, as it provides a way for customers to remotely review the daily menu, check ingredients, and submit feedback or new recipe ideas. The intention was to design a simple, fail-safe, aesthetically stimulating interface without confusing or frustrating users with excessive choices or information. Users have commented on the ease and directness of use as a motivator for regular visits.

Another feature of the café is a large plasma monitor in the center of the booth seating area. Although this monitor predated the café, we gave it an additional function by turning it into a Web access point using the Steam Web site as its home page. The idea was to create a place for public discussions about Web content—an alternative to the tendency for individuals to huddle around tiny screens or, more commonly, to work in isolation when online. The café provided the opportunity to turn the Web into a public space beyond the virtual. Patrons or passersby can now listen or watch while impromptu discussions about Web content take place.

Blanketing this area is MIT's signature ubiquitous wireless network. Because people can use wireless anywhere, the café's special features become that much more important in influencing where people choose to congregate.

What Makes the Space Successful?

Steam Café succeeds largely because of the
- ▶ enthusiasm of users and staff,
- ▶ delicious healthy food offered,
- ▶ innovative, thoughtfully designed space, and
- ▶ ongoing student initiative and participation.

Steam Café thrives because of the people who take varying levels of ownership for it, from the first-time patron to the foodie who submits a recipe to and interacts with the chefs and managers. At any given time visitors might encounter students from any program on campus, as well as professors, administrators, plumbers, and even the president of MIT. Steam sees a constant flow of people mixing, talking excitedly, meeting formally or informally, and eating in the booths. Ideas are developed and consumed here in even greater quantity than the food!

Food is a great motivator, however, and Steam provides a healthy alternative that draws people from across campus. Steam embodies the idea that the quality of the food we eat has a direct consequence in our daily lives, as well as having longer-term personal and societal health implications. Part of the café's mission was to give voice to a growing awareness that universities should be leaders in conveying this message. Steam functions both as an expression of these values and as a type of physical resource that more and more students demand.

Most of the students involved in the design process were architects with a commitment and sensitivity to the physical environment. Despite the extremely tight construction budget, the design team contemplated every detail of the space to determine how it might contribute to the project's underlying goals. Customer flow, materials, lighting, ergonomics, maintenance, serviceability, and "urban" connectivity were all seen as part of creating a space that worked at many levels. This rigorous design process was led by students with real-world experience and intimate knowledge of the institution, guided by the realities of schedule and budget.

A key strategy behind Steam was building a sense of ownership and empowerment. Initiated by students, the project continued to have student involvement at every level of implementation. The design of the menu, Web site, seating booths, food-service island, product selection, and hours of operation all involved students in discussion with the administration and corporate sponsors. Students even constructed the countertops of the café in the MIT hobby shop by recycling old conference tables slated for the dump.

The Web site serves as a critical tool to extend the original spirit of participation into Steam Café's ongoing life. While the physical infrastructure probably won't change much over the next few years, the food changes every day, offering a great way to engage new students on a regular basis.

What Principles Were Behind the Design?

The design team developed key objectives for Steam Café and then explored numerous ways of achieving them given the many limitations. We wanted the space to have a magnetic quality that would encourage dense occupation, thus fostering connectivity and collaboration. We wanted the theme of healthy food to be expressed as a guiding principle We also wanted to take advantage of open source as a design concept, but one that could be guided by strong leadership.

Magnetism: Drawing people together into a common space was an underlying goal and guiding principle. Food provides the initial pull, but an equally important attraction is the people who come for the food. As good urban spaces demonstrate, people attract more people. This magnetic "watering hole" concept keeps the dialogue flowing at Steam Café and makes it more than a place to simply get food.

Density and collaboration: Once we had attracted people to the space, we wanted to seat them close together—a principle also key to maximizing the small amount of space available for seating. The booths' backless design cuts down on the space needed but also allows people to turn and socialize with those at adjacent tables. This proximity puts people into regular and serendipitous contact. This made its "Main Street" location critical to ensure a constant stream of new faces. The booths take advantage of this central location as well. Seating and table height are elevated 10 feet, providing an overlook of the area. This brings the eye level of seated patrons close to that of passing colleagues and encourages more spontaneous conversation between the stationary and the mobile visitors. Collaboration is further supported by the built-in chalkboard in each booth. The board encourages brainstorming and informal learning discourse. Notes left behind add to the texture and culture of the place. (See Figure 3.)

Open source and leadership: The principle of participatory design was central to the Steam Café process, and we felt from the beginning that it was best embodied by the open source model. We also felt, however, that leadership was critical: individual ideas, expertise, and oversight set direction and standards. A common confusion about open source is the assumption that the mere fact of participation guarantees success, or that self-organization necessarily produces desirable results. We felt the need to establish clear values in the beginning of the project that could guide progress and provide benchmarks for evaluation. To this end, an ongoing role for individuals exists at many levels, to take responsibility for the direction and outcome even after the founders of the project have moved on.

Figure 3. Booths with Chalkboards

What Is Unique or Noteworthy?

Steam Café offers benefits to MIT that exceed its original goals by offering a new business model, expanding to host evening and weekend events, aligning with the university's mission, and spawning new initiatives

Creating a new business model: Not only does Steam provide a community service to the MIT campus, it also became a profitable business model for the Sodexho Corporation. Steam replaced an existing café in the same location, and within the first two weeks of its operation, revenue close to tripled.

Expanding beyond intended use: Since its opening, the Steam location has become a desirable place for evening and weekend events, including receptions for world-class lectures and visiting school groups. The movable booth tables can be rearranged in a more social configuration or removed to configure a bar or counter in any location; the stationary booth seating remains as casual perches for sitting or resting a drink.

Aligning with university mission: The Steam Café project received support from several key administrators who had studied the need for greater informal and spontaneous interaction on the campus. Isaac Colbert, dean of graduate students at MIT, had recently developed a report[1] that identified the "priceless encounter" concept, describing the kind of diverse off-the-grid interaction that MIT's graduate students felt were fundamental to their education but not always provided on campus. Steam Café tapped into these visions and values in a direct way, offering a pragmatic and expressive contribution to the ongoing dialogue of campus development.

Spawning new initiatives: Steam Café was the first project initiated by the student group Culture Lab. Steam's success prompted an outpouring of demand for similar projects on campus. Since the Steam Café opening in 2004, the Culture Lab has involved more than 50 students in designing seven innovative projects on campus, including a nap room, an A/V theater, and a schematic proposal for a major visitor center building on Massachusetts Avenue in Boston. Several of these projects have already been implemented.

Acknowledgment

The Steam Café project was led by Scott Francisco and Nick Senske of MIT. Both were completing their master's of science in architecture studies at the time.

Endnote

1. Isaac Colbert, "Making the Case for Graduate Community," *Journal for Higher Education Strategists*, vol. 2, no. 2 (2004).

About the Author

Scott Francisco is a senior consultant with DEGW North America in New York City, focusing on the relationships among space, community, and organizational culture.

CHAPTER 28

Flyspace
North Carolina State University

Hal Meeks

What Is It?

Flyspace (http://www.ncsu.edu/flyspace/) is a simple design for a meeting space for five to six students. It is intended to be inexpensive, modular, and compact. Keeping room sizes small fosters an intimate area for collaboration and makes it more likely that other rooms can be built around a campus with chronic space shortages.

Dot-com startups inspired Flyspace. These companies grew so quickly that they couldn't house all their employees, sometimes replacing offices with laptops and an open room with lots of flat work spaces. Offices with doors were converted into scheduled spaces for client meetings, brainstorming, or simply a quiet space to work. This nontraditional use of space fostered creativity and collaboration among employees.

Flyspace offers just enough technology to foster collaboration; technology is not the main feature of these rooms. The emphasis is on flat work areas, including extensive use of whiteboards along all walls.

The basic technology infrastructure is inexpensive to build and expand. Flyspace uses a basic design consisting of two computers with displays mounted on articulated arms and connectivity (data, video, and audio) for four laptops. A large flat-panel display allows users to share their desktops with others. A centralized pod contains all data and power connectors for equipment in the room, making it easy to connect equipment and minimizing the cost of running conduit for data, media, and power. Wireless networking is also available. Students can make on-campus calls or report problems by phone, and the speakerphone makes it possible for off-campus students and faculty to participate in Flyspace meetings. Perhaps the most important feature of Flyspace is an open scheduling system that lets any registered student schedule a space for a meeting or group project. (See Figure 1.)

©2006 Hal Meeks

Figure 1. Room Scheduling Puts Students in Charge

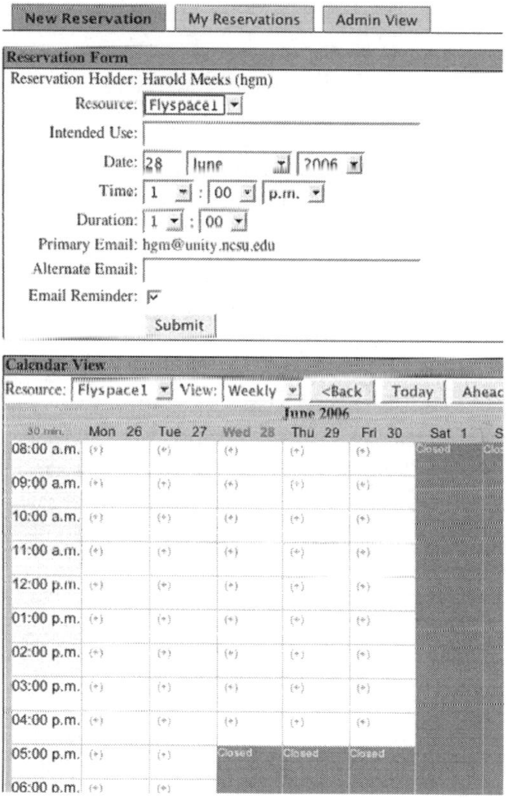

Beyond some basic assumptions about group dynamics and collaboration, Flyspace is pedagogically neutral—faculty and students determine how best to use these spaces for learning. The Flyspace project at North Carolina State University will study how faculty and students use this space for academic projects, resulting in a better understanding of the value of group projects that will shape future versions of Flyspace.

North Carolina State University is North Carolina's largest public university, with more than 7,000 full-time employees, 30,000 students, and degrees in 100 fields of study. Located in Raleigh, North Carolina, NC State is a land-grant university with extension offices in all 100 counties and the Cherokee Reservation. NC State's Centennial Campus serves as a national model of university-business collaboration and incubation.

What Happens Here?

Flyspace supports coursework, meetings, basic computing, and nonacademic activities.

Faculty who require their students to work in groups suggest Flyspace as a place to have their meetings. Students can schedule time in the rooms as needed. Because of Flyspace's open scheduling policy and a chronic shortage of meeting space, staff have begun to use Flyspace rooms for their own meetings. Centrally located on campus in the Student Center, the spaces are convenient for everyone.

The two computers in each of the Flyspace rooms replicate the standard campus software environment with immediate access to networked file space. Students can check e-mail, look up information on the Web, use high-end applications, or just relax. The 32-inch LCD display makes Flyspace a great place for students to get together to watch a movie. The central location makes it easy for students to buy snacks, meet after working out in the gym, or stop by between classes. The rooms are open a large part of the day and into the evening.

How Is Technology Used?

Flyspace facilitates collaboration, brainstorming, and various pursuits unlimited by rules on the rooms' use. An open, Web-based scheduling system lets users see if the space is available immediately, without having to authenticate, and they can schedule space without having to ask permission. Because every user in the room has access to the room-control system from his or her computer, seamless switching between participants is possible. No one person controls who has access to the screen; it is truly a collaborative experience. Moreover, the large amount of whiteboard space and markers allow students to brainstorm—with or without technology.

Flyspace rooms are "neutral territory"—they are not owned by a single academic unit on campus. Everyone can participate, and there are no restrictions on how the rooms are used. Students can use them for coursework, meetings for student groups, or simply to watch a movie. Staff can use them as spontaneous meeting spaces when their own departmental meeting rooms are unavailable. Because staff experience the same environment as students, they can appreciate the value of the space.

What Makes the Space Successful?

Flyspace succeeds because It works the way students want it to work. It does not require them to use technology they would not normally access, such as high-end equipment they can't afford. The support model is heavily oriented toward self service. Rooms use common, familiar technology. No staff or technical experts are needed nearby to assist students; they can do it themselves. The scheduling for the rooms is simple enough that students can reserve one on a moment's notice. Since scheduling for Flyspace is via the Web, students can schedule meetings spontaneously.

The focus has been on the bare essentials that students would need, while using as much functionality as possible with the equipment furnished. Originally, the rooms were furnished with DVD/VCR units, but the PCs themselves offered DVD playback, and it was not apparent that students wanted or needed the ability to play back VHS tapes, so they were later removed.

Flyspace's success has opened a campus dialogue about learning and public computer spaces. As the number of commuting students increases, the need for computing labs has changed, since they require space to work, connect, and meet. Flyspace has shown that other options exist beyond computer labs for our learning and public computing spaces. The model has already been copied by others—another sign of success.

What Principles Were Behind the Design?

The Flyspace design relied on
▶ simplicity,
▶ a commodity perspective,
▶ affordability,
▶ leveraging the existing technology infrastructure, and
▶ simplified support and room controls.

It makes no sense to design a space that is so expensive it cannot be easily replicated in several locations on campus. Many pieces of technology included in the initial Flyspace plans were thrown away, leaving what was essential for collaborative student work. Stripping Flyspace of equipment that could only be used for one activity resulted in an affordable, expandable, and replicable space. Students immediately know how to use the equipment provided. (See Figure 2.) The rooms are designed as the antithesis of high-end conferencing rooms. Flyspace is intended to be a commodity resource that can emerge all over campus and be used by anyone.

Figure 2. Simple Design with Whiteboards Everywhere

A central piece of Flyspace is not the room itself but an open scheduling system that uses the campus's investment in Oracle Calendar. Flyspace rooms show up as a campus resource that can be scheduled by anyone, whether student, staff, or faculty. Instead of using expensive videoconferencing hardware, Flyspace uses Web-based conferencing tools, which require less technology and align better with the ways students collaborate. An echo-canceling microphone connected to one computer allows everyone in the room to be heard; no expensive, dedicated videoconferencing equipment is needed.

Student employees provide room support. They also maintain the technology-enhanced classrooms. Problems reported are remedied in an hour or less. Also, the rooms are checked on a daily basis for unreported equipment malfunctions.

Room-control systems add not only to the cost but also to the complexity of the room itself. Flyspace has a unique Web-based control system that uses the computers in the room itself, allowing everyone in the room, including laptop users, to control equipment.

What Is Unique or Noteworthy?

Flyspace benefits from open scheduling, a unique funding model, and HTML-based room control.

▶ The rooms are for use by anyone on campus. This is not a technology innovation; it is a policy innovation. By using Oracle Calendar as the back end for scheduling, users only need a valid campus user ID; they do not even need an Oracle Calendar account to schedule a room.

▶ Flyspace was initially funded as a collaborative effort of the Student Center, which provided the space and money for renovation, a campus-wide learning technology project fund (http://litre.ncsu.edu/), and money and personnel from the campus information technology department. The experimental space allowed us to discover space-management problems, determine the critical mix of technology, and determine how to use technology in ways truly useful to students.

▶ Room-control systems are typically expensive and proprietary. Much of the labor cost of Flyspace went to the back-end programming required to create an inexpensive Web-based room-control system. With that initial investment, we could build room-control interfaces with Macromedia Dreamweaver, which helped us economize on that cost. (See Figure 3.)

Figure 3. Room Control in a Web Browser

About the Author

Hal Meeks is a computer consultant at North Carolina State University.

CHAPTER 29

SCALE-UP
North Carolina State University

Robert Beichner

What Is It?

A SCALE-UP classroom looks like a restaurant, with 7-foot-diameter round tables that each seat three teams of three students. (SCALE-UP stands for Student-Centered Activities for Large-Enrollment Undergraduate Programs.) Each team has a laptop to support their learning, as well as ready access to laboratory equipment in surrounding closets. Computer projection screens sit at opposite ends of the room. Large whiteboards cover the walls. A teacher station, with document camera and possibly a Tablet PC, is usually located near the center of the space.

Although SCALE-UP rooms can be found at various institutions, they were originally designed for research universities that offer large introductory classes. Several models hold 99 students taking introductory physics or chemistry for science and engineering majors. Some rooms are larger, but most are smaller. Pictures of a few of the classrooms can be seen at <http://www.ncsu.edu/per/SCALEUP/Classrooms.html>. Other courses taught this way include mathematics, biology, and even comparative literature.

Figure 1 shows 4 of the 11 tables in the SCALE-UP classroom at North Carolina State University. Normally, each table would have one laptop per team, but the room is also used as a computer lab, so in this view each seat has a laptop.

North Carolina State University is North Carolina's largest public university with more than 7,000 full-time employees and 30,000 students and degrees awarded in more than 100 fields of study. Located in Raleigh, North Carolina, NC State is a land-grant university with extension offices in all 100 counties and the Cherokee Reservation. NC State's Centennial Campus serves as a national model of university-business collaboration and incubation.

Figure 1. SCALE-UP Classroom at North Carolina State University

What Happens Here?

Tables in SCALE-UP rooms facilitate interactions among students as they work on activities. Most of the time students work in their assigned teams. Tasks are classified as tangibles, ponderables, or labs. Tangible activities involve hands on observations or measurements and typically take no more than 15 minutes to complete and discuss. Equipment used is typically quite simple, like meter sticks or racquetballs. Ponderables allow groups to work together on complex, real-world problems involving approximations, assumptions, and often some Internet sleuthing. These also typically take approximately 15 minutes to complete. Laboratory activities take place in the same classroom space, but several characteristics distinguish them from tangibles: they take longer to complete, they are usually hypothesis-driven, and they frequently require some type of formal write-up.

The room layout allows the instructor and teaching assistants to reach every student and engage them in Socratic dialogues as they work. All students have name tags, so hiding or remaining anonymous is impossible. The Web is used to collect student answers to questions raised by the instructor, and histograms of student responses are displayed for discussion. (This is similar to the use of a "clicker" student response system.) Students are encouraged to take risks and challenge each other. The surrounding whiteboards act as public thinking spaces. Students can see what others are doing and engage each other in discussion. When students work on activities where everyone is likely to take a similar approach, they work on smaller lap-sized whiteboards. That way, their work remains visible within the team and to the roaming instructor, but not to other groups.

How Is Technology Used?

Originally, the word *technology* meant "systematic treatment." Based on that idea, the round tables are the most important instructional technology in the classroom. The ideal size was found after experimentation with half a dozen table geometries. The 7-foot diameter permits table-wide conversations while being both large enough to avoid crowding and small enough for efficient use of space. Tables that are too large actually discourage table-wide discussions.

Each team of three students has a dedicated laptop with Internet access. (We tried one, two, and three computers for each team. One computer per team works best. We also found the smaller footprint and lower screen height of laptops offer definite advantages over desktop computers.) Students use these laptops to find information relevant to the task at hand, whether they need to know the atomic mass of aluminum or the mass of a racquetball. The course Web site is always available, along with access to a Web-based question delivery system (WebAssign). We use the laptops to present questions to groups and provide directions for class activities. They also serve as computer programming platforms.

We developed VPython, a 3D output extension to the Python programming language (http://www.vpython.org/). Students create objects such as spheres and arrows, give them physical properties (mass and velocity, for example), and then "teach" them to interact according to physical laws. Although there are no output statements, the programming environment automatically generates output in a realistic world of three dimensions, with hidden surfaces, zooming, rotating, and so on. When student work is somehow unique or representative of a good solution, we can easily display it for the entire class to see. Similarly, we can share the instructor's screen on the student laptops.

What Makes the Space Successful?

Group interactions are the key to making this instructional space work. We have seen dramatically decreased failure rates for minorities and women (down to one-quarter the failure rates in traditional classes). We believe this success results from the social interactions and risk taking the room design and instructional approach promote. Also, we carefully and deliberately created our learning objectives, which included not only content but also communication and technology skills. From those objectives we crafted each aspect of the learning experience, from homework assignments to room layout. Along with each objective we developed methods of assessing whether we succeeded in accomplishing the chosen goals. In other words, the instruction was deliberate and intentional.

Whiteboards along the SCALE-UP classroom's walls provide a "public thinking space." Figure 2, for example, shows a whiteboard where three teams at table 7 have sketched graphs of the height of a bouncing ball. Even the equipment closet doors have whiteboards for student use (see Figure 3).

Figure 2. Whiteboard with Sketches of Bouncing Ball Height

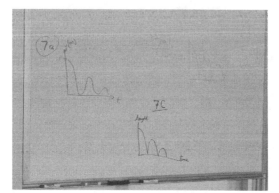

What Principles Were Behind the Design?

Social interactions are central to the SCALE-UP pedagogical approach. Vygotsky's social cognition[1] is a major component of what we try to make happen. The table shape and spacing, along with the surrounding whiteboards, promote active discussion and debate.[2] The curriculum incorporates well-known aspects of collaborative learning (individual accountability, positive interdependence, face-to-face interaction, appropriate use of interpersonal skills, and group self-assessment).[3] The instructor circulates about the room, engaging students in Socratic dialogues.[4] These factors challenge students to work at the upper levels of Bloom's taxonomy, synthesis and evaluation.[5]

Figure 3. Whiteboard on Door of Equipment Closet

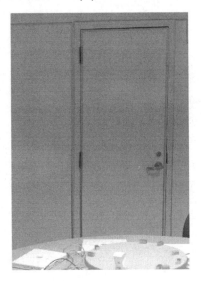

What Is Unique or Noteworthy?

We were very deliberate in designing the learning environment. Everything from the seating to assignments to interactions between students and instructors is part of the "technology" of the room. Starting from objectives, we could craft instructional sequences and assess whether they succeeded. This information was then fed back into revising the curriculum, pedagogy, and environment. Just like the restaurant setting it resembles, a SCALE-UP classroom is a friendly, comfortable space. People interact while focusing on physical phenomena (instead of food) and can accomplish much more than they could working alone.

Endnotes

1. Lev S. Vygotsky and Alex Kozulin, *Thought and Language* (Cambridge, Mass.: MIT Press, 1986; originally published in 1934).

2. Richard R. Hake, "Interactive-Engagement Versus Traditional Methods: A Six-Thousand-Student Survey of Mechanics Test Data for Introductory Physics Courses," *American Journal of Physics*, vol. 66, no. 1 (1998), pp. 64–74.

3. David W. Johnson, Roger T. Johnson, and Karl A. Smith, *Cooperative Learning: Increasing College Faculty Instructional Productivity: ASHE-ERIC Higher Education Reports, No. 4* (Washington, D.C.: The George Washington University, School of Education and Human Development, 1991).

4. Richard R. Hake, "Socratic Pedagogy in the Introductory Physics Laboratory," *Physics Teacher*, vol. 30, no. 9 (1992), pp. 546–552.

5. Benjamin S. Bloom, *Taxonomy of Educational Objectives, Handbook I: The Cognitive Domain* (New York: David McKay, 1956).

About the Author

Robert Beichner is an Alumni Distinguished Undergraduate Professor of Physics at North Carolina State University.

CHAPTER 30

The Information Commons
Northwestern University

Bob Davis and Denise Shorey

What Is It?

Northwestern University is a private doctoral research institution just north of Chicago with a full-time enrollment of 15,700 students. Northwestern University's Information Commons, or InfoCommons, is a new type of learning space that exemplifies technology and space design working to encourage and enhance research and collaboration. The library already supports spaces for teaching and learning. The InfoCommons does not replace these spaces; instead, it provides modular furniture, a group project room, staffing support, and a new sense of purpose for students. As a joint venture between the library and Northwestern University Information Technology (NUIT), it promotes cross-departmental cooperation.

During the design phase, groups providing input considered factors such as the ability for different sizes of groups to work and feel comfortable; the flexibility of the space; and the relationship of the InfoCommons to already established departments within the library and Academic Technologies (a division of NUIT). The 5,100-square-foot InfoCommons offers a variety of configurations: individual workstations, group presentation areas, booths for group study, and a small-group project room, permitting students to choose different level of interactions with their peers in a technologically rich yet informal environment.

What Happens Here?

The InfoCommons provides a technologically rich and welcoming environment that supports and encourages many new practices in scholarship, teaching and learning, and electronic publishing. It offers a solution to the problems that students often face when trying to work or study in an area that lacks adequate technology, is physically uncomfortable, or makes collaborative work difficult. Within the InfoCommons, students write class papers; work collaboratively on class projects with peers (onsite or virtually); hold impromptu meetings near their workstations; e-mail friends, professors, and others; and use the location as a first stop for their research needs. The workstations, booths, presentation stations, project room, and flexible furniture make this a space where people and technology comfortably intersect.

Group Work

The InfoCommons supports both formal and informal groups. The furniture arrangement allows students to work comfortably by themselves, but its flexibility encourages small groups to gather around a single workstation by moving chairs or monitors. Many larger groups find the two presentation stations convenient for working on class projects. (See Figure 1.)

Figure 1. Flexible Furniture for Group or Individual Study

The project room supports more formal work. It is scheduled by groups that need a slightly different setting for presentations or discussions, while still feeling they are part of the InfoCommons. For example, teaching assistants regularly schedule the room for review sessions with their classes.

How Is Technology Used?

The InfoCommons contains more than 50 high-end computers, wireless access, and data ports at strategic locations. Students have the option of printing to a color or two black-and-white printers as well as saving their work online for easy access at a later date.

General area: Students engage in individual or spontaneous group work. The furniture setup enables easy collaboration. Three, four, or five students sitting together in a booth can use the resident computer or connect their laptops to do joint work; many students use available tables for wireless laptops. (See Figure 2.)

Figure 2. Modular Furniture and Ample Work Space

The 52-inch plasma screens work with a resident computer or a connected laptop. They face into the general area and are available for group projects, papers, and presentations. The large screens are valued both for group collaboration and individual use. (See Figure 3.)

Figure 3. Plasma Screens

Small-group project room: The state-of-the-art technology in the small-group project room includes two digital whiteboards, a projector, a computer, comfortable chairs, and network connections for interactive presentations, projects, and study sessions. Students can also connect a laptop and turn the whiteboard into a presentation screen, allowing them to combine images and annotation that they can ultimately print (in color, if they choose) or save as separate files to be shared or reviewed later.

What Makes the Space Successful?

A number of features contribute to the area's success.

No boundaries: No barriers separate the InfoCommons from the main library corridor, yet the space successfully creates small enclaves of privacy in a completely open area. The InfoCommons provides spaces that allow students to work together—to solve problems, exchange ideas, and work collaboratively. The casual passerby can view activity and easily become part of it. Particularly in the booths (see Figure 4) and at the presentation stations, students remain unaware—or perhaps uncaring—of passersby, opening their lives and work to all who might see.

Figure 4. Enclaves of Privacy

Challenging and changing cultures: The concept of a learning space such as the InfoCommons can challenge those with traditional views of "learning" and "space." Library staff accustomed to following long-established routes to their offices and departments through the busy InfoCommons, for example, now view it differently. The high visibility of the area's social and learning capability is often a new idea, especially for visitors and prospective students (who embrace it with enthusiasm).

A social space: The InfoCommons is a first stop for many students entering the library. (See Figure 5.) It offers a welcoming social environment where they engage in independent inquiry, participate in small group interactions, or sip coffee from the nearby café.

Figure 5. A First Stop for Many Students

Informality: The project room was initially envisioned as a glassed-off formal conference room, complete with a large table surrounded by chairs, distinguishing it from the rest of the InfoCommons. By contrast, the room's actual success can be attributed to the shift away from this planned formality to a relaxed setting rich in technology that blends unobtrusively, versatile and comfortable chairs, and a surprisingly low "coffee table" with a wireless keyboard, data, and power ports—at the right height for feet. (See Figure 6.)

Staffing: Administratively, the InfoCommons is part of the library's Reference Department, but joint staffing is provided by Academic Technologies, ensuring that assistance (by students or staff) for research, technology, and other needs is always available.

Figure 6. Group Project Room

What Principles Were Behind the Design?

The vision of the InfoCommons was that of a learning environment to support the growing institutional focus on interdisciplinary programs for undergraduates. The technologically rich InfoCommons supports different needs and priorities, encourages collaborative learning, and is sufficiently flexible to accommodate changing requirements. David Bishop, the university librarian, said,

> If academic libraries are to remain vital as places, students must want to use them, even though they can access electronic resources remotely. The Information Commons was conceived as a focus for undergraduate activity. It provides a facility that enables and encourages collaboration, and is a place where students can get answers to questions about both library resources and computers. Student needs and preferences will undoubtedly change over time, so a key to the success of the Information Commons will be to reinvent it as needed.

What Is Unique or Noteworthy?

Four characteristics distinguish the InfoCommons:

▶ **The whole is greater than the sum of its part(ner)s.** The InfoCommons is just one example of continuing partnerships between Academic Technologies and the library that cross many boundaries. The vision of the

InfoCommons was to move beyond traditional computer labs and computer spaces. The result has been a successful partnership that enhances the undergraduate experience.

▶ **Spaces evolve.** Digital resources, new programmatic needs and directions, and advances in learning theory all form part of our changing environment. As these elements emerge and develop, reflecting changing characteristics of the institution, the InfoCommons will continue to evolve and redefine its role.

▶ **Location, location, location contributes to the site's success.** The InfoCommons is a destination of choice for students. Viewing it as more than "the library," they value its welcoming feel, its casual yet supportive atmosphere, its dynamism and energy, and the exceptional technology and resources that it provides as they engage in learning.

▶ **The InfoCommons has been replicated elsewhere.** The overwhelming acceptance and success of the InfoCommons as a unit and also as an innovative learning space has encouraged the university library and Academic Technologies to replicate similar spaces and concepts elsewhere in specialized or branch libraries.

About the Authors

Bob Davis is the associate director of academic technologies, Northwestern University Information Technology, and **Denise Shorey** is the head of the reference department, Northwestern University Library, at Northwestern University.

CHAPTER 31

The Digital Union
The Ohio State University

Victoria Getis, Catherine Gynn, and Susan E. Metros

What Is It?

The Digital Union (http://digitalunion.osu.edu/) was established in 2004 at The Ohio State University (http://osu.edu/) as a partnership between the Office of the CIO and the University Libraries (http://library.osu.edu/). The leaders of these organizations envisioned a centrally located space that would serve as a test bed for multidisciplinary, experimental projects involving technology in teaching and learning, as well as creative and scholarly activities. The underlying premise is that experimentation in a dynamic environment is necessary for the university to prepare for tomorrow's technologies. In addition, the academic community needs a place to conduct low-risk trials and evaluate emerging technologies to make informed decisions. The Digital Union provides a place to test-drive emerging technologies prior to making large resource and financial investments.

Centrally located on campus in 2,000 square feet of space in the Science and Engineering Library, the Digital Union (see Figure 1) is dedicated to investigating technology solutions, providing access to new media technology, showcasing emerging technologies, building academic collaborations, and fostering interdisciplinary partnerships among researchers. Plans are being made to expand its size and add additional staff and services. The Digital Union engages the university community and its leadership in the exploration of technology in academic environments and in society as a whole.

Organizationally, the Digital Union staff report to the deputy CIO, who oversees the Technology Enhanced Learning and Research unit (http://telr.osu.edu/). Formal collaborations exist between the Digital Union, WOSU Public Media, and the Americans with Disabilities Act (ADA) Coordinator's Office. The Digital Union receives input from advisory panels representing users, technology, research, and external partners.

Figure 1. The Digital Union

The Digital Union provides students, staff, and faculty with:

▶ Consultation with professionally trained instructional designers and technologists; technical advisors; usability, videoconferencing, and media production experts; graphic and Web designers; Web programmers; grant writers; and library specialists

▶ Space for technology-rich experimentation and new media production

▶ Videoconferencing delivery and support

▶ Collaborative work areas

▶ Demonstrations of multifunctional and ergonomically correct work spaces including stations with assistive and adaptive technologies

▶ Support for communities of practice on distance education, knowledge management, programming, and visual communication

▶ Workshops and one-on-one tutoring for software and hardware innovations in new media technologies

▶ Educational presentations and demonstrations on emerging technologies and practices

For a tour of the Digital Union, visit <http://digitalunion.osu.edu/Resources/DUVirtualTour/>.

Ohio State's main campus is in Columbus, Ohio, the state capital and one of the fastest growing cities in the Midwest. The Ohio State University system includes four regional campuses and the Agricultural Technical Institute. Ohio State is a Research I land-grant institution with an enrollment of 58,000 students; 3,400 regular, clinical, and research faculty; and 14,000 professional staff.

What Happens Here?

The Digital Union supports research, project development, and videoconferencing. In addition, Digital Union staff consult on a wide variety of implementations, provide support for faculty using multimedia in their research, and offer technology training workshops. The space is also used for demonstrations, conferences, and working sessions.

Research: The Digital Union supports undergraduate, graduate, and faculty research, as well as creative and scholarly activities through classes, events, technology support, and grants. Examples include open source initiatives such as Open Source Portfolio Initiative (OSPI) and Pachyderm (a suite of authoring tools), cross-disciplinary projects on Web accessibility and digital storytelling, and numerous teaching with technology grant projects (funded externally or internally).

Consulting: Digital Union staff consult with Ohio State personnel on a diverse range of technology implementations such as how to use information technologies to enhance the classroom experience. Staff members are available to answer questions concerning electronic theses and dissertations, online library research, podcasts, clickers, course lecture streaming, and so forth.

Project development workspace: Faculty and students use the space for team meetings and production work. Spread throughout the many reconfigurable workspaces are 15 desktop workstations that support single and multiple users. In addition, users can borrow laptops and other mobile devices or use their own. Digital Union staff provide additional training to students working on academic projects.

Faculty support: The Digital Union supports faculty who use multimedia in research and teaching. Faculty have access to technology tools and information, server space for pilot projects, technology components required for grants, and training for research teams.

Course support: Faculty can schedule the Digital Union's flexible meeting space when the course's learning outcomes rely on student familiarity with technology tools, collaboration, or videoconferencing. The Digital Union staff develop and deliver educational programs for students who need specific skills for coursework.

Technology workshops: Faculty, staff, and students from across the five campuses participate in workshops, seminars, and classes on a variety of topics including multimedia applications, video, audio, and photography; using the course management system or learning object repository; improving library research techniques; understanding computer and laboratory ergonomics; and incorporating educational technologies into teaching. Staff also train clients to use specialized, discipline-specific software.

Showcases, demonstrations, conferences, and working sessions: As a centrally funded experimental facility, the Digital Union is positioned to bring stakeholders together to address issues related to the use of new and emerging technologies in education. The Digital Union meets the needs of both administrative and academic units by offering both online and in-person showcases, demonstrations, and conferences featuring academic and corporate experts in specific topical areas. The Digital Union also serves as a gathering place for formal and informal communities of practice.

Videoconferencing: Faculty and staff can use the Digital Union's videoconferencing suite to host or participate in professional meetings, have a guest or instructor join a class remotely, or conduct grant application, graduate admissions, and search committee interviews. Students also use the facilities to defend dissertations. Portable videoconferencing units are available on loan to faculty traveling or working off site.

How Is Technology Used?

The Digital Union offers technology for experimentation and practical applications such as videoconferencing.

Experimentation: Proof-of-concept projects are undertaken in a low-risk environment that provides a safety net of technical support. The Digital Union has its own server and storage as well as system administration staff that understand the need for managing a short-term use, nonproduction, "sandbox" environment.

Equipment for loan and evaluation: The Digital Union maintains more than 50 laptops for loan to groups or individuals to enable technology projects. Digital cameras (still and video) and small peripheral equipment such as iPods, PDAs, Tablet PCs, and digital audio recorders are available for short- or long-term loan for evaluation and/or project work (see Figure 2). Thanks to the generosity of corporate sponsors, the Digital Union can cycle in beta software and just-released products, providing clients a place to test-drive new and emerging technologies prior to making large resource and financial investments.

Figure 2. Equipment Available for Loan and Evaluation

Videoconferencing: Videoconferencing capabilities allow users to connect with others around the globe using desktop video resources and H.323.

Wireless: The entire facility is supported with wireless high-speed Internet access. Digital Union researchers serve on the university's wireless implementation team to explore the pedagogical implications of wireless in the university's informal and formal learning spaces.

Digital conversion: Equipment for digitizing analog materials such as slides, text, or video is available along with staff guidance to enable faculty and students to convert materials.

What Makes the Space Successful?

Several factors contribute to the success of the Digital Union, from collaboration and innovation to support and assessment.

Collaborative design: The development of the Digital Union brought together multiple stakeholders and fostered collaboration among several university offices—the University Libraries, Office of the CIO, WOSU Public Media, ADA Coordinator's Office, and Department of Industrial, Interior, and Visual Communication Design—and the university architect, as well as local and national hardware, software, and furniture companies.

Interdisciplinary leadership: The Digital Union is a centrally administered facility governed by an interdisciplinary leadership team comprising the director of libraries and the CIO, with advisory panels of students, faculty, staff, and external partners who represent a wide variety of emerging technology interests. Active participation by advisory panels representing a wide constituency inside and outside the university guides projects and planning.

Innovative student programs: Two student programs are run out of the Digital Union. The first, Research on Research: Student-Faculty ePartnerships, responds to the president's leadership agenda goal to support undergraduate research. This innovative, interdisciplinary summer program pairs faculty and undergraduates to work on a research project. The deliverable is a publicly accessible, multimedia-rich, online portfolio chronicling the research effort. Projects include everything from researching cancer to discovering fossils to studying violence in online gaming. (See <http://digitalunion.osu.edu/Research/CurrentProjects/>).

The second program, Technology Education and Multimedia Skills (TEAMS), builds technology skills among undergraduate and graduate students. In addition to the hands-on, skill-based courses, students gain knowledge about intellectual property, universal design and accessibility, and the pedagogical uses of technology.

Technology and instructional support: The Digital Union is part of a larger central unit, Technology Enhanced Learning and Research, whose mission is to enhance teaching and learning through the thoughtful integration of innovative instructional technologies. E-learning course consultants are available to work with faculty. Student assistants trained at the Digital Union provide project or long-term technical assistance for building online course content and components. A partnership with the Office of Faculty and Teaching Assistant Development focuses on the efficient and effective use of technology in the classroom.

Assessment: The Digital Union conducts focus sessions, usability testing, and surveys to determine how best to design services to respond to changing campus needs. Evidence-based management encourages innovation and provides opportunities to experiment, and assess technologies and techniques in a low-risk environment.

What Principles Were Behind the Design?

Initial concepts for the facility were derived from the academic plan's call for Ohio State to become a national leader in integrating information technology into learning, discovery, outreach, and collaboration. The planners envisioned interior architecture and environments that were reconfigurable to accommodate multiple uses in a fixed space. Tables can be set up in conference or theater style (see Figure 3), and equipment such as video-conversion stations on rolling carts provide mobility. Comfort, safety, and efficiency were foremost in the design and selection of the furnishings and equipment. Beyond seating, desk height, and equipment placement, the planners considered appropriate lighting as well as climate and sound control.

Figure 3. Ergonomic, Reconfigurable Furniture

The Digital Union succeeds largely because of the proximity of expert staff and students to the users. Staff offices and student help stations are integrated into the main area of the facility, allowing users to seek help from their workspaces and encouraging open communication and problem solving among users and staff. The environment benefits everyone, including people with disabilities and different learning styles, as showcased through the use of touch-screen monitors, closed captioning equipment, and ergonomic, accessible furniture.

What Is Unique or Noteworthy?

If you visit the Digital Union, you will see students working on wireless laptops, taking advantage of the comfortable furnishings. Teams gather around production workstations, building media rich Web sites and producing digital movies. Faculty consult with Digital Union staff or student interns to decide, for example, what technologies might best engage learners.

Digital Union visitors may participate in a vendor-led product showcase or join a hands-on workshop on topics ranging from podcasting to making course content accessible to students with special needs. Also, visitors will find a state-of-the-art videoconferencing suite where students in Palestine, Israel, and Ohio State debate—virtually and in real time—their cultural similarities and differences.

Above all, you will see the excitement on the faces of students, staff, and faculty as they experience the "Aha!" moment when they achieve something new and learn more about themselves at the same time. The Digital Union is the promise of technology fulfilled.

About the Authors

Victoria Getis is the interim director of the Digital Union at The Ohio State University. **Catherine Gynn** is the CIO at The Ohio State University Newark and Central Ohio Technical College. **Susan E. Metros** is the deputy CIO, the executive director for eLearning, and a professor of design technology at The Ohio State University.

CHAPTER 32

Academic and Olin Centers
Olin College of Engineering

Joanne Kossuth

About Olin

Olin College is a four-year, independent, undergraduate engineering institution that provides full-tuition scholarships for all students. The curriculum takes an interdisciplinary, project-based approach emphasizing entrepreneurship, liberal arts, and rigorous science and engineering fundamentals. Olin College prepares future leaders through an innovative engineering education that bridges science and technology, enterprise, and society. Skilled in independent learning and the art of design, Olin graduates are prepared to make a positive difference in the world. The college currently enrolls 300 resident undergraduate students and graduated its first class in May 2006.

Olin College had the unique opportunity to create a new campus from scratch, a rare occurrence in today's academic environment. (See Figures 1 and 2.) Even so, the slate was not 100 percent clean. The Olin Foundation (founder of the college) had hired program planners and consultants to provide initial campus designs prior to staffing the college. General building space, classroom, and lab sizes were already determined; moreover, local building codes and restrictions regarding use and height were already taken into consideration.

As an engineering institution, the college required a robust technological infrastructure that allowed for 24 x 7 student access as well as production and experimentation environments. Olin College runs a fully converged network. Voice, video, data, building security, and building controls all run over a strictly IP network. The college also provides a ubiquitous campus-wide wireless overlay that supports 802.11b and 802.11g Wi-Fi.

Classrooms, labs, and research spaces are equipped with power and wired data to every seat. In the case of labs, many of the connections are supplied through ceiling-mounted towers. All spaces are also outfitted with single- and multimode fiber for future use.

Figure 1. Aerial View of Olin College of Engineering

Photo: © Mark C. Flannery

Figure 2. View of Olin College from the Great Lawn

Photo: © Mark C. Flannery

All classrooms were designed with motorized screens and the ability to transmit or receive signals to and from any space on campus. They are prewired for an audiovisual control station with speakers and lighting controls, eliminating the need to cut into floors and walls when the construction was completed, since the A/V infrastructure was phased in to accommodate changing technologies and the requirements to support the curriculum. The A/V stations include

- ▸ Crestron control panels,
- ▸ DVD players,
- ▸ multiformat VCRs,
- ▸ audio connections,
- ▸ laptop connections, and
- ▸ other peripheral connections for document cameras.

All A/V equipment can be controlled from the stations, handheld devices such as iPAQs, and Web pages based on access controls. E-Crestron controls (Ethernet based) allow for remote control including shutoff and help desk support. Training sessions familiarize all faculty, staff, and students with the equipment, and IT staff are cross-trained in providing A/V service support.

A key consideration of the campus design is mobility. Ubiquitous connectivity is required because virtually all classrooms contain mobile furniture to accommodate diverse teaching styles. Comfortable lounge chairs with reversible tablet arms, knife tables (see Figure 3), puzzle tables, oval tables, and folding shopping-cart chairs populate these spaces. The majority of classroom spaces have whiteboards (and a few blackboards) on two or four walls along with moveable whiteboards. Classrooms and labs are used for projects, collaborative team work, collaborative design, presentations, seminars, research, and student work space as well as scheduled internal and external meetings. Figure 4 shows a project lab.

Figure 3. Mobile Classroom Design with Knife Tables

Figure 4. Reconfigurable Project Lab

Type of Learning Spaces

Olin College encompasses tiered (step down) classrooms, an auditorium, a computer lab, and the library/knowledge lab.

Tiered classrooms: Tiered classrooms are designed so that students can work on projects on the front portion of the desk space and work on their computers on the back desk space when they turn around. (See Figure 5.) The instructor can then be aware of what the students are working on. These spaces are used for collaborative design and projects, lectures, presentations, and seminars as well as internal and external group meetings.

Figure 5. Tiered Classroom Desks Support Project and Computer Work

Auditorium: The auditorium is the largest teaching space on campus. A theater-like, two-story room, it features an A/V production booth in the rear for managed events and a fully outfitted podium (the same design as the classroom podiums for ease of use and instruction) at the front of the room for self-service events. (See Figure 6.) The room is equipped with IP-based videoconferencing and the ability to simulcast events to a mezzanine for in-building overflow or to any of the classrooms, labs, or dining halls for out-of-building overflow. The space hosts speaker panels, theater productions, vocal and instrumental presentations, assemblies, student events such as viewing the presidential debates, student elections, seminars, and just about anything else requiring a large space.

Figure 6. Auditorium

Computer lab: The computer lab has 24 x 7 access for community members and contains high-end equipment, which is possible because the students have a mandatory laptop program. The lab contains a Ricoh color copier/printer, HP Design Jet plotter, AVID video editing workstation, ProTools Audio editing workstation, scanning workstation, and 10 high-end workstations capable of supporting graphically intensive applications such as 3D modeling. The lab also contains at least one of each laptop currently in use for faculty testing to ensure compatibility.

The computer lab is used for education and training, project work space, video and audio production, collaborative team work, seminars, poster development, and printing. Internal and external group meetings and research are also conducted here. (See Figure 7).

Figure 7. Computer Lab

Library/knowledge lab: The Olin library/knowledge lab space includes 5 group study rooms, 22 study carrels, tables and computer seating for 21, and lounge seating for 24. Four public workstations augment the college laptop program. Network drops and wireless access points are available throughout the space.

Innovation and creativity are critical factors in the school's curriculum and mission. The laptop program frees the library from the necessity of housing large numbers of computers in its physical space. This freedom has created the opportunity to rethink physical space in an academic setting and to emphasize support for discovery.

Because of Olin's emphasis on design and hands-on learning, collections emphasize creativity, design, and pedagogy in addition to curriculum and research. One collection includes building toys, modeling clay, drawing pads, pencils, drafting kits, chess, magnetic poetry, puzzles, and LEGO Mindstorms. These objects serve as tools for inspiration, brainstorming, and distraction. The library/knowledge lab space is used for group study, team work, individual quiet work space, research, and demonstrations. (See Figure 8.)

Success

The success of the learning spaces is evidenced by the fact that the demand for fully media-equipped classrooms has increased; faculty and students now advocate outfitting additional facilities. Increased use of all facilities as measured through statistics from the scheduling system as well as greater staff and student use of A/V support services provide additional indicators of success.

Figure 8. Comfortable Group Work/Meeting Space in the Library/Knowledge Lab

Principles

Mobility, interchangeability (flexibility), accessibility (anytime, anywhere, any way), technological sophistication, and usability are the driving factors in the design and use of the academic facilities at the college. All spaces strive to demonstrate Olin's philosophy of continual improvement by leveraging emerging technologies, space-design practices, and ongoing feedback to serve Olin and the broader learning community. Learning spaces are designed to offer students, faculty, and staff comfortable choices. Multiple configurations support the hands-on, project-oriented, "do-learn," collaborative, team-oriented curriculum.

About the Author

Joanne Kossuth is the associate vice president of development and CIO at the Olin College of Engineering.

CHAPTER 33

Smeal College of Business
The Pennsylvania State University

Peter Nourjian

What Is It?

Smeal College of Business is the largest academic building on the Penn State University Park campus, the third largest classroom building, and one of the largest business school complexes in the country. It adds 55,000 square feet of academic space for business programs—increasing space available for students and faculty by 35 percent.

The building features specialized instructional studios including a trading room and e-incubator lab, research laboratories, 150-seat auditorium, team study rooms, 22 classrooms, faculty and graduate student offices, interview rooms, executive space for visiting experts, a 100-seat café, administrative offices, and a four-story atrium lobby that offers a central gathering space—all configured to trigger discussions across disciplinary boundaries and mirror developments in the business world.

On the upper floors, instead of a long, narrow hallway, a wide, well-lit thoroughfare contains lounge pods where collaborative discussions occur. Conference rooms are scattered throughout the building. Faculty and business research areas are located in close proximity to the executive, leadership, and administrative areas to encourage dialogue among all faculty groups, research centers, and external constituents, including business partners, alumni, and friends. Even Smeal's exteriors, courtyards, and two terrace balconies are designed to bring minds together. (See Figure 1.)

The school is part of the east subcampus, a plan that puts Smeal beside the Food Science and Forest Resources buildings and diagonally across from the future site of the law school—a layout that physically embodies the links between research and commerce and the litigation issues between business and ethics. The adjacent construction underscores the trend toward "subcampus" environments designed to encourage interdisciplinary interaction among faculty and students. Construction began in August 2003 and was completed a month ahead of schedule in July 2005. (Take a virtual tour at <http://www.smeal.psu.edu/>.)

Figure 1. Smeal College of Business

©2006 Esto Photographics

The Smeal College originally was founded as the Department of Commerce and Finance in the College of Liberal Arts. Today, Smeal offers undergraduate degrees in accounting, actuarial science, economics, finance, management, management information systems, and marketing, as well as supply chain and information systems. The college's undergraduate enrollment exceeds 4,500. Nearly 150 students are pursuing MBA degrees and about 75 are studying for their PhDs. The college also offers executive education courses in University Park and around the world.

Smeal offers teaching, research, and learning spaces to create a "home" where faculty, staff, students, and alumni can connect. Common areas promote and enable communications among the Smeal academic community, corporate recruiters, and the outside community.

All of the college's academic needs are met under one roof. The building features versatile classrooms for instruction, state-of-the-art laboratories for research, comfortable study lounges for reading, and even a coffee shop. Undergraduates manage a $4.5 million investment fund in the trading room, guest speakers share their insights in the auditorium, careers are kicked off in the building's interview rooms, and the spacious atrium plays host to a variety of special events, from career fairs to dinner receptions. Innovation and knowledge can be found in every corner. (See Figure 2.)

Figure 2. The Four-Story Atrium Lobby

How Is Technology Used?

Technology is integrated throughout—Smeal is hardwired with the latest CAT 6-E system, and wireless capabilities energize every space within and outside the building. Soon the block of academic buildings that populate the subcampus will also have wireless access. In the classrooms, connectivity reaches every seat. The podiums integrate technology, and global messaging is available through an A/V system. To maximize communications for both the campus and the external community, a kiosk in the atrium features a display screen that can locate a dean's office, provide details about an accounting program, or give the who, where, and when of a lecture series.

The trading room epitomizes the building's technological advances, mimicking the reality of a Wall Street brokerage firm. Two 48-square-foot projector screens and three plasma television screens broadcast the latest business news from around the world on CNBC and Bloomberg News. Students track their stocks' performance on two 64-block ticker boards and a streaming ticker, each updated continuously with live data feeds from Reuters and Bloomberg. The room's 54 dual-monitor desktop computers each feature dual

Pentium 4 processors and 512 megabytes of RAM, ensuring Smeal students have access to the same tools and technology available to financial brokers in Manhattan. (See Figure 3.)

Figure 3. The Trading Room

©2006 Esto Photographics

What Makes the Space Successful?

One-stop shopping makes the space successful. A student can lounge in the atrium space, get something to eat in the café, go to class, interview for an internship in the corporate relations area, do research in the trading room, meet with a faculty advisor to plan courses for next semester, and meet with a student organization—and never leave the building!

When there's a special event, an elaborate dinner, or a career fair, furniture is moved; multiuse flexibility allows quick and easy reconfiguration of the space. Even the new mailroom plays a role: faculty and staff who would seldom cross paths are now channeled into a space that lets them pick up their mail and gather some interdisciplinary ideas at the same time.

What Principles Were Behind the Design?

Driving Smeal's design was the belief that community, connectivity, and curiosity can be powerful catalysts to learning. By creating interesting, flowing spaces that bring people with different interests into close proximity, an exchange of ideas and cultures occurs that makes the educational experience even more rewarding and enriching.

The walls separating departments in today's corporations are being torn down. Real business problems aren't solved by marketing or accounting alone. Rather, they require the collaborative efforts of several departments. Accounting may find a shrinking bottom line, which can be turned around with a new marketing campaign, an improved supply chain, and perhaps some human resource maneuvers. Smeal's business building fosters this kind of collaboration in teaching and research, aiding its faculty in producing cross-discipline research that is truly relevant to today's businesses and preparing the college's students for the challenges they will encounter in their careers.

What Is Unique or Noteworthy?

Friends and alumni have invested more than $4 million in the Nittany Lion Fund, which undergraduate students manage by investing the money in the stock market. They're accountable for its profitability (so far exceeding the Standard & Poor's index) and must make the case for their stock selections to investors.

A supply-chain research lab uses IBM software, server, and storage technology to connect Smeal's number-one-ranked supply-chain department with several other universities around the country as well as in Europe and Asia. The interconnected grid lets faculty and students at these universities collaborate in studying, simulating, and testing the key relationships in an end-to-end supply chain. The unique supply-chain simulations help IBM and other companies build dynamic supply chains that can sense and rapidly respond to changing customer demands and market conditions.

All in all, Smeal offers students the knowledge, the experience, and the interdisciplinary exposure that will ensure their success in a tough-minded global economy.

About the Author

Peter Nourjian is the corporate marketing editor at Gilbane Building Company.

CHAPTER 34

Center for Teaching and Learning
St. Lawrence University

Sondra Smith and Kim Mooney

What Is It?

The Center for Teaching and Learning (CTL) is a resource center serving 180 faculty at St. Lawrence University (http://www.stlawu.edu/), a private, liberal arts institution founded in 1856. Located in Canton, New York, this rural, residential campus for 2,100 students is bordered by the St. Lawrence River to the north and the Adirondack foothills to the south. St. Lawrence University is the oldest continuously coeducational institution of higher learning in New York State.

St. Lawrence faculty are respected scholars in their fields and known for their love of teaching. The CTL is designed to meet the pedagogical and technological needs of faculty at all stages of their careers. The first multipurpose space on campus to become wireless, the center includes a laptop training lab, a small project lab, a large conference room, two administrative offices, and a small kitchen on the ground floor of a student residence. (See Figure 1.) For a virtual tour of the CTL, visit <http://www.stlawu.edu/ctl/>.

What Happens Here?

The CTL's mission is to provide ongoing faculty development that promotes innovative teaching practices and course design. To achieve that mission, CTL hosts a rich variety of programs such as the yearlong new faculty orientation. Eight follow-up sessions throughout the remainder of the year help new faculty prepare for upcoming pedagogical responsibilities. The CTL also hosts a mentor program that supports first- and second-year faculty. Mentors are colleagues who have successfully struck a balance among their teaching, scholarship, and service responsibilities and who can offer a sounding board to newer faculty.

Figure 1. CTL Renovation Drawings

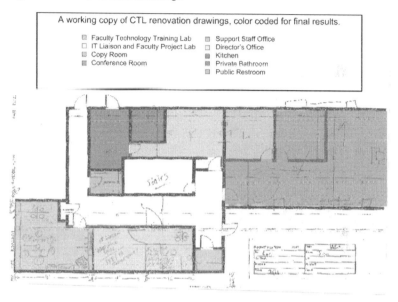

A working copy of CTL renovation drawings, color coded for final results.

- Faculty Technology Training Lab
- IT Liaison and Faculty Project Lab
- Copy Room
- Conference Room
- Support Staff Office
- Director's Office
- Kitchen
- Private Bathroom
- Public Restroom

The IT division plans all faculty technology development programming in close coordination with the CTL. Ongoing educational technology offerings include an annual four-day faculty technology festival and a two-day back-to-basics event.

Throughout the year, educational technologists provide one-on-one consultation and training through liaison hours typically held in the project lab. (See Figure 2.) Often, faculty learn or refresh their working knowledge of a particular technology. Conversations during liaison hours are often a precursor to a CTL technology grant application; the CTL provides grant funding for innovative teaching practices and for the integration of technology into teaching and learning.

Figure 2. Floorplan for CTL Faculty Training and Project Labs

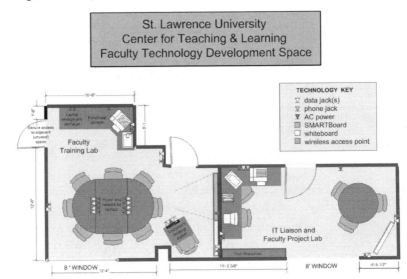

How Is Technology Used?

The entire facility is equipped for wired or wireless networking and Internet access. The conference room is a favorite location for formal presentations and meetings and is also used for faculty social gatherings. (See Figure 3.)

Figure 3. Conference Room for (a) Informal Gatherings and (b) Formal Meetings

A mobile presentation cart (data/video projector, laptop docking station, VHS player, and speaker) and a portable projection screen are frequently used. Workshops or training for groups larger than eight use this space; laptops from the training lab or elsewhere are easily deployed. (See Table 1 on the Web.)

The training lab, which mimics our standard smart classroom, features a SMART Board with wall-mounted speakers installed on either side; a ceiling-mounted data/video projector; an instructor's podium with laptop docking station, VHS player, and network, Internet, and cable TV connectivity; a wireless mouse and keyboard; and a networked printer. (See Figure 4.) A small conference table is hardwired for network/Internet connectivity and AC power for eight laptops. Laptops are stored securely and continuously recharged, enclosed in a glass and steel cabinet. Peripheral equipment (power cables, network cables, mice, a variety of storage media, digital and video camera equipment, and an Elmo presentation device) are shelved nearby. (See Table 2 on the Web.)

Figure 4. Faculty Training Lab

Faculty have unlimited access to the adjacent project lab through an ID card security system. The project lab features a high-end computer, a variety of software (Adobe Photoshop, InDesign, ImageReady, Illustrator, GoLive; Macromedia Flash, Freehand, Fireworks; QuickTime Pro), a flat-panel display, and peripherals not often available in faculty offices (for example, a document/object camera, flatbed scanner, and color networked printer). (See Table 3 on the Web.)

What Makes the Space Successful?

Upon entering the CTL for the first time, faculty express pleasant surprise at the welcoming environment. A warm color palette, rich woodwork, nicely appointed furnishings (including a gas fireplace in the conference room), and tastefully selected patterns and textures enrich the space. Student and alumni artwork, professionally matted and framed, adorn each room.

Each room within the space serves multiple purposes. The conference room is used by faculty and administrative staff for a variety of meetings, and the training and project labs routinely double as small meeting rooms or breakout rooms during workshops. The kitchen simplifies the ability to serve food—anything from coffee and cookies to catered dinners.

Faculty feel valued in this space, and they value the resources available to them here. The space is clearly understood by the campus community to be dedicated faculty space. Faculty may access the building and enter the project lab at their convenience. Conference room and training lab space may be reserved for almost any faculty event, with preference for events supported and coordinated by the CTL.

What Principles Were Behind the Design?

Throughout the project, we were cognizant of the faculty preference for small group interactions; face-to-face contact is critical to the culture of teaching and learning at St. Lawrence University. We were also aware of the fairly widespread reluctance to integrate technology, complicated by historical barriers in faculty-IT working relationships. The CTL was designed to bridge the gap between IT and academic affairs, a neutral space used to reset institutional memory.

At the outset, the educational technologies unit established a low faculty-to-trainer ratio (maximum 10:1, ideally 6:1) and designed technology training spaces that would hold us accountable to that standard. A long, narrow room was divided into two small spaces with distinctly different purposes. One-half became the training lab, the primary space where small groups of faculty meet with IT staff. We purchased comfortable office-style chairs on casters and well-proportioned tables and equipped the space with technology to mimic the typical smart classroom experience. The other half became the project lab, a space where faculty meet one-on-one with IT staff, work independently, or collaborate with colleagues while accessing a range of technology. Tables and chairs are easily repurposed or repositioned throughout the facility, allowing flexible combinations and multifunctional capabilities.

What Is Unique or Noteworthy?

Many projects are launched with a "build it and they will come" philosophy, designing space to meet anticipated needs. The CTL is unique in that CTL programming preceded CTL space. Faculty were consulted broadly via focus groups about the vision of the center, and programming evolved before space allocations or renovations occurred.

Another unique feature is the interdisciplinary nature of the space. The CTL is the only space on campus truly dedicated to the faculty, and the only space where faculty from the full range of academic disciplines routinely interact, engaging colleagues in pursuit of excellence in teaching.

A third unique feature of the space is unhindered access to professional educational technologies staff. Small group workshops and one-on-one interactions during liaison hours have helped change the nature of faculty-IT working relationships. Historical barriers have disintegrated as faculty have found instructional technologists ready, willing, and available to help.

Also noteworthy is the manner in which the mission of the CTL aligns with university goals: "The university is committed to the goal of fostering excellent teaching in its faculty and to assisting its members to realize their full potential as teachers."[1] CTL programming is highly collaborative and not perceived as remedial. All workshops reflect the landscape of higher education and the local culture. Faculty attend CTL events at any stage in their teaching career at their own discretion, as they pursue teaching excellence.

Endnote

1. *St. Lawrence University Faculty Handbook* (revised August 2005), p. 9, <http://www.stlawu.edu/acadaffairs/handbookrevisedaug2005.pdf>.

About the Authors

Sondra Smith is the director of educational technologies and co-CIO for information technology and **Kim Mooney** is the director of the Center for Teaching and Learning and an associate professor of psychology at St. Lawrence University.

CHAPTER 35

GroupSpaces
Stanford University

Richard Holeton

What Is It?

Stanford University (http://www.stanford.edu/) is located on the San Francisco peninsula midway between San Francisco and San Jose on 8,200 acres. It is a private research institution serving about 6,500 undergraduates and 8,000 graduate students. Nearly all undergraduates and a majority of graduate students live on campus.

GroupSpace (http://groupspace.stanford.edu/) is the name for several group collaboration spaces deployed at Stanford. The physical spaces consist of one or more large computer displays, custom furnishings, and nearby whiteboards for two to six people doing group work. Installed on a host server(s) in each location is TeamSpot collaboration software from Tidebreak, Inc. (http://www.tidebreak.com/). TeamSpot facilitates team work for walk-up laptop users by allowing them to alternate or share control of the large display(s), share files or copy and paste text and images among the connected users, annotate the shared display screen, and record a log of session activities.

Stanford currently has three public GroupSpace installations:

▶ **Meyer Library GroupSpace:** Located in the 24-hour lobby of Meyer Library, a computer-enhanced study and teaching facility in the heart of campus, Meyer GroupSpace seats up to six at angled "teardrop" tables. (See Figure 1.) It is adjacent to other study spaces, kiosks, and computer stations. The GroupSpace is defined by banners and a 6 x 10-foot rolling whiteboard.

▶ **Toyon Hall GroupSpace:** This GroupSpace is located in a dedicated group study and multimedia room in Toyon Hall, an all-sophomore undergraduate residence for 200 students. The GroupSpace is available 24 hours for Toyon residents and their guests. Seating handles up to three at a custom-designed quarter-round table. (See Figure 2.) The group study room is also equipped with an analog-digital conversion station, LCD projector for presentation rehearsal, and soft seating with tablet arms.

Figure 1. GroupSpace at Meyer Library

Figure 2. GroupSpace at Toyon Hall

▶ **Freshman-Sophomore College (FroSoCo) GroupSpace:** The third GroupSpace location is in the residence computer cluster of FroSoCo, home of 185 freshmen and sophomores interested in broad intellectual exploration of the liberal arts and sciences. The space is available 24 hours for FroSoCo residents and their guests. Seating for up to three is available in the same configuration as the Toyon GroupSpace. It is integrated into the existing computer cluster, which is equipped with eight PCs and Macs, a laser printer, a scanner, and whiteboards.

What Happens Here?

Laptop users can work together using the following capabilities of the TeamSpot software:

▶ **Control the shared display:** Users can take turns or share control of the large public display(s). They scroll their mouse pointer off the top of their laptop screen into the shared display, where they can control the host machine like any other computer.

▶ **Share files or Web pages:** Users drag selected files or URLs to the Cross-Warp icon and drop them onto the name(s) that appear in a drop-down menu. They can choose to share with one or all, including the host computer driving the shared display.

▶ **Copy and paste to the shared display:** Users can copy and paste text or images from within an application onto the shared display.

▶ **Annotate work in the shared display space:** Users can mark up the public display, whiteboard-style, using colored electronic "pens" (the annotated screen is not yet savable and exportable as a file).

▶ **Track session work:** Users can capture and view logs of collaboration session activities, such as CrossWarped files and URLs, and add comments to the log. Examples of using these functions include:

▶ **Academic coursework:** Students use the GroupSpaces for collaborative research using online and library resources. They can also compose and rehearse group PowerPoint presentations for courses across the curriculum. Other activities facilitated by GroupSpaces are study groups and section meetings for large undergraduate introductory courses (for example, chemistry or human biology), collaborative editing and peer review for writing courses, team computer programming, or team design projects (for example, for mechanical engineering).

▶ **Academic support and tutoring:** Small group tutorials with teaching assistants or peers are facilitated in GroupSpaces.

▶ **Residential education:** Small groups of residential staff and/or residents working on community-building projects such as dorm Web sites, social or educational events, videos, or slideshows use GroupSpaces.

▶ **Student organization projects:** Stanford has more than 500 registered student organizations, which increasingly need to produce collaborative multimedia projects such as videos and Web sites.

- **Casual student use:** Multiplayer gaming or simply watching videos or other entertainment in small groups happens in GroupSpaces. These activities have lower priority than academic tasks.

How Is Technology Used?

GroupSpaces take advantage of large displays, servers, client and logging software, and wireless capability to support users.

Large shared displays: The Meyer GroupSpace uses two 42-inch plasma displays, and the two residential GroupSpaces each use a single 23-inch LCD display, mounted on steel standards.

Host server computers: A host machine (we use both Dell towers and Apple Mac minis) drives each display, delivers the client application to users, and manages user information and interaction. The server application provides configuration and service options and downloadable configuration profiles. Only physically present users can connect for a session ("room-based authentication"), though remote users may be supported in the future. Socket-layer encryption protects cross machine communication over the network. Our host machines provide the same robust suite of productivity and courseware applications that we deliver in our public and residential computer clusters, making these applications available for users in the TeamSpot shared work space.

Client computers: Walk-up laptop users (PCs or Macs) download the TeamSpot client the first time they use any GroupSpace. With the client, they can start working together by just clicking a few buttons. (See Figure 3.)

Logging software: A beta application uses XML templates to capture "events" (actions) in every TeamSpot session. These event logs provide data about how student groups use the TeamSpot software. We have configured the application to protect user privacy; a privacy policy is under development as part of the GroupSpace project.

Wireless networks: Users connect in each GroupSpace and to one another via wireless or cabled (CAT5) networking.

What Makes the Space Successful?

Initial user studies[1] conducted in the Meyer GroupSpace found that:
- Students quickly adapted to the metaphor of shared versus personal workspace.

Figure 3. The TeamSpot Client

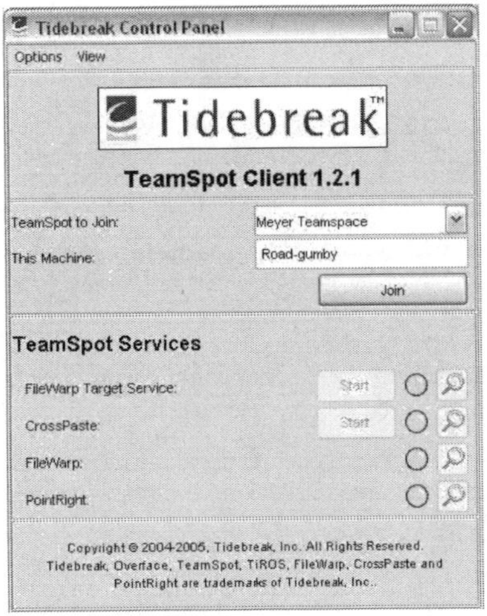

▶ Groups that were already acquainted and had a real-world project to work on developed social protocols to work effectively in the space more quickly than groups given an experimental task by the researchers.

▶ Most students found the software helpful in facilitating their collaboration. Evaluations under way in 2006 are exploring:

▶ What students use GroupSpaces and the TeamSpot software for (including analysis of logging data).

▶ The efficacy of multimedia demos for educating users about the usefulness of TeamSpot for specific academic projects (for example, group PowerPoint presentations or collaborative writing).

▶ Self-reported learning outcomes.

▶ Differences in usage and learning outcomes between public and residential deployments.

What Principles Were Behind the Design?

The GroupSpace design aligned with perceived learning needs, Nct Generation needs, and university academic needs. Learning and social cognition research, for example, suggests that opportunities for social and collaborative work enhance learning. Moreover, today's Net Gen students have a bias for working collaboratively and for social uses of technology. Finally, a new university writing requirement includes a course that focuses on the written, oral, and multimedia presentation of research and that assigns group projects—emblematic of a trend across the curriculum. GroupSpaces support all these needs.

The three GroupSpaces all have different physical designs, exist in different social contexts (public and residential), and take different approaches to managing "noisy" group work near adjacent "quiet" individual study areas, according to the design team's evaluation of the preferences for users in each context. All of the spaces offer TeamSpot software, which works across platforms and requires near-zero administration. TeamSpot, which evolved from the TeamSpace open source software project,[2] aims to keep barriers low for users and to be as intuitive and low-maintenance as possible.

What Is Unique or Noteworthy?

Two factors stand out in GroupSpaces at Stanford: the spaces fill institutional gaps, and they demonstrate the results of human-computer interface (HCI) research combined with advances in classroom technology.

Filling institutional gaps: Specifically oriented to group learning, GroupSpaces integrate an installed collaboration software technology with physical spaces designed for teams. Except in a very few high-tech classrooms, students have lacked access to such environments. Residential GroupSpaces, in addition to supporting the academic mission, also facilitate community-building and social uses of technology for today's Net Gen students.

Rolling out classroom technology and HCI research: The software behind TeamSpot began in the computer science research labs of Stanford University's Interactive Workspaces Project (see <http://iwork.stanford.edu/> and Figure 4) and evolved into, first, the production "iSpace" technology in the classrooms of Wallenberg Hall (see chapter 36 and <http://wallenberg.stanford .edu/>); second, TeamSpace, an open source, lightweight client-server application scalable for large public deployments; and third, the commercial TeamSpot product—a model of knowledge transfer within and beyond the institution.

Figure 4. Standford Interactive Workspaces Project

Endnotes

1. Clara C. Shih et al., "Teamspace: A Simple, Low-Cost, and Self-Sufficient Workspace for Small-Group Collaborative Computing," CSCW 2004 Interactive Poster, Chicago, Ill., November 2004, <http://hci.stanford.edu/research/teamspace_CSCW.pdf>.
2. See the research papers available at <http://iwork.stanford.edu/>.

About of the Author

Richard Holeton is senior strategist for student computing and associate director of academic computing, part of Stanford University Libraries and Academic Information Resources at Stanford University.

CHAPTER 36

Wallenberg Hall
Stanford University

Dan Gilbert

What Is It?

Wallenberg Hall (http://wallenberg.stanford.edu/) opened in 2002 to showcase Stanford University's commitment to advancing learning. Originally completed in 1900, the interior was completely redeveloped with a generous $15 million grant from the Knut and Alice Wallenberg and Marcus and Marianne Wallenberg Foundations in Sweden. (See Figure 1.)

Figure 1. Student Breakout Group Outside Wallenberg Hall

Five advanced resource classrooms occupy the first floor of Wallenberg Hall: four classrooms that can host up to 25 students and the Peter Wallenberg Learning Theater, which handles classes up to 50 students and small performances. (For details, see <http://wallenberg.stanford.edu/classresources/details.html>). These spaces can be used individually or in combination to support a myriad of learning activities. All the classrooms contain multiple display screens, laptops,

©2006 Dan Gilbert

wireless networks, flexible furniture, and multiple writing surfaces to support a wide range of learning activities. (For more on classroom technologies, see <http://wallenberg.stanford.edu/classresources/technologies.html>). The first floor also contains unscheduled breakout spaces designed to support small group work with booth seating, whiteboards, and wireless Internet access (http://wallenberg.stanford.edu/classresources/rooms/breakout.html). The building's third floor hosts 15 centrally scheduled classrooms, each with a ceiling-mounted projector, a DVD/VHS player, and speakers.

Stanford University (http://www.stanford.edu/) is located on the San Francisco peninsula midway between San Francisco and San Jose, California, on 8,200 acres. It is a private research institution serving about 6,500 undergraduate and 8,000 graduate students. Nearly all undergraduates and about 60 percent of graduate students live on campus.

What Happens Here?

Wallenberg Hall hosts regular class sessions, meetings, lectures, conferences, student gatherings, expositions, and other special events, along with four research organizations.

Classes: More than 20 departments, from history to environmental engineering to the School of Medicine, have sponsored undergraduate and graduate courses in Wallenberg Hall. Professors and instructors who use Wallenberg Hall commit to teaching their lectures, seminars, project-based classes, and arts classes with at least one pedagogical innovation. In general, the innovations fall into three categories:

▶ *Expanding the social world of the classroom:* Videoconferencing over high-speed data networks opens up the classroom to outside participants, including students and experts located elsewhere (http://wallenberg.stanford.edu/teachresources/examples/videoconf2.html). See Figure 2.

▶ *Supporting segmented and distributed work:* Modularizing key classroom technologies, from furniture to computing resources, supports flexible organizing of classroom interactions and attention into small or large groups (http://wallenberg.stanford.edu/teachresources/examples/transitions.html).

▶ *Enabling complex information retrieval, display, and inscription:* A suite of technologies, including large-scale displays and electronic whiteboards, enables rich and flexible display and capture of information (http://wallenberg.stanford.edu/teachresources/examples/webster.html).

Figure 2. Sharing Field Experience Through Videoconferencing

Meetings and student gatherings: Throughout the year, Wallenberg Hall hosts events ranging from PhD defenses to research meetings held via videoconference. Planning sessions from university and industry groups also are held in Wallenberg Hall.

Lectures, conferences, expositions, and other special events: Wallenberg Hall hosts the Stanford Center for Innovations in Learning's lecture series Future of Learning (http://scil.stanford.edu/events/index.html). The series is designed to inform members of the Stanford community and local citizens about developments of critical importance in education today.

Research: Wallenberg Hall is home to four research organizations that have sponsored a broad variety of interactive media research projects such as:

▶ The Stanford Center for Innovations in Learning (SCIL): <http://scil.stanford.edu/>
▶ Stanford Humanities Lab: <http://shl.stanford.edu/>
▶ Media X: <http://mediax.stanford.edu/>
▶ Wallenberg Global Learning Network (WGLN): <http://www.wgln.org/>

How Is Technology Used?

The entire facility is supported with wireless high-speed Internet access. In addition to the examples listed above in "What Happens Here," the Wallenberg Hall Web site lists multiple case studies of innovative uses of classroom technologies (http://wallenberg.stanford.edu/teachresources/experiences_summary.html).

Multiple large-screen displays: Instructors and students use multiple screens to compare and add context to their work (see a case study at <http://wallenberg.stanford.edu/teachresources/examples/multimedia.html>).

CopyCams: Teams use CopyCams to capture work done on whiteboards to document their processes as well as to continue work outside class (see a case study at <http://wallenberg.stanford.edu/teachresources/examples/copycams.html>).

Laptops with iSpace collaborative software: Students use experimental software to share Web sites and files from their personal laptops with the entire class. Students also author documents and media in small groups on collaboration stations.

What Makes the Space Successful?

Three characteristics contribute to Wallenberg Hall's success:

▶ Network convergence
▶ Changing instructor roles
▶ Multiple roles for academic technology staff

Convergence of networks on campus, in Silicon Valley, and campuses globally: Wallenberg Hall is in the geographic center of Stanford's campus, and Palo Alto is in the heart of Silicon Valley. This location provides many critical opportunities for interactions among people who ordinarily wouldn't cross paths, resulting in a loose network that supports innovative practice beyond the classroom.

Changing roles of instructors and students: Teaching in Wallenberg Hall forces instructors to think creatively about their pedagogies. In Wallenberg Hall's highly instrumented spaces that support collaboration and interactive technologies, instructors often act as a "guide by the side" instead of a "sage on the stage." (See Figure 3.)

Academic technology staff play multiple roles: The staff that runs the first floor of Wallenberg Hall have a broad skill set to support the design, execution, and evaluation of innovative learning activities. The academic technology specialists (ATSs) who work in Wallenberg Hall and across campus have training in both pedagogical theory and advanced technology. The ATS team helps bridge the gap between faculty's wishes and needs and the technology team's ability to deliver resources.

Figure 3. Configuring Furniture for Teamwork

What Principles Were Behind the Design?

Interactivity, flexibility, collaboration, and acquisition of resources to support reflection contributed to the design of Wallenberg Hall.

Learning first: At every chance, the design team tied learning goals and practices into the design of the spaces themselves. By developing scenarios with instructors that focused on what they and their students would actually do in class, the design team could choose technologies that created new opportunities for instructors.

Flexible spaces to encourage innovation: These learning spaces contain mobile furniture, laptop computers, and portable whiteboards to facilitate multiple learning activities. (See Figure 4.) Additionally, the building has a minimum of load-bearing walls to support future redesigns of the entire floor.

Support for collaborative work practices: Webster digital whiteboards, Huddleboards, flexible furniture, breakout spaces, and experimental software work together to support collaboration in the Wallenberg Hall spaces. The classrooms also include collaboration tools to support remote guest speakers and work practices among distributed teams.

Facilitate capture for archive and reflection: Video cameras and microphones, Webster interactive screens, CopyCams, and easily accessible USB ports are all designed to capture interactions in class for future review by students and instructors.

Figure 4. Folding Tables, Stools, and Mobile Chairs in the Classroom

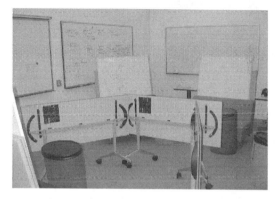

What Is Unique or Noteworthy?

Wallenberg Hall hosts courses that tie research together with learning. Lessons learned there about prototyping tools and effective practices benefit the rest of campus

Research into learning: Wallenberg Hall was designed as a loop that connects scholarly research in learning with the practice of instruction. Experiments and prototypes are developed in the fourth floor's research labs, then tested in the first floor's spaces. The best innovations can be put into practice in the general-purpose classrooms on the third floor and throughout campus.

Prototyping tools and practices: Campus groups ranging from residential computing to language centers to research spaces have used the lessons learned from Wallenberg Hall to guide the design of their own spaces. Stanford's Residential Computing, Academic Computing, and other departments have worked with the SCIL team to design other learning spaces on campus that take advantage of the knowledge generated in Wallenberg Hall.

About the Author

Dan Gilbert is an academic technology specialist at Stanford University, working with faculty and instructors to design, carry out, and evaluate learning activities in the experimental spaces of Stanford's Wallenberg Hall.

CHAPTER 37

Manuel Pacheco Integrated Learning Center
The University of Arizona

Christopher Johnson

What Is It?

The University of Arizona (http://www.arizona.edu/) in Tucson, Arizona, serves 28,000 undergraduate and 9,000 graduate students. It is a public land-grant Research I institution that boasts a heritage as Arizona's first university with leadership in a variety of research areas.

The Manuel Pacheco Integrated Learning Center (ILC) serves as a home to first-year students at the University of Arizona. The 118,000-square-foot facility houses 14 classrooms, a 300-computer information commons, and a variety of other spaces. The ILC is designed to provide first-year students with state-of-the-art instructional materials, academic advising and student support services, and access to information resources. When not providing these services to first-year students, the ILC is used by a broad spectrum of classes on campus.

The ILC provides students and faculty with the following services:

▶ Technology-rich classrooms
▶ Study, meeting, and social spaces
▶ Wireless networking
▶ Midlevel computing for course assignments and high-end computing for multimedia development
▶ A variety of information resources such as reference tools, tutorials, guides, and course-related materials (http://www.library.arizona.edu/help/tutorials/index .html) and a variety of digital exhibits (http://www.library.arizona.edu/exhibits/).
▶ In-depth one-on-one multimedia development support
▶ Technical and instructional support services
▶ Academic advising and exploration of majors for undecided students, and tutoring specifically focused on lower-division math/science courses

Classrooms: Each of the 14 classrooms is equipped with technology and projection systems with wired and wireless access for faculty and student laptops. For more information on the four lecture halls (one holding 300 students and three accommodating 150 students), four midsize classrooms (60 students), and six small classrooms (30 students), see <http://www.ilc.arizona.edu>.

OSCR Underground: The Office of Student Computing Resources' main help desk, known as OSCR Underground, provides on-site assistance for student owned hardware and software (http://www.oscr.arizona.edu/underground).

Information commons: The information commons (http://www.library .arizona.edu/ic/) provides access to desktop computing and a variety of library resources. (See Figure 1.)

Figure 1. Information Commons

Multimedia Zone: The Multimedia Zone, another OSCR support location for students, provides high-end computing for multimedia projects.

University College: University College (http://www.universitycollege .arizona.edu/) is one of the university's 15 degree-granting undergraduate colleges. It is housed in the ILC and provides academic advising, tutoring, and other support for new students, especially transitional, interdisciplinary, and/or exploratory students.

Courtyard: The courtyard serves as a meeting place and is often used by faculty for outdoor class activities. (See Figure 2.)

Figure 2. Courtyard

What Happens Here?

The lecture halls and classrooms support instructional activities for a variety of courses. The building primarily supports courses in the university's general education program. When not used by these courses, graduate and upper division courses also use the facility. (See Figure 3.)

Figure 3. Lecture Hall

The ILC provides access to a 300-student responder system, which can be divided into smaller groupings. In addition, networked laptop computers allow students to respond and interact during classes. A 150-student lecture hall equipped with video capture allows classes taught in this room to be digitized and logged to create a searchable transcript and streamed via the Web (http://www.svl.arizona.edu/).

The information commons provides access to a variety of different information tools from the university's library system (reference material, digital exhibits, tutorials, and so on). It also provides hardware and software to create digital materials to support class work. The information commons is open 24 hours a day, five days a week, with reduced hours on weekends. Group study rooms placed around the periphery of the commons are available for students to use for individual or group study. The commons purposely provides two chairs for every desktop computer to promote group work. These chairs move throughout the commons as students come together to work on projects. In addition, the courtyard is used for a variety of formal and informal gatherings; students congregate in a number of areas.

How Is Technology Used?

The ILC features wireless high-speed Internet access throughout. It also provides access to a 300-student radio frequency responder system that can be configured for use in the large lecture hall (300 students), the smaller lecture halls (150 students in two halls at a time), or three simultaneous uses in smaller numbers.

The Office of Student Computing Resources supports more than 100 laptop computers. Forty-five of these systems are permanently placed in one of the midsize classrooms; the rest are delivered to classrooms in laptop carts. In addition, each classroom has a teaching station that provides access to a desktop computer and connection for a laptop. The stations have a separate touch panel to control computer and video input, audio, and lighting. Each station has a visual presenter (electronic overhead), VCR, and DVD player. The desktop computer is equipped with a screen that doubles as an electronic whiteboard. OSCR also provides high-end multimedia workstations for students in the Multimedia Zone.

What Makes the Space Successful?

Four factors contribute the success of the ILC: a collaborative design process, shared oversight of the facility, technology and instructional support, and ongoing assessment.

Collaborative design: The initial design process solicited input from a broad spectrum of users. The design team consulted faculty and students along with experts in teaching and learning, technology-enhanced instruction, information sciences, networking, and facilities design to develop a set of guidelines for the facilities. These guidelines were then communicated to the architect who, in the words of many on the design team, "got it" in terms of the mission of the facility. These guidelines have been used to monitor the progress of the different types of activities that occur in the building.

Shared oversight: The ILC is not associated with an academic college or unit, as is common with other facilities on campus. A management team of representatives from instruction, computing, academic advising/tutoring, and the university library governs the activities in the building. This team communicates regularly with the vice provost for academic affairs, CIO, and dean of the libraries to ensure that the activities in the ILC mesh with other instructional activities.

Technology and instructional support: Members of the management team are responsible for equipment services and OSCR Underground. Personnel from each unit are housed in the ILC, providing immediate access to technical and instructional support.

Assessment: The management team conducts annual surveys to determine if current resources meet the users' instructional needs. This data allows the management team to adjust services and direct resources to maintain and update the infrastructure.

What Principles Were Behind the Design?

Four principles went into the design: agility, multifunctional use of the spaces, transparency, and seamless access. The systems in the ILC can be easily reconfigured based on data collected from student and faculty surveys, and the different spaces in the ILC support individual, group, and class work in quiet and semi-quiet environments. The technology resources are designed to allow faculty to experiment and implement a variety of different instructional strategies.

The design committee, working with the architect, decided that the ILC should provide a level of transparency to permit users of the information commons and courtyard to see what goes on in these spaces. In addition, access to the Internet, library, and other campus resources is designed to be as seamless as possible.

What Is Unique or Noteworthy?

The design committee collected input from a variety of campus constituents, architects, and space planners during the design process, and the management team continues to solicit this input through online surveys and a variety of other data collection techniques. The design team chose to locate the ILC completely underground, allowing the facility to be in the center of campus without violating the sacrosanct space of the mall and Old Main, the original campus building. The instructional facilities link to the university library through the information commons. (See links to the courtyard and the mall at <http://www.ilc.arizona.edu/>.)

The ILC provides first-year students with a single location for important support services as well as a rich instructional environment. This assists the campus in meeting a prime university goal of increasing student retention by providing the best resources possible to first-year students. The general education courses supported by the ILC are multidisciplinary in nature and provide students with a broad foundation of courses in English, math, foreign languages, natural sciences, individuals and societies, and traditions and cultures. Faculty in general education courses are encouraged to collaborate with instructors of other courses. The ILC provides locations where faculty can meet.

While all instructional spaces on campus are controlled through central scheduling, many academic units feel a sense of ownership of the rooms within their buildings. Since the ILC does not "belong" to any academic unit, it can serve as a university wide resource. Management of the ILC by the management team provides a broad perspective in its use and maintenance.

About the Author

Christopher Johnson is a consultant and an adjunct assistant professor at the University of Arizona South.

CHAPTER 38

The Irving K. Barber Learning Centre

University of British Columbia

Simon Neame and Cyprien Lomas

What Is It?

The Irving "Ike" K. Barber Learning Centre (http://www.ikebarberlearningcentre
.ubc.ca/) is the newest addition to the University of British Columbia Library system. Located at UBC's Vancouver campus, the Learning Centre provides access to library facilities, learning resources, services, and innovative teaching spaces. Among the services the Learning Centre provides are:

▶ Access to print and digital research collections
▶ Study, meeting, and social spaces
▶ Access to programs that promote knowledge and innovation for students, faculty, staff, and the general public
▶ Space for future growth and preservation of collections in an environmentally controlled environment

The Learning Centre is not only a focal point of education for students and faculty at UBC but also supports lifelong learning by people throughout British Columbia by providing virtual access to the rich collections and resources of the library and university, using technology to connect British Columbia's geographically diverse population.

The Irving K. Barber Learning Centre was designed to provide a variety of learning and study spaces that support new approaches to accessing print and digital resources. The physical facility is a blend of 40,000 square feet of refurbished space and 200,000 square feet of new construction. (See Figure 1.) A 3D walkthrough of the Learning Centre is available at <http://www
.ikebarberlearningcentre.ubc.ca/view1.html>.

©2006 Simon Neame and Cyprien Lomas

Figure 1. Ike Barber Learning Centre

UBC (http://www.ubc.ca/) is a public research institution located in Vancouver, British Columbia, that serves 30,000 undergraduate and 20,000 graduate students. UBC has a long history of excellence in teaching and is continually experimenting with new teaching methodologies and technologies.

What Happens Here?

The Learning Centre includes a lecture hall, classrooms, and seminar rooms designed to encourage and support innovative teaching and learning activities. A variety of unique spaces provides venues for events such as lectures, concerts, and symposia. Videoconferencing capabilities allow users to connect with others around the globe, including those at UBC's other campuses, such as UBC Okanagan. Web-based and on-site displays and exhibitions make rare books and special materials available to visitors.

A café and informal seating areas encourage students and others to use the Learning Centre as a place for informal gatherings and small group work, as well as a place to study in a relaxed atmosphere. (See Figures 2 and 3.) More formal study spaces are also available. (See Figures 4 and 5.)

Figure 2. Comfortable, Portable Furniture

Figure 3. Rolling Furniture for Easy Reconfiguration

The heart of the Learning Centre's facility is the Chapman Learning Commons, a space that combines academic resources, technology, and expert assistance within a space that offers seating for individual and group study. The learning commons is also home to various special-purpose rooms, including the Dodson Room, where events such as concerts and lectures are hosted.

Figure 4. Study Room

Figure 5. Study Nook

A multimedia room provides innovative space in the Learning Centre that allows students, faculty, and staff to work on multimedia projects, develop presentations, and collaborate on group projects that require shared technologies.

How Is Technology Used?

The entire facility is supported with wireless high-speed Internet access. In addition, videoconferencing capabilities allow users to connect with others around the globe using H.323.

The Learning Centre is home to a number of digitization projects with a focus on British Columbia history. These projects help showcase the wealth of historical materials in the UBC Library collection and allow people from around the province and beyond to learn more about British Columbia's rich history. The Learning Centre's Webcast program provides free online access to events such as lectures, seminars, and concerts, all of which are archived on the Learning Centre's Web site. The Learning Centre is also working with a number of professional groups to provide online information services to members located throughout the province.

The automated storage and retrieval system (ASRS) provides high-density, climate-controlled storage for up to 1.8 million items from the UBC Library and other BC library collections. The first of its kind in Canada, the ASRS uses industrial technology to store and retrieve rare and low-use materials. The robotic cranes store and retrieve items in the ASRS and respond to user requests for materials initiated through the library's online catalogue.

What Makes the Space Successful?

To create traditional quiet study spaces, flexible learning spaces, and storage for an extensive collection, the university adopted an open model with flexible and modular furnishings. These furnishings are playful yet at the same time help to create a new space that also honors the tradition of previous spaces such as the Ridington Reading Room, named after the first university librarian. (See Figure 6.) Lessons learned from the learning commons housed in the previous main library building greatly influenced the design process of the Learning Centre, especially with the goals of blending technology with learning resources and staff assistance.

The existing patrons and staff were consulted extensively to help create the design principles. Those most familiar with the library and its activities were surveyed to identify the needs in the existing commons and library. Student workers identified common problems of the existing space and offered suggestions on how to resolve them, such as areas to support collaborative study, quiet, and semi-quiet activities.

Figure 6. The Ridington Reading Room

The space can be considered successful in that it appears to satisfy the needs and desires of the previous space inhabitants. The space supports transparency and easy movement between different areas of the Learning Centre. Ongoing focus groups are being conducted to determine how to meet the needs of the extended community that will use the space in the future.

What Principles Were Behind the Design?

The architects and design committee decided that the Learning Centre should provide a level of transparency to permit those outside the building to observe what goes on inside the library. Inside, the study spaces were conceived to support many different types of quiet, semi-quiet, individual, and small group interactions. Access to resources including the Internet and library collections was designed to be as seamless as possible. Multiple modes of activity as well as the rapid and unobtrusive transition from one functional area to another were primary requirements. The Learning Centre achieves this balance of different requirements by introducing transition zones where patrons can quickly and easily move from one region to another. (See Figure 7.)

To properly fulfill its role within the community, the Learning Centre must serve a diverse set of constituents whose needs may change depending on the task. The ability to act as a meeting place, study space, or social place required a high degree of flexibility. Different zones within the Learning Centre were set up as

Figure 7. Transition Zone

flexible or less flexible spaces to encourage movement to the space appropriate for the desired activity. (See the floor plans at <http://www.ikebarberlearningcentre.ubc.ca/images/concourse.jpg>.)

What Is Unique or Noteworthy?

The designers of this space went to great lengths to reconcile traditional library spaces and the activities supported with the changing nature of modern collections and information services. (See Figure 8.) Great effort went into encouraging

Figure 8. The Ridington Reading Room

and collecting the input from existing, past, and potential users. Rethinking the library and the research services offered in the face of the increasing importance of digital resources was important. The design committee had the difficult task of merging the feedback collected in informal evaluations and comments from those that used the space with new requirements.

The space embodies several of the goals of the university, including an ongoing commitment to research and student exposure to primary research, including offering students the best resources available. The importance of multidisciplinary studies is emphasized through the prominence of multiple transition zones built throughout the library and the inclusion of a diverse set of academic programs including Arts One, Science One, and the School of Library, Archival, and Information Studies. Also, the Fine Arts and Science and Engineering Libraries have collections and service points in the building.

About the Authors

Simon Neame is coordinator of programs and services for the Irving K. Barber Learning Centre, and **Cyprien Lomas** is an ELI scholar in residence and director of the Learning Centre in the Faculty of Land and Food Systems at the University of British Columbia.

CHAPTER 39

Collaboration and Multimedia Classrooms
University of Central Florida

Ruth Marshall

What Is It?

Multimedia classrooms (http://www.oir.ucf.edu/MultimediaClassrooms.asp) at the University of Central Florida (UCF) (http://www.ucf.edu/) are technology-rich learning spaces designed to promote the innovative use of learning resources in teaching and learning. Our greatest strength is not the technology system but the creative faculty and staff who designed the systems and guide and train UCF faculty to use the technologies and learning environments in innovative ways.

The faculty and staff of the UCF Karen L. Smith Faculty Center for Teaching and Learning (FCTL) are using five of the multimedia classrooms to encourage faculty adoption of interactive pedagogical practices to create rich learning environments. (See Figure 1.) Students in the collaboration classrooms are

Figure 1. Multimedia Classroom for Interactive Pedagogy

©2006 Ruth Marshall

assigned in-class problem-solving activities so that the faculty can assess their learning progress early enough in the semester to allow for adjustments to meet students' learning needs.

Multimedia and collaboration classrooms are managed through a partnership between the Office of Instructional Resources (OIR) (http://www.oir.ucf.edu/), which is part of the Information Technologies and Resources Division (http://www.itu.ucf.edu/), and the FCTL, which is part of the Division of Undergraduate Studies. Both units are part of the Division of Academic Affairs

The collaboration classrooms provide faculty with a full set of resources that are available in standard multimedia classrooms, as well as student work areas where students work together in teams. (See Figure 2.) Technologies in the collaboration classrooms also include classroom response systems, wired and wireless computers, and software to view the outcome of student learning activities on the centralized multimedia classroom system. Because of the configuration of the workspace, the students can very quickly switch from listening mode to collaboration mode to individual activity.

Figure 2. Student Team Work Areas

The FCTL has 13 personnel who provide room support, training, and administrative assistance for the faculty who use the five collaboration classrooms OIR has 32 personnel involved in various classroom support activities for the 240 technology-rich classrooms on a campus of 45,000 students and 1,500

full-time and part-time faculty. The FCTL and OIR directors are advised by representatives from the faculty senate and faculty members from each of nine colleges who are actively involved in their units' activities and services.

The University of Central Florida began offering classes in the fall of 1968 and now has the seventh largest enrollment of any university in the United States. The university provides 92 baccalaureate programs, 94 master's programs, three specialist programs, and 25 doctoral programs. UCF receives more than $100 million in research funds annually and just received authorization to create a new school of medicine. Facilities are currently located at the main campus in Orlando, the Florida Solar Energy Center in Cocoa, and 12 regional campus locations. Multimedia classroom systems are used to support instruction at all of these locations. Integrated multimedia systems are in place in nearly 100 percent of all UCF classrooms. (See Figure 3.)

Figure 3. Integrated Multimedia Classroom

What Happens Here?

In addition to providing multimedia classrooms, the university supports faculty through training, continues planning classrooms, and makes space available for faculty work on projects.

Teaching and learning: Technology-rich classrooms at UCF support faculty and student interaction with high-speed data networks and multimedia tools. Faculty have multiple delivery options for communicating with students; instructional systems tools are designed to meet faculty priorities. Well-trained support personnel help faculty use instructional strategies and tools to their best advantage.

Classroom planning and design: Key personnel from IT&R, facilities planning, and physical plant meet regularly to review the status of UCF construction and renovation projects and confirm that all projects meet UCF guidelines (http://www.fp.ucf.edu/guides/design/Division16.htm#telecommunications). IT&R also created the Classroom Improvement Project, which provides $300,000 to $400,000 annually for classroom renovations and system upgrades aligned with the guidelines.

Faculty support: OIR provides training and one-on-one support to faculty for multimedia, digital media, and various video-based technologies in classroom settings. The majority of faculty support is provided by the FCTL. Faculty apply to have their courses held in the collaborative rooms, and the FCTL staff trains them in the effective use of technology in the collaborative environment. Preparation for using these environments includes understanding alternative instructional models that create different roles for faculty and students. Training is offered through a funded, semester-long workshop series and through one-on-one mentoring. Technical staff and FCTL staff are available to support the learning environment as needed.

Faculty Multimedia Center: The Faculty Multimedia Center (FMC) in OIR provides an innovative space where graduate students, faculty, and staff can work on multimedia projects, develop presentations, and collaborate on group projects that require shared technologies. OIR personnel bring II experts and company representatives to the FMC to conduct "shoot outs" of their new products and to allow faculty and staff to consider various academic applications.

How Is Technology Used?

These classrooms provide faculty and students with access to essential visual, oral, graphic, and digital media. Technology includes:

▸ LCD video projectors
▸ Computers with a network connection and VGA connection to the projector
▸ Laptop ports with VGA connection to the projector
▸ VHS and DVD players
▸ Wall-mounted whiteboards and/or electronic whiteboards
▸ Ceiling-mounted overhead document cameras
▸ Electrically operated projection
▸ Audio systems that include microphones, mixers, distribution amplifiers, and speakers

- Lighting control systems
- Console and equipment racks to hold the equipment, PC, DVD and VCR player, laptop port, and extra USB ports
- Crestron touch-panel control systems that let faculty easily switch media between various sources and link to a university-wide Web-based maintenance and security system

Chair layout varies from "case study rooms" with fixed seating, to tablet arm chairs that can be moved or fixed tables and chairs in various configurations with PCs for individual and team-based projects.

For the past two years, the FCTL and OIR have helped faculty evaluate and use wireless radio frequency classroom response systems (CRS). Now that the evaluation is complete, the FCTL provides guidance on CRS applications in large multimedia classroom settings. A standardized model has been selected so that faculty and students can use them reliably from room to room. For example, some faculty are using the CRS system to prepare case studies on student learning for their promotion and tenure portfolios, and they conduct classroom research on various methods of teaching and learning.

Innovative pedagogies in specific disciplines are supported by the FCTL. For example, a language pack is installed so that students studying modern language use the computers in the language that they are learning, enhancing their written and verbal skills.

Classroom research has focused on developing new interventions and new learning outcomes for these environments and their effects on technology literacy, teamwork, and critical thinking. Surveys of students in these classrooms over a two-year period ($n = 1,337$) indicate:

- **Technology literacy:** We discovered that class year makes a difference in student learning. The more advanced the student, the more likely he or she is to report an increase in skills over the course of the semester. Across all levels, however, 53 percent of respondents reported an increase in their technology skills over the course of one semester. Females are more likely to report an increase in skills than males.
- **Teamwork and collaborative learning:** About one-third of respondents reported increased learning due to debates, group presentations, group tests, online discussions, peer evaluations, and team research. Two-thirds reported gains from in-class discussion groups.

▶ **Critical thinking:** Using Bloom's taxonomy of educational objectives[1] to evaluate critical thinking in these classrooms, twice as many respondents reported engagement with the highest outcome level as the lowest (30 percent at the "evaluating" level versus 14 percent at the "knowledge" level). Forty-four percent reported working at the "synthesis" level, with 32 percent at the "comprehension" level.

What Makes the Spaces Successful?

Three major characteristics factor into the multimedia classrooms' success.

Commitment to supporting faculty: UCF is committed to supporting student and faculty success in teaching and learning. The development of reliable, technology-rich, diverse classrooms brings in the outside world. Students can experience real-life situations and develop critical thinking and problem-solving skills that cross disciplines. Faculty are supported in the development of innovative pedagogies that enhance student learning. Faculty innovations in teaching and learning are supported by trained staff and reliable technologies. (See Figure 4.) The integration of the efforts of the OIR and FCTL create a seamless support system for all faculty and students at UCF.

Figure 4. Support for Technology

A rapidly growing university: UCF has developed from a relatively small college of 1,948 students in 1968 to one of the fastest-growing universities in the nation with 45,000 students in 2005. Constant growth has made innovation and creativity essential in the design and development of multimedia and collaboration classrooms. Enrollment growth has been matched by growth in the support of effective teaching and learning practices enabled by technology. (See Figure 5.)

Figure 5. Enabling Technology

Accumulation of evidence: Faculty are using the research that has come from their collaborative classroom case studies to enhance their promotion and tenure portfolios and earn teaching awards. They are also documenting increased student learning outcomes in their student evaluations.

What Principles Were Behind the Design?
UCF President John C. Hitt's goals and strategic plan for the university (http://www .spc.ucf.edu/SPCMission.html) emphasize the importance of providing student and faculty seamless access to resources that facilitate success. The multimedia and collaborative classrooms provide:
▶ Transparency so that all types of learning interactions can occur in the classrooms
▶ A variety of environments that support different learning pedagogies
▶ Flexibility so that environments can adapt to new ideas and technologies
▶ Seamless integration and support of technologies

- Support to ensure that faculty and students can use the environments effectively
- Training to keep the faculty and students current
- Information fluency to give students the lifelong learning skills that they need to be effective in the workforce

What Is Unique or Noteworthy?

The multimedia classroom plan embodies several of the university's strategic goals, from an ongoing commitment to research to student exposure to primary research, including offering students the best resources available. In fall 1996, the faculty senate mandated that all new classrooms be designed with multimedia systems in place. Student learning evaluations show a strong student preference for receiving instruction in multimedia classrooms rather than in classrooms without multimedia technology. The Student Government Association even donated funds to renovate an older classroom with multimedia technology. UCF launched the online initiative and the integrated multimedia classroom system and created the FCTL at the same time. Faculty took the next step by integrating all three resources into teaching and learning.

The diverse classroom environments were developed *by* faculty *for* faculty, based on research into effective learning environments and the technologies that support them. UCF integrates the traditional with the innovative, using technologies that support student and faculty research, teaching, and learning. Faculty experience in online, collaborative, and multimedia classroom delivery are developing into blended modes of teaching and learning. We plan to implement the lessons learned from innovative activities and incorporate more formal methods of assessment with the scholarship of teaching and learning. We will continue to enrich our classroom environments and encourage faculty and students to actively use our collaboration model.

Endnote

1. Benjamin S. Bloom, *Taxonomy of Educational Objectives* (Boston, Mass.: Allyn and Bacon, 1956).

About the Author

Ruth Marshall is the director of the Office of Instructional Resources in the Division of Information Technologies and Resources at the University of Central Florida.

CHAPTER 40

The USITE/Crerar Computing Cluster and Cybercafé
University of Chicago

Shirley Dugdale and Chad Kainz

What Is It?

The USITE/Crerar Computing Cluster and Cybercafé (http://nsit.uchicago.edu/academic/usite/crerar.shtml) is a public computing laboratory within the John Crerar Library at the University of Chicago. The story of its development is a testament to design that goes beyond seats and square feet to a vision based on response to user needs.

USITE, once merely an acronym for the terminal room of the central computer users' site, evolved beyond one space to represent a new kind of technology-enabled learning environment. The team that developed the new USITE model looked beyond the "seat problem" in 1998 and challenged the campus notion of the public computing lab. They asked:

▶ Could a space reflect the University of Chicago's academic practice of small group interaction and collaborative research?

▶ Could several different kinds of academic needs across multiple disciplines be met within one space and its management framework?

▶ Could a lab offer a welcoming, technology-based destination for all members of the campus community, not just students?

The team believed that space and technology should adapt to users, rather than the users adapting to the limitations of space. This led to a concept of space that offered many kinds of user-friendly activity areas, a variety of technology options, and compelling, comfortable, and adaptive settings for collaborative work. The study results were presented in December 1998; construction was approved in June 1999; and USITE/Crerar opened in May 2000. By the end of that month, nearly 1,000 users were visiting the site every day.

The USITE/Crerar concept encompassed seven different spaces (see Figure 1):

▶ A cybercafé with 24-hour to access to Web and e-mail kiosks (since branded as WebStations), tables, and lounge seating
▶ Multipurpose staffed computing space arranged in a variety of individual and group work configurations
▶ A dedicated digital media "wall" of stations for digital video and scanning projects
▶ A semi-enclosed collaborative area that includes data projectors, banquette seating, and seminar tables
▶ A visualization classroom
▶ A videoconferencing facility
▶ A separate consultation area for teaching assistants, faculty, and librarians

Figure 1. Plan Diagram

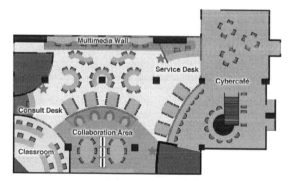

USITE/Crerar has become a model for computer lab and technology-enhanced space design in facilities such as the Cox Computing Center at Emory University (see chapter 8), Arc Technology Center at Washington University in St. Louis, and Christopher Center for Library and Information Resources at Valparaiso University.

What Happens Here?

Students, faculty, and staff use the cybercafé space for studying, conversing, and informal meetings. Windows workstations along one wall transform the area into a 24-hour academic space for students, and a shop at one end sells drinks and snacks. (See Figure 2.)

Figure 2. Cybercafé with Shop and WebStations

Photo: Roberto Marques, University of Chicago

In the general computing area students work independently or in small groups on projects that require access to specialized software and multiple computer platforms. Larger individual work spaces let students spread out materials or work together. Figure 3 shows the main computing space looking toward the consultation/service desk; the media wall is on the right side of the photo. Along the 40-foot media wall, eight MacOS workstations provide the technology foundation for digital video, scanning, and audio projects—whose demands have grown over the past few years.

Figure 3. Main Computing Space with Media Wall

Photo: Roberto Marques, University of Chicago

Dubbed the "boardroom" by students, the glass-enclosed visualization classroom functions both as a quiet lab space and a 10-seat teaching space. (See Figure 4.) The curved tables focus attention on a large screen often used by the visual arts department for digital video production classes. The classroom also serves as a campus videoconferencing facility; it has been used for events ranging from thesis defenses and provost-level meetings to joint course offerings with Northwestern University and a live performance of a Chicago-based blues harmonica player and his guitarist over Internet2 to a class at the University of Wisconsin–Madison.

Figure 4. Visualization Classroom

Photo: Roberto Marques, University of Chicago

The seminar area hosts classes and seminar groups, small study groups, computer-based lab sessions, and teams working on projects. (See Figure 5.) Activities range from statistics workshops and IT training programs open to the campus community to final project presentations within an African Studies course.

The four restaurant-style collaboration booths within the seminar area allow up to three people to work together around a single monitor in a casual, comfortable, nest-like setting. (See Figure 6.) There are not enough booths to keep up with demand, as students camp within and hand off the booths throughout the day.

The consultation desk provides a place for users to sit down with teaching assistants, librarians, or staff who have office hours within the cluster. This space is also used by others who periodically provide services to students, such as helping international students prepare their taxes. The student staff at the service desk manage the space and provide assistance on computer-related issues. The

Figure 5. Seminar Area with Projection Screens

Photo: Roberto Marques, University of Chicago

Figure 6. Banquette Team Seating

Photo: Roberto Marques, University of Chicago

original student-developed touch-screen printing system has been replaced by a commercial product that functions in a similar manner; both color and high-speed black-and-white laser printing are available to any user on campus.

People use computing labs in unexpected ways, so the space was designed to accommodate novel purposes. Because of USITE/Crerar's size, the planning team included a public address system for the space. The team assumed that at some point a student would reverse-engineer the sound system in order to play music over the room speakers. Rather than limit such behavior, the team agreed to include a way to hook up a CD player to the PA system. Within a year, an undergraduate employee who was a part-time DJ hosted his iPod-based "Dance Night Fridays" for an audience of medical school students. Together, they reconfigured the general-purpose computing space into a dance floor—while other students continued to work in the lab.

How Is Technology Used?

Although USITE/Crerar is managed by the central IT organization and provides capabilities expected of a computer lab, technology is not the focus. Primary consideration went to the work environment and its users; the technology flows from that. Spaces were designed to allow technology to evolve over time, adapting to the community's ever-changing needs. The facility is used

▶ As a test bed
▶ As an application of enterprise computing
▶ For multiple uses of platforms and equipment
▶ To produce digital media
▶ For teaching and team learning
▶ To visualize complex data or use simulation software
▶ For distance learning and videoconferencing
▶ For advanced collaboration
▶ To check e-mail and conduct Web searches

When USITE/Crerar opened in 2000, it was one of the most advanced computing facilities on campus, with more than 80 percent of the technology new and untested in a public environment. Today, the technology has matured, but the environment continues as a test bed for new approaches, services, and infrastructure. For example, flat-panel LCD displays were a radical idea in 1999. Because they are smaller and easier to move than regular desktop displays, LCDs were integrated in the space to facilitate collaboration and increase usable desk space.

Likewise, the network is a critical enabler established with the belief that rapid and reliable access to information would be crucial to scholarship. USITE/Crerar became an experiment for CAT6 cabling, alternate switching schemes, and a planned exploration of gigabit-to-the-desktop capabilities.

Technology consistency and stability resulted from applying enterprise desktop management principles to public computing. All computing clusters on campus offer identical software; only the physical environment and extended capabilities such as scanners, video equipment, displays, and so on change to meet local needs. Workstations offer Windows, MacOS, Linux, and UNIX operating systems; a full suite of software including statistical packages, Adobe products, and department-sponsored applications; and color laser printing. The continuous counter along the media wall provides flatbed and transparency scanners, studio monitors, digital video decks, and digital photo and video editing software. This variety encourages inventive uses, such as collaboration while using several types of adjacent workstations to run data while packaging a presentation.

Faced with the challenge of creating the Internet equivalent of the classic phone booth within the cybercafé, the team decided to adopt Sun Ray thin clients from Sun Microsystems. The 16-seat thin-client deployment became the model for the WebStation service that now boasts more than 70 kiosks in approximately 10 locations across campus. In addition, users needed an easy way to connect their laptops to the Internet. Although data jacks were installed throughout the space, hardwired connections are not always convenient. As a result, the first public wireless access point on campus was installed in USITE/Crerar. Visitors to the cybercafé stations can quickly check their e-mail and conduct Web searches using wired or wireless access.

Both the classroom and seminar area can be used for teaching, team presentation rehearsal, and group information analysis. The classroom is equipped with a projector and 10 workstations equipped for graphics, simulation programs, and digital media applications. The classroom's videoconferencing facilities can be used by classes or any other groups interested in conversing with remote collaborators, students in the university's Paris Center, or other institutions. Plans are under way to equip the classroom with an AccessGrid node that would be open to all members of the campus community.

What Makes the Space Successful?

Multiple factors contribute to the success of USITE/Crerar, from clarity of mission to extensive use of technology, variety of work settings, ingenious design, attention to detail, and department-store-style management.

The mission of USITE, and Crerar in particular, is to provide access to technologies, applications, and resources normally out of reach of the average user but necessary for scholarly success. The space succeeds because it blends the needs of its users seamlessly with the physical and technological environment. Color and high-speed black-and-white laser printers, large-screen displays, data projectors, slide-capable flatbed scanners, professional-grade digital video decks, removable FireWire hard drives, headphones, and a host of other technologies as well as academic software meet users' needs.

The center offers a wide range of computer-equipped settings, providing users with different places to work, either in small groups or independently. Variety was part of the design. Corners, curves, open spaces, and partitions fill the lab, allowing users to select a work environment that matches their styles. Carefully selected materials and elements break down the scale of the space. For example, the variety in ceiling heights and treatment creates a different character in the main space than the more intimate collaboration area. The "found" space below the landing of the entry stairs was exploited to create an intimate cluster of stations with a low ceiling, in contrast with the high ceiling of the main lab.

Inspiration came from many sources, such as restaurant design. Banquette seating and decorative pendant lighting call to mind comfortable cafes. These banquettes for three provide a table with a flexible arm supporting the monitor above the table surface and the CPUs tucked unobtrusively below. A prominent translucent curved wall defines a separate area without actually partitioning it off and helps give a sense of closure to the area it defines. A fritted pattern of fine vertical stripes on the glass allows staff at the desk to see into the enclosed space, yet it is perceived as translucent from other angles.

The goal was to create a single space that could serve multiple groups with myriad needs—from undergraduates and instructors to medical students and administrators—under one management framework. Using a department-store-type management approach, USITE/Crerar successfully addresses needs ranging from computer access to remote collaboration.

What Principles Were Behind the Design?

Some key principles went into the design:

▶ **Collaboration:** A primary driver for the design was to provide a variety of settings for collaborative work with technology tools to support those activities. Figure 7 shows movable whiteboards in a collaborative work area.

Figure 7. Collaborative Work Zone with Movable Whiteboards

Photo: Roberto Marques, University of Chicago

▶ **Transparency:** The transparency throughout the center makes activities taking place there visible to users and easy to supervise.

▶ **Choice:** To break away from the traditional "church pew" computing center layouts, the center sought to provide a wide variety of choice in workstations and seating areas.

▶ **Flexibility:** Furnishings were selected to be inviting and comfortable—and movable, so users could rearrange their work areas. Figure 8 shows the main computing space with its variety of seating arrangements.

What Is Unique or Noteworthy?

One of the most unique aspects of this project was the visionary planning process. The planning team spent a year—and the initial funding—on wide consultation and thoughtful planning and design, gambling that the strength of the concept would serve as a springboard for future projects. The team looked for ideas outside the institution, visiting coffee shops, restaurants, bookstores,

Figure 8. Main Computing Space

Photo: Roberto Marques, University of Chicago

subway stations, and other places where people gather and work, both formally and informally. These ideas coalesced into design concepts. Ultimately, the planning process proved so successful that the study produced a fully funded space and changed the paradigm for future technology-equipped spaces. The computing center has prompted considerable cultural change at the University of Chicago. Although a venue for students, USITE/Crerar has become a destination for administrators, visitors, and classes. Similar facilities are now viewed as extensions of the learning experience, not merely a required, centrally provided resource.

Because technology and user needs change more often than built space, the computing cluster was built on raised flooring with flexible furnishings such as whiteboards on casters so that users could move furniture around as desired, reconfiguring the space without additional construction. The plan also matched technology carefully to program needs. The use of thin clients as Web and e-mail kiosks is a prime example of understanding a programmatic need and letting the technology flow from that.

Another benefit of the design was the repurposing of underutilized library space. The basement space directly accessible off the entry stairs gained a new energy, and the lab is credited with increasing traffic through the John Crerar Library.

Acknowledgments

VMC Architects of Chicago worked with the design team in planning the USITE/ Crerar Computing Cluster and Cybercafé. A special acknowledgment to the late Kathleen Zar, former head science librarian at the John Crerar Library, who was instrumental in shaping the vision for USITE/Crerar from a library perspective, tirelessly worked to ensure the project was a success, and quietly helped transform the model of learning environments at the University of Chicago.

About the Authors

Shirley Dugdale is the director of learning environments at DEGW North America, LLC. **Chad Kainz** is the senior director of academic technologies at the University of Chicago.

CHAPTER 41

The Student Learning Center

The University of Georgia

William Gray Potter and Florence E. King

What Is It?

The Student Learning Center (SLC) at the University of Georgia (UGA) opened in August 2003. Encompassing more than 200,000 square feet, it integrates general classrooms with an extensive electronic library or information commons (http://www.slc.uga.edu/). (See Figure 1.)

Figure 1. Student Learning Center

Led by the university architects (http://www.maps.uga.edu) and Cooper Carry, the design architect (http://www.coopercarry.com/), several university departments collaborated on the design of the facility and continue to service it: the University of Georgia Libraries (http://www.libs.uga.edu); the Center for Teaching and Learning (CTL) (http://www.ctl.uga.edu/), which provides classroom support and instructional support for faculty; and Enterprise Information Technology Services (EITS), UGA's computing services (http://www.eits.uga.edu/). Other partners include the Office of the Vice President for Instruction and the Office of the Vice President for Student Affairs.

Geared toward undergraduates, the SLC consists of two interlocking components: classrooms and the Electronic Library.

The classroom component, managed by the CTL, includes:

▶ 26 general classrooms varying in size from 24 to 300 seats, with a total of 2,200 seats

▶ Offices for staff who support the classrooms

▶ An interactive computer lab dedicated to faculty technology development

▶ Three faculty preparation rooms providing a work space away from the faculty member's office

The Electronic Library, managed by the UGA Libraries and EITS, includes the following:

▶ 2,300 seats in a variety of configurations, including single- and double-carrel seating, study tables and chairs both in and outside a group study room, soft seating, and four computer labs

▶ Three state-of-the-art computer classrooms dedicated to teaching electronic research, information literacy skills, and technology

▶ 500 PC workstations

▶ 96 group study rooms with 6 to 10 seats each

▶ A pervasive wireless network and 2,000 data ports

▶ A traditional reading room for quiet study

▶ Four information/reference desks

▶ A coffee shop (see Figure 2)

The SLC is comprised of four floors of approximately 50,000 square feet each. The building is designed to integrate the two components (classrooms and the Electronic Library) so that students can quickly shift from classroom activity to research or study. Floor plans are located at <http://slc.uga.edu/facility.html#floorplans>. Photos of the SLC and a QuickTime video are available at <http://slc.uga.edu/press/educause.html>.

The first state-chartered university in America, UGA is a research institution with approximately 24,814 undergraduate and 8,386 graduate/professional students. Fifteen colleges and schools, with auxiliary divisions, conduct the university's programs of teaching, research, and service.

Figure 2. Jittery Joe's Coffee Shop

What Happens Here?

The classrooms are equipped with state-of-the-art presentation technology and computers. The CTL Classroom Support Center in the building provides support for classroom technology. The CTL's other units also provide workshops and seminars on various teaching technologies for faculty and teaching assistants (http://slc.uga.edu/technology/generalclass.html).

The Electronic Library offers access to 500 research databases and 30,000 full-text journals and newspapers. Microsoft Office and other course-specific software programs are available on each of the 500 PCs, with additional Web design software on 20 multimedia PCs. Research, reference, and computing help are available at four information desks in the building. Because of the integrated nature of the classroom and library environment, librarians at the SLC have an unusual opportunity to promote information literacy. EITS also offers courses in various software packages to the general student population.

Currently under design, a digital media lab will provide students with workstations, media, and Web development software as well as on-site support and training to help them create their own digital multimedia projects for courses. The UGA Writing Center offers on-site walk-up services that have proven to be very popular (http://www.slc.uga.edu/students.html#writing). The UGA Tutorial Program also takes advantage of the facility by offering free tutoring in core-level math, science, language, and business courses by appointment and on a drop-in basis.

After 5:00 p.m., the SLC classrooms are heavily booked as meeting spaces for registered student groups and campus departments, and several areas in the SLC can host events that encourage collaboration between faculty and students or allow departments to host small conferences, presentations, or speakers (http://www.slc.uga.edu/policy/eventspace.html). The SLC has become a host site for freshmen and transfer orientation sessions held throughout the summer featuring parent receptions, testing, and course registration.

The SLC offers a light-infused environment with comfortable seating, student-focused services, and an open food and drink policy. Feedback from faculty and students is that Jittery Joe's Coffee Shop, the group study rooms, the open table environment, and the soft seating areas promote both informal discussions and study sessions.

How Is Technology Used?

The building uses technology to offer research, teaching, and computing services in an integrated learning environment. More than 500 PCs are provided as well as a pervasive wireless network and more than 2,000 physical connections. Technology is also used for building monitoring, including automated access control, motion detection, and lighting control.

Each classroom is equipped with state-of-the-art presentation technology. With its classroom control software, CTL can maintain, monitor, and assess all classroom equipment use centrally.

More information is available at <http://www.slc.uga.edu/facility.html #technology>.

What Makes the Space Successful?

The SLC provides a one-stop shop with classrooms and library research sources located in one facility. In addition, the computer software and technology create a common interface. Based on usage alone, we believe the space is successful. Approximately 8,000 students use the facility a day, with 1.5 million visitors in 2005. Even UGA's president noted that the SLC is "now truly the signature academic building on campus, filled at all hours with students, faculty, and staff engaged in the full range of academic activity."[1]

Part of the integration of the SLC comes from a new focus on the library as "process." The SLC integrates learning in class, gathering information, and consulting with research professionals, using SLC computers to complete assignments or a group study room to practice a presentation. The SLC gives faculty and students the opportunity to teach and to learn in a technology-enhanced environment.

The simple building design with light-filled, open spaces, and student/faculty-driven policies and protocols creates a pleasant environment. Advanced technology combined with traditional library furnishings such as solid cherry tables and chairs by Thos. Moser Cabinetmakers (http://www.thomasmoser.com/library/) invites students to linger. (See Figure 3.) In addition, the space is flexible. Classrooms can be used in the evenings for student meetings, tutoring, or other activities, and the building has become a location of choice for a variety of student pursuits. Flexibility is built into the design; the space can adapt to new user needs as they arise.

Figure 3. SLC Reading Room (a) Furniture and (b) in Use

(a)   (b)

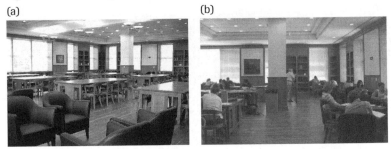

The building partners' shared oversight and collaboration has created a solid management and operations structure to guarantee that the building continues to serve student and institutional needs. In addition, SLC staff training, a clear service philosophy, and performance expectations ensure that student needs are met and the facility is well utilized. Success is further measured by a formal assessment process that involves student input via structured focus groups. Informal assessments include on-site observation of how students use the space, soliciting suggestions, unsolicited suggestions to our SLC e-mail box, and letters to the editor in the school newspaper.

What Principles Were Behind the Design?

Four principles informed the design:

▶ **Integration:** The SLC was designed to integrate services, both online and physically. For example, great emphasis was placed on integrating classrooms, technology, and the Electronic Library.

▶ **Adaptability:** The SLC adopted a 50-year building concept that begins with a basic structure but assumes it will change as needs change.

▶ **Centrality:** A location in the center of campus makes the SLC both a place to move *through* and a place to move *to* on campus.

▶ **Collaboration:** The SLC provides spaces that encourage group study and allow group work on projects.

What Is Unique or Noteworthy?

To our knowledge, the SLC is the only facility at a research university to combine a large number of general classrooms with the information commons concept. The university architects coordinated the building program and sought input from many campus units while working closely with the building partners, which ensured buy-in and knowledge of the building from all constituencies who would be using the building and led to it being viewed as a university-wide resource rather than one controlled by any single department or unit. The SLC offers general classroom space to all disciplines; thus, students and faculty alike have the opportunity to interact with colleagues who they might not normally see.

According to UGA President Michael F. Adams:

> The opening of the Student Learning Center may have had the greatest impact on the intellectual climate of this institution since Old College was constructed (in 1806).... Every time I am there the place is alive with academic activity.... I do not know of another facility on this or any other campus where design so fully meshes with function.... For decades to come, the Student Learning Center, with its combination of Electronic Library and classroom spaces, will be a defining experience for almost all UGA students.[2]

Endnotes

1. University of Georgia President Michael F. Adams, "2005 State of the University Address," January 13, 2005, <http://www.uga.edu/presofc/pdfs/speeches/SoUGA2005.pdf>.

2. University of Georgia President Michael F. Adams, "2004 State of the University Address: A Community of Learners," January 15, 2004, <http://www.uga.edu/columns/040120/news13.html>.

About the Authors

At the University of Georgia, **William Gray Potter** is the university librarian and associate provost, Main Library, and **Florence E. King** is the assistant university librarian for human resources and director, Student Learning Center Electronic Library, University of Georgia Libraries.

CHAPTER 42

The Math Emporium
Virginia Tech

Barbara L. Robinson and Anne H. Moore

What Is It?

Virginia Tech's Math Emporium (http://www.emporium.vt.edu/) is an open, 60,000-square-foot laboratory with 550 Macintosh computers serving more than 8,000 math students each semester. The facility occupies renovated, leased space in an off-campus shopping mall. (See Figure 1.) Spurred by the need to accommodate thousands of students and to improve learning outcomes, the emporium opened in 1997 to improve the quality of large-enrollment math courses in the face of growing resource constraints. Today, 11 courses have been redesigned to take advantage of the emporium, with demonstrable improvements in student learning and significantly reduced costs for staffing and space.

Figure 1. Street View of the Math Emporium

In addition to the open area where computers are arranged in six-station circular pods (see Figure 2), the Math Emporium has space for large orientation sessions, small conferences and tutoring, a math education lab, quiet study areas, and student lounges. The facility is open 24 x 7 and staffed days and evenings by math faculty, graduate students, and advanced undergraduate students who offer personal assistance when students request it. Peer group projects, collaboration, and tutoring are also encouraged. The combination of online courses and various sources of assistance offer students a wide variety of learning opportunities that they can tailor to meet their needs and preferences.

Figure 2. Open Area with Six-Station Computer Pods

Founded in 1872 as a land-grant institution, Virginia Polytechnic Institute and State University (http://www.vt.edu/) serves the Commonwealth of Virginia as one of its largest research universities. With the main campus located in Blacksburg, Virginia, Virginia Tech educates more than 27,000 students. It operates extension centers, experiment stations, and teaching and research centers across Virginia.

What Happens Here?

The Math Emporium supports a variety of activities:

▶ Active, independent learning through locally developed, self-paced online math courses designed to let students learn on their own schedules, while providing immediate feedback and sufficient structure to ensure students understand expectations and meet required milestones.

- One-on-one coaching by professors, graduate students, and advanced undergraduates who are available 15 hours a day to assist students having difficulty with material, in a comfortable, less-threatening environment than a faculty office.
- Proctored online exams, from which most of a student's grade for target math courses is derived.
- Group projects and help sessions, facilitated by comfortable, easily moved chairs and generous work space around each computer.
- Online video lectures for students who prefer that format.
- Independent study by anyone in the Virginia Tech community who wishes to take advantage of the high-end computers or the quiet study environment.

How Is Technology Used?

Technology is important at the Math Emporium primarily because it supports a unique Web-based teaching and testing system based on Mathematica templates, Java server pages, and Oracle databases. The system permits the use of streaming video, audio recordings, and other interactive tools to explain concepts. The focus, however, is on practice quizzes that cover all the skills a student is expected to learn in a course. These quizzes, generated on demand, offer a large number of random variations for each problem. This allows the 8,500 students registered in the system each semester, if they so desire, to practice until the program's immediate feedback indicates they have truly learned the particular skill.

Tests for credit are generated by the same system. Students who have mastered all the practice quizzes are assured they'll find no surprises in the tests. This emphasis on active performance rather than listening to lectures results in the delivery of 750,000 mathematics quizzes and tests each semester, with demonstrably improved understanding of material.[1]

What Makes the Space Successful?

Factors ranging from high-end hardware and software to a collaborative environment make the space successful.

High-end Mac OS X computers: Students are quick to complain when technology fails to meet their performance expectations. Computers and software in the facility are updated regularly, and lower support costs for Macs allows a single support person to maintain the equipment at high performance levels.

A friendly, nonthreatening, collaborative environment: While most students can learn the majority of the material independently, the math department staffs the emporium 15 hours a day with faculty, graduate students, and advanced undergraduate students who provide immediate one-on-one assistance. Thus, resources target specific times when personal interaction is most useful, as opposed to the less-efficient lecture model. The system also effectively removes faculty from the testing process, mitigating the potentially adversarial faculty/student relationship that might discourage positive interaction.

Local software development: Good software did not exist for courses to be taught at the emporium, requiring local development. Other systems were created to perform housekeeping chores such as assigning students to computers, tracking student performance, and even offering online, real-time information on emporium use so that students can determine if they will need to wait in line to use a computer.

Proctored testing: While learning occurs best when student-centered, there still exists a need for evaluation. No system yet developed efficiently and effectively performs accurate online evaluations without human supervision. While students can work on their math courses anywhere if they don't need personal assistance, they are required to take formal exams under supervision at the emporium.

Reducing the cost of a quality education: Courses converted to the emporium learning paradigm have reduced costs about 75 percent, primarily because the personal assistance offered at the emporium requires far fewer and lower ranked personnel than the traditional lecture format. Studies of student performance in courses downstream of emporium classes show students do as well or better than students from traditional math classes.

Flexible design: Carpeted flooring tiles raised 3 inches span the 60,000-square-foot learning laboratory for easy wiring deployment over time. The carpeting, in combination with special acoustical ceiling tiles, makes for a quiet study environment even when the emporium is filled to capacity. Long interior walls surrounding the emporium's open working spaces invite arts-and-crafts displays from the community (see Figure 3); scattered supporting columns display large-scale, locally designed, computer-generated graphics inspired by the space itself.

Figure 3. Wall-Mounted Community Art

Institutional support: No project this size can succeed without strong support at higher administrative levels as well as within sponsoring departments. Factors that smoothed the way for the creation of the Math Emporium included reduced budgets, a culture of innovation, and the desire to improve undergraduate teaching, particularly in the large introductory math courses that serve nearly all students at the university.

What Principles Were Behind the Design?
Space design reflects the openness and flexibility of the designs for learning in which math faculty are engaged; they can redesign learning spaces as learning needs change over time. In particular, emporium faculty employ the following tenets in their learning designs:
▶ Technology can be used to individualize a student's experience in a course, improving instruction. Allowing students to progress at their own pace, review material, and take practice quizzes as much as they like, while getting personal help only when desired, is a cost-effective way to improve the learning experience.

▶ Active learning, as opposed to the traditional lecture model, improves outcomes. Faculty and other coaches provide just-in-time assistance using techniques designed to allow the students to discover answers themselves.

▶ A course must clearly delineate expectations and provide comfortable and effective mechanisms to support learning. However, students gain other valuable real-world skills beyond course content, including self-discipline and organization, when entrusted with responsibility and authority to manage their own learning.

What Is Unique or Noteworthy?

The Math Emporium has improved math education at Virginia Tech while reducing costs by using an innovative learning paradigm with new expectations and motivations. The system is supported by locally developed software and made possible by the unique organization of space, complemented by high-end technology. Important features include:

▶ Taking advantage of the bottom-line orientation of many students ("What do I need to know to pass the test?")

▶ Replacing broadcast education with one-to-one coaching and programs that allow students to succeed at their own pace

▶ Tracking performance and providing immediate feedback

▶ Converting students from passive spectators to active participants in learning

Community Asset

The Math Emporium resides in a renovated off-campus space, making cost-effective use of the leased space. By designing numerous emporium-based learning activities, the math department freed many on-campus spaces for other uses. Furthermore, the renovation of a large, empty space (formerly a department store) anchoring one end of a shopping mall where a university bookstore was the anchor tenant at the opposite end helped revitalize a community asset that had been in decline for years. The community bus service, which many students use to get around town and campus, runs continuously and provides easy access to this off-campus site. (See Figure 4.) For those who prefer to drive, parking is readily available in lots surrounding the shopping mall. The mall's landlords are currently implementing plans to establish multifamily housing units and more small shops on the land occupied by the newly rejuvenated mall.

Figure 4. Math Emporium Bus

Endnote

1. Michael Williams, "A Technology-Based Model for Learning," *Journal on Systemics, Cybernetics, and Informatics,* vol. 2, no. 6 (2005).

About the Authors

Barbara L. Robinson is the director of test scoring services for learning technologies and **Anne H. Moore** is the associate vice president for learning technologies and director of information technology initiatives at the Virginia Polytechnic Institute and State University.

CHAPTER 43

Torgersen Hall
Virginia Tech

J. Thomas Head and Anne H. Moore

What Is It?

Founded in 1872 as a land-grant institution, Virginia Polytechnic Institute and State University (http://www.vt.edu/) serves the Commonwealth of Virginia as one of its largest research universities. With the main campus located in Blacksburg, Virginia Tech educates more than 27,000 students and operates extension centers, experiment stations, and teaching and research centers across Virginia.

Named after the Virginia Tech president who called for a facility that would advance and demonstrate the university's strategic initiatives in technology, Torgersen Hall is an advanced communication and information technology center. Designed as a student-centered learning environment at the heart of campus, this high-tech center connects to the university's library via a bridge over University Mall, a major entrance to the university. (See Figure 1.) A symbolic bridge between

Figure 1. Torgersen Hall Bridge Exterior

old and new, town and gown, the facility offers opportunities for collaborative learning, research, and service activities that leverage the potential of computing, communications, and information technologies.

The 150,000-square-foot facility has:

▶ Wireless connectivity throughout
▶ Wired classrooms with state-of-the-art audiovisual systems and computer-controlled lighting preset for different teaching scenarios
▶ Classrooms configured for interactive video distance learning
▶ High tech auditoriums
▶ Observation booths for studying experimental teaching techniques
▶ A computer-automated virtual environment for 3D virtual reality
▶ Electronic reading rooms and study courts
▶ A media center
▶ Office and laboratory spaces for research activities
▶ 30 miles of fiber-optic cable and 75 miles of copper cable

Torgersen Hall serves as a physical gateway to digital library assets, research in a myriad of technology arenas, and a complex of activities supported by the university's Learning Technologies division (http://www.it.vt.edu/organization/lt/). The vaulted bridge connecting to the university library is a heavily trafficked space where students gather to collaborate, access digital content, purchase software, and borrow laptops or Tablet PCs. (See Figure 2.) Ten classrooms function as test beds for determining effective and efficient ways to integrate technology in teaching and learning.

Figure 2. Torgersen Hall Bridge Interior

The electronic study court is a focal point for students and faculty engaged in experiments in technology-enriched learning. Adjacent to high-tech classrooms, the study court fosters flexible space use in formal and informal learning activities with support for students collaborating on projects. For example, students and faculty may convene in a classroom to introduce a topic, then adjourn to the study court to work in groups or to the New Media Center on the same floor for assistance with multimedia development. (See Figure 3.)

Figure 3. Torgersen Hall Study Court

A university resource for all departments and schools, Torgersen Hall also brings together faculty and students engaged in research on the application of technology in areas such as digital library materials, collaborative learning, human-computer interaction, distributed and distance education, scientific visualization, multimedia development, fiber optics, and wireless communication.

What Happens Here?

Ten classrooms serve more than 10,000 students daily. These classrooms support a variety of pedagogical needs including distance-learning classes, computer-integrated classes requiring specialized software, and flexible spaces that encourage experimental approaches to teaching and learning. Three distance-learning classrooms with videoconferencing capabilities allow students and faculty to interact synchronously with students and faculty in Virginia Tech's three distributed graduate centers, other learning sites across Virginia, and beyond. (See Figure 4.)

Figure 4. Torgersen Hall Classroom

The New Media Center supports a suite of spaces designed for multimedia production that includes recording studios, video editing equipment, and specialized production software for student projects (See Figure 5.) To keep the community abreast of the latest multimedia production techniques and to support collaborative projects, this space also contains a training center supported by center staff (http://www.nmc.vt.edu/).

Figure 5. New Media Center

Students use the electronic study court and the bridge to collaborate on team-oriented projects using wired and wireless connectivity that pervades the facility. These informal spaces are in close proximity to experimental classrooms, the New Media Center, software distribution stations, and student support services. The building design promotes informal interactions leading to serendipitous research collaboration. For example, researchers in pervasive computing have joined with applied services staff in nearby assistive technology labs to collaborate on products that will benefit learners with disabilities.

The library partners with the neighboring digital imaging production unit to digitize materials for the university's digital repositories. The physical proximity of these collaborating units is especially important when handling fragile collections (http://spec.lib.vt.edu/).

The 3D computer-automated virtual environment (CAVE) provides a rich learning and research space for exploring concepts across such disciplines as interior design, engineering, chemistry, physics, and entomology (http://www.cave.vt.edu/).

The award-winning Faculty Development Institute provides year-round opportunities for faculty to explore the benefits of integrating technology in their teaching and research activities (http://www.fdi.vt.edu/). A three-credit seminar offered through the Graduate Education Development Institute introduces graduate students to critical pedagogies, e-portfolios, and other resources that might assist them with their professional development (http://www.gedi.vt.edu/). The assistive technologies lab ensures that all students and faculty have access to course content regardless of physical or cognitive disabilities, and the lab hosts a research and development team for advancing the frontiers in learning technologies. The Center for Human Computer Interaction studies people using various technologies to help improve the usability and effectiveness of technology (http://www.hci.vt.edu/).

How Is Technology Used?

Torgersen Hall incorporates a variety of technologies to support students, faculty, and staff.

Laptop computers: Laptops are available for checkout for ad hoc use by students, and Tablet PCs are available for distribution by faculty to students in class for testing new pedagogical approaches.

Wireless and wired: The entire facility is supported with wireless high-speed Internet access. Optical fiber is routed at a central point through glass brick cylinders that allow for easy adjustment and secure display.

Multimedia classrooms: All classrooms are equipped with a touch-panel interface for using the latest technology. Lighting controls provide several levels of lighting for a variety of learning and discovery activities.

Computer-integrated classrooms: Classes with specialized software requirements meet in these rooms throughout the day and in the evening hours.

Videoconferencing: Heating and cooling systems for these classrooms are designed to register very low noise coefficient ratings so that interactive distance-education activities occur without undue background noise. Also, lighting controls and the acoustical characteristics of materials on the floors, walls, and furniture support distance-education audio and video requirements.

Digital collections: The digital imaging group provides high-quality professional services for creating digital content in collaboration with academic departments. Faculty use these services to digitize instructional content for classes and archives.

What Makes the Space Successful?

Faculty, instructional technologists, and creative architects joined in extensive consultation on innovative and practical considerations for the facility. As ideas turned into drawings, architects continuously gathered feedback from university stakeholders. These conversations resulted in an admired, well-used edifice. University support, through on-site training and technology services as well as competitive grants to faculty for integrating technology in learning activities, encourages experimentation with pedagogy. Students, faculty, and the community at large may receive just-in-time support for instructional and research projects by walking into the New Media Center.

What Principles Were Behind the Design?

The guiding principle in the building design was to create an open learning environment with the flexibility to accommodate the evolving needs of learning in the foreseeable future.

Transparency: Classrooms are located at ground level with large windows to allow the broader community to see inside. These rooms ring a three-story atrium where daylight filters through without heat gain or glare. The balconies ringing this space allow for visual contact vertically and horizontally to promote openness and chance encounters among students, faculty, and staff.

Transitional zones: The electronic study court promotes teaming before and after classes and in round-the-clock general use with comfortable, well-designed, and inviting furniture arrangements. The court also acts as surge space for adjoining classrooms.

Multifunctional: Learning, discovery, and engagement activities range across quiet study spaces, training and multimedia production suites, and experimental classrooms (flexible rooms and large auditoriums). Advanced research suites include digital library research, development, and implementation spaces.

Flexibility: Classrooms have raised access floors twelve inches high to accommodate rewiring efficiently. These rooms also have low-voltage lighting controls to allow for flexible, independent control of lighting setups and to encourage pedagogical innovation. The rooms are bay sized (30 x 40 feet), accommodating a broad range of uses. With no vertical mechanical or electrical elements within the bay walls, spaces as large as 210 x 40 feet could be created. Exposed vertical ducts in the atrium help achieve this flexibility, since they are exterior to the room spaces and also allow other infrastructure that might have run vertically in walls to run horizontally in ceiling plenums.

Groups may comfortably gather in numerous informal nooks. The bridge's more formal study space has help stations and classrooms at either end. Through careful placement of stairs and circulation routes, the bridge may operate on a 24-hour basis without opening adjacent spaces.

What Is Noteworthy?

Outside, a gray-stoned, gothic exterior maintains the integrity of the prevailing campus architecture (see Figure 6), even as a mall-spanning bridge and glass-topped atrium portend a new age. Overstuffed chairs on the bridge offer comfort and support the idea that technology can exist in warm, inviting spaces with views in many directions—to the past, present, and future. Torgersen Hall proves its architect's thesis: if one of information technology's benefits is the freedom to accomplish many things differently, then technology-enabled spaces should express as much in form and function.

Inside Torgersen Hall, students and faculty creatively blend traditional and new approaches to learning and discovery. Researchers investigating uses of smart materials and sensing devices collaborate with colleagues in assistive technology on applications that help disabled students better navigate the campus. Human-computer interaction researchers scrutinize the usability of these and other innova-

Figure 6. Torgersen Hall

tive applications developed around the building. Faculty and students work easily with resident instructional designers and digital imaging specialists to improve the quality of digital materials they are developing and archiving. Interdisciplinary, technology-enriched teaching and research projects unfold by design as well as from informal encounters in the building. The synergies and emerging communities Torgersen Hall's planners envisioned are being created. (See the e-book resource Web page for short videos of interviews with Virginia Tech Professors Carol Burch-Brown and Kerry J. Redican about teaching in Torgersen Hall.)

About the Authors

J. Thomas Head is the director of administration and chief of staff for learning technologies and **Anne H. Moore** is the associate vice president for learning technologies and director of information technology initiatives at the Virginia Polytechnic Institute and State University.

Index

G

H

Torgersen Hall
Virginia Tech

J. Thomas Head and Anne H. Moore

What Is It?

Founded in 1872 as a land-grant institution, Virginia Polytechnic Institute and State University (http://www.vt.edu/) serves the Commonwealth of Virginia as one of its largest research universities. With the main campus located in Blacksburg, Virginia Tech educates more than 27,000 students and operates extension centers, experiment stations, and teaching and research centers across Virginia.

Named after the Virginia Tech president who called for a facility that would advance and demonstrate the university's strategic initiatives in technology, Torgersen Hall is an advanced communication and information technology center. Designed as a student-centered learning environment at the heart of campus, this high-tech center connects to the university's library via a bridge over University Mall, a major entrance to the university. (See Figure 1.) A symbolic bridge between

Figure 1. Torgersen Hall Bridge Exterior

E D U C A U S E

Transforming Education Through Information Technologies

info@educause.edu   **www.educause.edu**

1150 18th Street, NW, Suite 1010   4772 Walnut Street, Suite 206

Washington, DC 20036   Boulder, CO 80301

202-872-4200   303-449-4430

202-872-4318 (fax)   303-440-0461 (fax)